CHALLENGE OF BATTLE

OSPREY
PUBLISHING

C90023826%

CHALLENGE
OF
BATTLE

THE REAL STORY OF THE
BRITISH ARMY IN 1914

ADRIAN GILBERT

First published in Great Britain in 2014 by Osprey Publishing,
PO Box 883, Oxford, OX1 9PL, UK
PO Box 3985, New York, NY 10185-3985, USA

E-mail: info@ospreypublishing.com

Osprey Publishing is part of the Osprey Group

A CIP catalogue record for this book is available from the British
Library

Adrdian Gilbert has asserted his right under the Copyright, Designs
and Patents Act, 1988, to be identified as the Author of this Work.

ISBN: 978 1 84908 859 6
e-book ISBN: 978 14728 0814 1
PDF ISBN: 978 14728 0813 4

Page design by Ken Vail Graphic Design, Cambridge, UK
Index by Sharon Redmayne
Cartography by Peter Bull
Typeset in Didot and Bembo
Originated by PDQ Digital Media Solutions, Suffolk
Printed in China through Worldprint

14 15 16 17 1 10 9 8 7 6 5 4 3 2 1

Front cover: Men of the Army Service Corps in England at Christmas
1914. (IWM, Q 53478)

Osprey Publishing is supporting the Woodland Trust, the UK's
leading woodland conservation charity, by funding the dedication of
trees.

www.ospreypublishing.com

CONTENTS

PART FOUR: DECISION AT YPRES

LIST OF MAPS

LIST OF IMAGES

14. Indian troops man defences near Wytschaete, October 1914. (IWM, Q 56325)
15. J Battery RHA, deployed at Wytschaete, 31 October 1914. (IWM, Q 56307)
16. 1st Cameronians, Cabbage Patch trench, La Boutillerie, 5 November 1914. (IWM, Q 51524)
17. 18-pdr gun crew, Armentières, 7 December 1914. (IWM, Q 51542)
18. 1st Cameronians, Houplines trenches, December 1914. (IWM, Q 51550)
19. 11th Hussars machine-gun section, winter of 1914–15. (IWM, Q 51194)
20. 2nd Scots Guards digging trenches, Armentières, late 1914. (IWM, Q 57380)

INTRODUCTION

'In every respect the Expeditionary Force of 1914 was incomparably the best trained, best organised, and best equipped British Army that ever went forth to war.'[1] With these words Brigadier-General J. E. Edmonds summed up the British Expeditionary Force in his introduction to the Official History of the First World War. Edmonds was the editor of this multi-volume series on the army's contribution to the war, an epic undertaking not completed until 1948.

The first two volumes, published in 1922 and 1925 respectively and directly compiled by Edmonds, described the army in the 1914 campaign, from the opening encounters at Mons and Le Cateau, through the great retreat and advance to the Aisne to the desperate battles in defence of Ypres. These initial works swiftly established a commanding presence as the definitive account of British Army operations in 1914, casting a long shadow over subsequent histories of the campaign.

James Edmonds was a gifted multi-linguist whose intellectual abilities saw him pass out top at the Staff College, Camberley in 1898. As the 4th Division's senior staff officer in 1914, he took part in the opening phase of the war, but the strain of work led to a breakdown in September 1914 and reassignment to GHQ for the remainder of the conflict. In 1919 Edmonds took over as head of the Historical Section of the Committee of Imperial Defence, then engaged in the preparation of the history of the war.

Subsequent volumes of the Official History became the subject of fierce controversy, but those devoted to 1914 were excluded from these debates. Yet, close examination of the 1914 campaign reveals flaws in Edmond's account that have distorted our view of the army in this period. Tribute must be paid, however, to the quality and depth of research conducted by Edmonds and his small team of historians. This will be evident to anyone who has examined the files in the National Archive at Kew and read the correspondence with key individuals, after-action reports and interviews with front-line officers. And yet, the question remains: what material was included and how was it used?

In some respects, Edmonds was producing his work too soon after the end of conflict – with little time for reflection – and he was certainly too close to its major figures, having spent most of the war in their company. Despite his personal, often waspish attitudes towards senior colleagues, he was reluctant to belittle them in public. And as a regular officer with a lifetime's attachment to the army, he was understandably protective of it from the threat of outside criticism.

The 1914 volumes comprised a chronicle of operations, with the emphasis on the actions of individual regiments, battalions or batteries. This had the tendency of turning the work into an enormous, composite regimental history, with limited room for historical analysis and the development of wider themes, leading the military theorist Basil Liddell Hart to quip that it was, '"official" but not "history"'.[2] Despite this limitation, Edmonds intended the Official History to have a definite instructional purpose. In a letter of 1932 he wrote: 'I want the young officers of the army who are to occupy the high places later on to see the mistakes of their predecessors, yet without telling the public too much.'[3] Consequently, where there was criticism, it was muted and oblique, and for most readers, all but invisible.

Considering the 1914 volumes it is possible to see significant instances of evasion and omission, and, on occasion, outright distortion. A striking example of this can be found in the chapters dealing with the battle of Le Cateau on 26 August. The Official History transformed a British tactical defeat into a successful delaying action fought against great odds. Those aspects of the engagement that raised uncomfortable truths were conveniently forgotten.

The virtual destruction of the 1st King's Own, from the 12th Brigade, was treated as bad luck rather than bad judgment, and the knowledge that the brigade's retreat across the Warnelle ravine was unauthorized and against the wishes of the divisional commander was ignored. Also overlooked was the rout of part of the 8th Brigade during the general withdrawal from the battlefield later in the day. There may have been some coded disapproval of the inept deployment of the 5th Division, although the passive voice adopted by Edmonds would seem to lay the blame elsewhere. But most damning to the veracity of the Official History's account was the unsupported and disingenuous assertion that British forces 'had turned upon an enemy of at least twice their strength'.[4]

Other examples of the Official History's coy attitude to British embarrassments included the discrete veiling of incidents such as the attempted surrender of two infantry battalions at St Quentin on 27 August and the collapse of the 1st West Yorkshire Regiment in the face of a German attack at Paissy on 20 September.

These shortcomings would be of less importance had the Official History not been so influential in defining the outlook of subsequent histories of the war. Although the analysis of the British high command before and during 1914 has been the subject of much illuminating research in recent years,[5] books published on the army at the tactical level – which include most popular accounts – have remained in the hands of those following the line set by Edmonds. Indeed, rather than challenging the Official History they have embellished it for greater effect.

To return to the example of Le Cateau, the historian John Terraine described it as 'one of the most remarkable British feats of arms of the whole war'.[6] George Cassar went half-a-step further: 'The stand of 4th Division and the II Corps in the delaying action at Le Cateau ranks as possibly the most brilliant exploit of the British Army during the whole war.'[7] A more moderate assessment of the battle by Antony Bird still maintained that the British commander had inflicted a 'smashing blow' on the Germans.[8]

British histories of the 1914 campaign typically adopt the emotionally comforting paradigm of the plucky Briton giving the overbearing foreign bully a bloody nose. Histories of previous wars helped establish this national military stereotype, whether the small band of English archers taking on the overwhelming mass of French knights at Agincourt, or Wellington's steadfast infantry saving the day at Waterloo. It was only a short move to view the soldiers of 1914 in the same light, red coats merging into khaki, firepower transferred from Brown Bess musket to Lee-Enfield rifle. Contemporary wartime histories understandably viewed the campaign through this prism, a perspective that has surprisingly continued over the years.

In this book my intention is to look afresh at the British Army during 1914. While paying due respect to the research that lies behind the Official History, I have not felt bound by its conclusions. My aim is not by any means to belittle the army's many achievements but to provide a more realistic assessment of the army set within a general narrative of the war in 1914.

My interest in the campaign was sparked in the reading room of the Imperial War Museum, when looking through the memoirs (subsequently published) of General Thomas Snow, the 4th Division's commander. Snow's unusually frank description of Le Cateau and beyond chimed with half-remembered books dealing with the same period by John Lucy and the future Field Marshal Montgomery. Their accounts made it clear that not all had gone well, describing incidents completely absent from the standard record. Further research suggested that there was another story to be told of the army's campaign in France and Belgium.

For reasons of space I have confined this history to the seven infantry divisions and cavalry of the original British Expeditionary Force, while acknowledging the contributions made by the Indian Corps and the Territorial battalions during the latter stages of the campaign.

I have made deliberate and extensive use of first-person narratives, drawing material from wide sources: published accounts (well-known and obscure) and unpublished memoirs, diaries and letters. I have also consulted official papers from the National Archives that include diaries, letters, reports and questionnaires. Together they provide vital evidence of how the battles of 1914 were actually fought, sometimes confirming the traditional view, sometimes not.

First-person accounts are, of course, essential in supplying the texture of the soldiers' experience, the sense of what it was like to gallop across open ground with swords drawn or to undergo the hell of an artillery bombardment. They also provide the human interest to what is one of the more fascinating episodes of World War I. The 1914 campaign marked the transition from a war of manoeuvre to the war of the trenches. This process would transform the British Army from a small colonial corps to the vast, industrialized force that would eventually assume a leading role in the defeat of Germany in 1918.

Adrian Gilbert,
Altrincham, Cheshire
March 2013

PROLOGUE:
FIRST BLOOD

In the midst of a heat wave, a scorching sun beat down on troopers and horses alike; some men rolled down the flaps from their caps to protect their necks, while the horses wore head fringes to shield their eyes from the ever-present swarm of flies. Major Tom Bridges, commander of C Squadron, 4th Royal Dragoon Guards, led his men through the Belgian town of Mons on the afternoon of 21 August 1914.

The Dragoon Guards were part of the cavalry screen protecting the advance of the British Expeditionary Force (BEF) from France into Belgium. Local civilians told stories of vast numbers of Germans pouring south from Brussels, laying waste to all they encountered. But the British reconnaissance patrols needed more precise information: what was their strength and where were they headed? Bridges was told that German cavalrymen had been seen in the vicinity of Soignes, a village a few miles north-east of Mons. Raising clouds of dust, C Squadron trotted forward to investigate.[1]

As darkness fell on the evening of the 21st the Germans remained worryingly elusive, and the four troops of C Squadron – around 120 officers and men – bivouacked for the night in a wood close by the main road to Brussels. At 6 a.m. the following morning they filed out of the wood in the hope of ambushing a German patrol.

Bridges deployed his squadron on the Mons–Soignes road. Two troops came under the command of Lieutenant Charles Hornby, his men mounted and out of sight of the road, while the other two troops were dismounted with rifles at the ready. British cavalrymen were armed with the same Lee-Enfield rifle used by the infantry, which provided superior accuracy and a faster rate of fire than the carbines used by their opponents.

Just before 7 a.m. five German horsemen was spotted slowly advancing down the road, lances slung and the officer leading them casually smoking a cigar. But 300 yards off, before the ambush could be sprung, the Germans were seen to stop, look around and, possibly sensing danger, turn tail.

Bridges shouted to Hornby: 'Now's your chance, Charles – after them with the sword!'[2] With a thunder of hooves, Hornby led 1st Troop in hot pursuit of the Germans, followed by 4th Troop. The Dragoon Guards caught up with the Germans in the village of Casteau, but as well as the patrol they were also confronted by a larger group of enemy cavalry. Undaunted, Hornby drew his sword and charged.

The horses slipped and skidded across the Belgian village's pavé stones and tramlines, but the Dragoon Guards were soon in the enemy's midst, and Hornby drove his sword into one of the German horsemen – inflicting the first casualty on the enemy by a soldier from the BEF. The Germans immediately retreated to the far end of the village, dismounted and took up fire positions. Hornby did likewise with his men, who were now joined by 4th Troop. The reinforcements included Corporal Edward Thomas, who would achieve another distinction, being the first British soldier to fire a shot in anger on the Western Front. He described his part in the action:

> Captain [sic] Hornby gave the order, '4th Troop, dismounted action!' We found cover for our horses by the side of the chateau wall. Bullets were flying past us and all around us, and possibly because I was noted for my athletic ability I was first in action. I could see a German cavalry officer some 400 yards away standing in full view of me, gesticulating as he disposed of his dismounted men. Immediately I saw him I took aim, squeezed the trigger and automatically, almost instantaneously, he fell to the ground.[3]

After a short fire-fight the Germans remounted and retreated back towards Soignes, pursued by the British. The Germans were caught a mile further up the road, and a full-scale mêlée ensued. Private Ted Worrell recalled the fight:

> I got a poke at a man but I don't know what happened to him. There was a fair old noise what with the clatter of hooves and a lot of shouting. The Jerries couldn't manage their long lances at close quarters and several threw them away and tried to surrender but we weren't in no mood to take prisoners and we downed a lot of them before they managed to break it off and gallop away.[4]

Several Germans were killed in the engagement but at least five were captured, and they and their lances were loaded onto carts and taken to the rear. Hornby's men then came under fire from a battalion of Jäger light infantry on a nearby ridge. At this point, Bridges arrived on the scene with the remainder of the squadron and returned the German rifle fire. From an interrogation of the prisoners, he realized he was facing the advance guard of the German 9th Cavalry Division; prudently he withdrew his small force, the Germans making no attempt to follow. The casualties suffered by the Dragoon Guards amounted to just one horse killed and three more wounded.

Hornby was the hero of the hour, and as he and the rest of the sweat-stained and begrimed troopers of C Squadron passed through the regiment's lines they received a resounding cheer. Captain Arthur Osburn, the Dragoon Guards' medical officer (MO), noticed that Hornby's sword was unsheathed, and 'about four inches near the tip was smeared with blood'.[5] The prisoners followed. Second-Lieutenant Roger Chance pondered their arrival: 'They stared back like animals in a cage – alive but taken, were they glad or shamed at an early release from war?'[6] Behind them came a cart pushed by the squadron sergeant-major containing the German lances; made from steel tubing and dismissed by British cavalrymen as 'gas-pipes',[7] their bent and battered appearance made a pathetic sight. Osburn attended to the wounded prisoners and found them little more than 'Bavarian ploughboys in German uniforms'.[8]

PART ONE

ADVANCE TO BATTLE

CHAPTER ONE

OPENING THE
WAR BOOK

As his train entered Berlin's Friedrichstrasse station on 30 June 1914, the writer and traveller Maurice Baring was startled to read newspaper headlines announcing the assassination of the Austrian Archduke Franz Ferdinand two days earlier. Baring's friends in Berlin believed the news extremely serious, but on his arrival in London, 'the whole population appeared to be thoughtless and gay, and rumours of war were forgotten. Nevertheless, every now and then one was reminded of the small cloud which refused to dissipate on the horizon. One was vaguely conscious that it was there.'[1]

During July the tensions between Europe's great powers increased, so that by the end of the month Baring's small cloud had developed into a gathering storm. Diplomacy gave way to the prospect of military action, with the Dual Alliance of France and Russia arrayed against the Central Powers of Germany and Austria-Hungary. Britain's position remained ambivalent. The rapid expansion of Germany's fleet had produced a bitter naval rivalry that, in conjunction with the increasingly bellicose attitude of Kaiser Wilhelm and his government, encouraged Britain to pursue an unofficial military partnership with France. But no formal treaty existed between the two countries, and Britain remained on the sidelines.

Towards the end of July the European armies began to mobilize. Britain was sufficiently alarmed at the deteriorating situation to institute its own defence measures on 29 July, consisting of a 'Precautionary Period' prior to a full mobilization. The uncertainty of the British government, whether to stay out of the European quarrel or go to war in support of France, was decided by the German invasion of neutral Belgium on 2 August. Britain – alongside Germany – had been a co-signatory of Belgian independence, and Germany's aggressive action provided both the justification and impetus for military action. When a last flurry of diplomatic activity failed to stem the advance of German troops into Belgium, Britain declared war on Germany at 11 p.m. on 4 August 1914.

The British public's reaction to the declaration was more complex than suggested by the simple flag-waving enthusiasm of the newsreels and press reports. This was also true of the British Army. That war was imminent galvanized all professional soldiers, and the realization that this would be the greatest military encounter in history was at once exhilarating and sobering.

Those soldiers who had experienced war at first hand were inevitably more cautious. A veteran of the Boer War (1899–1901), Company Sergeant-Major A. Boreham of the 2nd Battalion, Royal Welch Fusiliers, wrote: 'The men were jubilant, as is usual in such circumstances. I'm not afraid to place it on record that I was not; the South African war had taught me that there was nothing at all to get jubilant about.'[2] Captain James Jack of the 1st Cameronians (Scottish Rifles) echoed this view: 'All ranks are in high fettle at the prospect of active service. But hating bloodshed as I do, and having had a hard if not dangerous fifteen months in the South African war… I personally loathe the outlook. A queer soldier!'[3] Even less experienced officers saw the gravity of the situation. Arthur Mills recalled: 'It was going to be "a hell of a war". All agreed on that. There was no feeling of going off for a day's hunting about anyone. Men made their wills quietly, packed their belongings, and wrote letters of goodbye to their friends.'[4]

Cavalryman Robert Lloyd of the Life Guards maintained the insouciance of all members of his august institution: 'We received the news calmly. War was our business, our calling; and the latest move simply meant business.'[5] He drew unfavourable comparison with the tumult of excitement beyond his London barracks and his regiment's steady preparation for war:

> Outside in the streets we were acclaimed by civilians who wanted to treat us to everything. Most of us were repelled by this gush of favour. Our memories were not so short as to have forgotten in a couple of days that the great bulk of those who now hailed us publicly as heroes looked upon us forty-eight hours previously as outcasts, and would have been ashamed to be seen in our company. I have actually seen posted in places of public entertainment before the war the words: 'Soldiers and dogs not admitted'.[6]

And yet regular soldiers like Bob Lloyd and CSM Boreham represented a minority of the total war establishment: just over 60 per cent of the army was made up of reservists, who after seven years of service were now civilians but subject to recall in the advent of a national emergency.

For some, the call to arms was an unwarranted intrusion; for others, it was openly welcomed. F. A. Bolwell, a reservist in the 1st Loyal North Lancashires, wrote: 'I downed tools and, although a married man with two children, I was only too pleased to be able to leave a more or less monotonous existence for something more exciting and adventurous. Being an old soldier, war was more or less ingrained into my nature, and during those few days before the final declaration I was at fever heat and longing to be away.'[7] It was much the same for John McIlwain of the 2nd Connaught Rangers. He subsequently recalled his wife's plaintive comment on the arrival of his call-up papers: 'You seemed so eager to be away.'[8]

For Boreham – and for most other soldiers and officers – the transformation from peace to war had come 'with the suddenness of a thunderbolt'.[9] But to those in command of the army, the possibility of war with Germany had been under serious discussion for much of the previous decade.

Throughout the latter part of the 19th century, the British Army's role focused on the defence of Britain and the acquisition and protection of territories that made up the British Empire. As the Royal Navy was the most effective guarantor of the British Isles against hostile intervention, the army was primarily concerned with its colonial responsibilities. The emergence of Germany as a potential threat to British interests changed this, and at the end of 1905 Sir Edward Grey, the British Foreign Secretary, sanctioned the army high command to instigate private talks with the French.

These talks marked the beginning of the continental commitment, which would lead to the creation of a British Expeditionary Force (BEF) of six infantry divisions and one cavalry division for service in Europe. How this force might be best used became a matter of debate between deployment in France or Belgium.

Brigadier Henry Wilson, appointed to the influential post of Director of Military Operations (DMO) in 1910, enthusiastically championed the French option. The Francophile Wilson — who spent his annual leave cycling through northern France and Belgium to assess possible German invasion routes — readily accepted the French Army's suggestion to align the BEF alongside its left flank. This plan had many practical advantages but it inevitably subordinated the British to French strategic demands. Direct support for Belgium — using the port of Antwerp as a base — gave Britain more operational flexibility, but it was eventually vetoed because of the Royal Navy's inability to guarantee the protection of shipping sailing to Belgian ports, and through the Belgian government's insistence that its strict neutrality must not be compromised by any negotiations with a foreign power.

The War Office plan had been worked out in great detail by Wilson (in 1914 a major-general and sub-chief of the General Staff). The BEF would cross over to France and concentrate between the fortress of Maubeuge and Le Cateau, guarding the left flank of the otherwise exposed French Fifth Army. But rather than implement the plan without delay, the British Prime Minister Herbert Asquith — a reluctant warrior — called a War Council for the afternoon of Wednesday the 5th to discuss matters further. As well as civilian members of the Cabinet, the meeting included the senior officers of the British Army, with Field Marshal Lord Kitchener newly appointed as Secretary of State for War.

Field Marshal Sir John French — the designated Commander-in-Chief of the BEF — presented the War Office plan, and was joined by his chief of staff, Lieutenant-General Sir Archibald Murray, and two senior officers, Lieutenant-Generals Sir Douglas Haig and Sir James Grierson, with Wilson in attendance. To the dismay of Wilson and Haig, French suddenly veered off from the agreed plan to suggest the advantages of readopting the Antwerp strategy. While this idea was quashed, it precipitated a general discussion by the members of the Council, who in Wilson's eyes were 'mostly ignorant of their subjects' and who 'fell to discussing strategy like idiots'.[10] A second Council held the following day decided to uphold the original plan, although only four divisions would leave immediately for France (along with the Cavalry Division); a fifth would follow later, with the sixth held in reserve.

Kitchener also issued French with general instructions, which simultaneously called for him to support and co-operate with the French Army but to carefully husband his resources and maintain an independent command and not 'come in any sense under the orders of any Allied general'.[11] French would subsequently find himself torn between co-operation with his ally and the protection of his army.

As well as delaying mobilization, the War Council revealed the muddled thinking of the army and government, and pointed to the unsuitability of Sir John French to lead the BEF. French had established a reputation as a dashing cavalry commander during the Boer War and, in a modest fashion, was something of a military reformer, but in other important matters he was perilously out of his depth. Haig had been French's chief of staff in South Africa and provided an accurate if damning assessment of his superior immediately after the Council: 'I had grave doubts whether either his temper was sufficiently even, or his military knowledge sufficiently thorough to enable him to discharge properly the very difficult duties which will devolve upon him during the coming operations with the Allies on the Continent. In my own heart, I know that French is quite unfit for this great Command.'[12]

French's psychological volatility might have been held in check by an experienced and tough-minded chief of staff, but the newly appointed Archie Murray ('an old woman', according to Haig) proved unable to stand up to the Commander-in-Chief. This unfortunate combination was not helped by the presence of Wilson, who while knowledgeable and articulate did little to moderate French's fears and enthusiasm. Haig and Grierson – the two senior corps commanders – were, however, capable and professional officers, although the latter, a noted trencherman, would die of a heart attack shortly after his arrival in France.

The mobilization of the army was conducted through a comprehensive series of instructions collectively known as the *War Book*. First issued in 1912, the *War Book* was designed to provide a swift and smooth transition from peace to war. Apart from the tens of thousands of call-up telegrams despatched to the reservists, its provisions included the arrest of undesirable aliens, preparation of billets and the requisition of horses and motor vehicles from their civilian owners. Most important of all, the rail network was redeployed for the transport of the army, first to get the Territorials back from their summer camps and then to direct the front-line troops to their embarkation ports. In the years leading up to the outbreak of war, European armies had become masters of the science of mobilization, and in Britain, as elsewhere, the system worked exceptionally well.

In barracks and training camps across Britain, officers and NCOs worked feverishly to prepare their men for war. The mess silver and other accoutrements of peacetime soldiering were packed away, while weapons, uniforms and kit were issued to a growing numbers of reservists. The reliance on reservists was greatest in the infantry battalions; the 4th Royal Fusiliers had to integrate 734 former soldiers into its ranks to make up its war establishment of just over 1,000 officers and men.[13]

Some of the older reservists had never fired the new 'Short' Lee-Enfield rifle and almost all were confused by the recent organizational change to the battalion from eight to four companies. More to the point, the reservists were generally unfit and had soft feet that would be bloodied by their new boots. Officers did their best to help the new arrivals re-acclimatize to military life in the limited time available.

Captain Henry Dillon of the 2nd Oxford and Buckinghamshire Light Infantry received a modest £5 grant for his company: 'I spent this on nailing reservists' boots, buying dubbin to take out, also cotton wool lint, boracic powder and tincture of iodine for sore feet, clippers for hair – string for bivvies.'[14] Lieutenant Bernard Montgomery – the future field marshal who commanded a platoon in the 1st Royal Warwickshire Regiment – wrote to his mother: 'So every morning we go for a long route march to get their feet hard and finish up with some manoeuvres of sorts.'[15]

Despite these efforts the reservists would find the coming campaign, with its many forced marches, a terrible physical strain. The question of the unfitness of the reservists was related to a wider and more fundamental problem faced by the army. Much emphasis has been laid upon the apparent superiority of Britain's volunteer, long-service soldiers over those of the continental armies relying on short-service conscription. In reality, this was often far from the case.

Service in the British Army was generally unpopular; pay and conditions were worse than those of the poorest agricultural labourer or factory worker, and a continuing social stigma against military service existed among the 'respectable' working classes. The army remained chronically understrength; in May 1914 it was nearly 11,000 men short of its full peacetime establishment.[16]

Almost 50 per cent of recruits came from the unskilled, with 'town casuals' constituting the largest single category. According to Benjamin Clouting, half of the recruits to his cavalry regiment, the 4th Dragoon Guards, 'joined up because they had no work or money'.[17] That economic necessity was the prime mover in recruitment was amply confirmed in the Health Report of 1909, which went on to state that 'well over 90 per cent' of those taking the King's shilling were unemployed.

The poor physical condition of recruits from the urban poor had caused a scandal during the Boer War, but the situation pre-1914 was little better. Over half of those seeking to join the army were rejected on medical grounds that were far from stringent: in the infantry a man had to reach 5ft 3in., be 33in. around the chest and weigh at least 8 stone. In mitigation, the army worked to improve the physical quality of its recruits and even provided rudimentary educational facilities. Yet these measures could not disguise the fact that the armies of France and Germany were recruited from the nation as a whole, which provided them with the well-educated, physically robust individuals largely denied the pre-war British Army. Medical officer Arthur Osburn was unsparing in his criticism of the recruitment pool available to the army:

> In England the ranks of the Regular Army had always been a refuge for the man out of work, the man with no friends and no prospects, for the boy who could not find a job and had neither the energy nor the initiative to make one for himself, for the healthy man who was not a blackguard but a failure in civil life because he could not fight successfully against his fellows in a sternly competitive world. So it followed that many 'fighting men by trade' are anything but 'fighting men by temperament'.

It was easier in 1913, even if you hated fighting to enlist as a 'sodger' than to fight your own way in an overcrowded labour market. Certainly in pre-War days these men had not a great deal to fight for. Their country gave them social inferiority as a tradition, economic inferiority as a habit, subjection to a social system in which the hardest driven were almost invariably the worst paid and least thought of, as their birthright.[18]

One of the consequences of the physical and educational limitations of the British private soldier was the need for a higher level of supervision by officers and senior NCOs than was the case in other armies. This made other ranks unduly dependent on their superiors; at the end of his toughening-up route marches, Lieutenant Montgomery was required to 'inspect all the men's feet to see if they haven't got blisters etc, & also see that they wash them. If you left a man alone he would never wash his feet!'[19]

In most units the relationship between officers and private soldiers had a distinctly paternal aspect, where officers felt it their duty to look after the men's welfare in a way beyond the basic requirement for military efficiency. But the relationship was one without familiarity, the officers having little direct contact with the ordinary soldier, with senior NCOs acting as intermediaries between the two worlds.

The pre-war British officer corps was drawn from the upper and upper-middle classes, with the public-school ethos firmly entrenched in the officers' outlook on the world. Sports were encouraged at the expense of academic study, and character was seen to count for more than intellectual capability. Field Marshal Wolsey summed up a popular view when he declared in 1897: 'I hope the officers of Her Majesty's Army may never degenerate into bookworms. There is happily at present no tendency in that direction, for I am glad to say that this generation is as fond of danger, adventure, and all manly out-of-door sports as its forefathers were.'[20]

If Wolsey's comments were commonplace, there were other, dissenting voices, encouraging a professionalism that did include intellectual inquiry. Military journals, such as that of the Royal United Services Institute, acted as a showcase for new ideas, as did publisher Hugh Rees's popular Pall Mall Military Series, which included works on military theory and history by European as well as British authors. Admittedly, this strand was in the minority but it demonstrated that British officers were not quite as homogeneous in outlook as suggested by their stiff photographic portraits, complete with bristling moustaches. If the pre-war officer did share certain common values, they might be summed up by Robert Money, a lieutenant in the 1st Cameronians in 1914: 'Frugality, austerity and self-control were then perfectly acceptable. We believed in honour, patriotism, self-sacrifice and duty, and we clearly understood what was meant by "being a gentleman".'[21]

•

In an era when horses were still an integral part of the transport system their military importance was crucial. Aside from the cavalry regiments, horses were essential for artillery batteries and the supply trains that kept the front-line troops in being. Even an infantry division, marching to battle some 18,000 men strong, required the support of over 5,000 horses.

In peacetime, the War Office had instituted a scheme that on payment of a fee the army could requisition nominated horses from their civilian owners. This allowed some 120,000 animals to be swiftly transferred to the military. Captain Jack bemoaned the loss of two of his best hunters, but artillery officer Lieutenant Roderick Macleod, according to his father, had the best of both worlds: 'R. has sold "Be Early" to the Government for £70, but keeps her as his charger.'[22] Macleod's battery, part of the 5th Division based in Ireland, acquired 'two splendid heavy draught horses from Guinness's Brewery in Dublin. We called them "Lager" and "Pilsner", and they could have pulled anything.'[23]

A similar scheme was introduced for motor vehicles. Owners of cars and trucks were paid to keep their vehicles in a roadworthy state and then hand them over for a fixed sum in time of war. In 1914 the army possessed just 80 vehicles, but through the subsidy scheme it had the immediate use of 250 motor cars and 950 heavy vehicles. With time of the essence, they crossed the Channel in the state in which they were requisitioned, the trucks still painted in their homely commercial liveries.[24]

Motor vehicles and horses apart, the railway was the key to strategic mobility in Britain and continental Europe. Of the initial four divisions to be sent to France, the men of the 1st, 2nd and 3rd Divisions travelled by train to Southampton, while the 5th Division prepared to sail from Belfast and Dublin. The extensive railway system existing in 1914 was well able to cope with the demands of mobilization, and according to the Official History, during the busiest five-day period, 1,800 special trains were run to the embarkation ports.[25]

The well-ordered mobilization of the BEF was paralleled by a surge of martial enthusiasm from civilians and former soldiers determined to take part in the fighting. But the masses of volunteers queuing at recruitment centres would play no military role until 1915 at the earliest. The general consensus was that the war would be short and extremely violent, climaxing in what the Germans portentously called 'a battle without a 'morrow'. For those seeking an active and immediate role in the conflict, good connections were everything.

Despite former military service in the Rifle Brigade, C. D. Baker-Carr had a difficult time in booking a passage across the Channel. On arriving at the War Office on the morning of 5 August, he found it 'besieged by officers, active, retired, or on leave from foreign service, begging and beseeching to be employed'.[26] Realizing he had no hope of getting in through the front door, Baker-Carr used his friendship with a fellow rifleman, Quartermaster-General Sir John Cowans, to help him out. While there was no chance of direct military service, he was offered a position with the Royal Automobile Club (RAC), which provided cars and drivers to transport senior British officers once in France.

Maurice Baring cornered an old associate, Sir David Henderson, intending to offer his talents as a multi-linguist to the army, but on Henderson's appointment to command the Royal Flying Corps (RFC), Baring readily accepted the role of his private secretary. Baring had already 'ordered some khaki on which it was only necessary to put some badges of rank in order to make it into a kind of uniform'.[27]

But the 40-year-old writer's military career nearly foundered on his inability to put on the puttees that were a standard item of military dress. Six people attempted to help without success, until Henderson carefully wound them rounds his legs. The following morning Baring faced the same problem: 'I got up at half-past five, and went into a remote and secluded part of the country to put on my puttees at my leisure. This, although a long operation, was not entirely successful as, when it was finished, they were so tightly bound I could scarcely walk, but I did not dare undo them again.'[28] The unfortunate Baring hobbled onto the station platform to take the train to the embarkation ports, through which flowed the rest of the BEF on its way to France.

CHAPTER TWO

ACROSS THE
CHANNEL

On 9 August 1914 the first ships steamed into the English Channel, and over the next week over 80,000 soldiers and 30,000 horses of the BEF crossed to France. Protected by the Royal Navy, the transports – with officers on deck and the men packed in the hold – sailed for the ports of Boulogne, Le Havre and Rouen.

The 2nd Grenadier Guards – part of the 4th (Guards) Brigade – sailed to Le Havre on the night of 12/13 August, an incident-free passage described by Major Lord Bernard Gordon-Lennox: 'We sauntered quietly across the Channel, which was like a mill-pond and awoke to find a lovely morning and out of sight of land. We kept on slowly and as we neared the French coast we went close by several fishing boats and trawlers, the crews of which waved frantically at us and cheered us to the echo.'[1]

The enthusiasm shown by the French for the British arrival was almost universal. Among the welcoming crowd were French Territorial soldiers, second-line troops whose ill-fitting uniforms of bright-red trousers and blue coats surprised and amused the British soldiers as they disembarked. Flowers were pressed on the British officers and drinks of all kinds offered to the men; while among the younger female civilians a mania developed for souvenir hunting, with cap badges and buttons the most prized objects.

After disembarking at Le Havre, the Guards made their way to a rest camp above the port, described by Gordon-Lennox:

> It was the hottest march I have ever done and hope ever shall. Our rest camp was about five miles off and our way led us through numerous docks into the town. Here we had an even more enthusiastic welcome than ever, the inhabitants crowding round us and throwing flowers at us with the usual cries. With the sun on our backs and no air, everyone felt the heat very much, and the men started falling out, a few at first and then more. The inhabitants in their kindness were responsible for a good deal of this, as they persisted in giving the men drinks, among which was a very acrid form of cider, which had dire results. I have never seen march discipline so lax before, and hope I never shall again.[2]

The Guards were not the only troops to suffer in this way. On their march to the rest camp, the 4th Royal Fusiliers had 97 men fall out, most of them reservists unused to the rigours of marching in the sun.[3] The weather throughout August – and into September – was especially hard on the infantry: hot, humid conditions broken by intense rainstorms.

●

A select group crossed to France not on water but in the air. The Royal Flying Corps (RFC) had only come into being in 1912 and at the onset of hostilities deployed just four squadrons, with a total of 41 serviceable aircraft. The squadrons were ordered to assemble at Dover before flying to France. Aviation was in its infancy and every flight was still a dangerous adventure. Several aircraft crashed on their way to Dover – with two flyers killed – before the first wave of three squadrons took off from the Dover cliffs at dawn on 13 August.

The pilots and their aircraft were the cutting edge of the RFC, supported by the ground crews and administrative staff who went by sea. Before their departure, Lieutenant Louis Strange, a newly qualified pilot, recalled the odd sight of the requisitioned civilian transport vehicles:

The headquarters stores lorry was a huge, covered red van, with BOVRIL painted in black letters all over it; we may have laughed when we saw it go off, but we later blessed it because it was so easy to spot from the air on the frequent occasions we lost our transport. Our bomb lorry was originally destined for the peaceful pursuit of propagating the sale of Lazenby's Sauce (The World's Appetizer), while Peak Frean's Biscuits, Stephens' Blue-Black Ink, and the ubiquitous Carter Patterson were also represented.[4]

Strange followed the main force a few days later. He flew a Henri Farman F-20, a two-seat biplane with an 80hp engine capable of 60mph, a respectable speed for an aircraft of the time. But with a passenger, his kit and a Lewis light machine gun stowed on board, plus a head wind, the 70-mile flight to the assembly point at Dover took two-and-a-half hours, amounting to an average speed of just 28mph. Strange's flight to France was not without incident, either.

Landing on the bumpy airfield above Dover castle on the afternoon of 15 August, Strange broke a longeron, which he replaced during the night – only completing the repair job at 6 a.m. Making matters more difficult was the realization that his transport-driver passenger, terrified of flying, had fortified his resolve with large quantities of whisky. Before departure he had to be tracked down to a public house in the town, and then ordered onto the aircraft, which took off at midday with weather conditions deteriorating. Strange's crossing to Gris Nez took a full 45 minutes:

> I had some worried moments over the water. As the visibility was not more than about half a mile and no shipping was to be seen, I began to wonder whether I was not running up alongside the coast of Belgium. Suddenly the visibility became even worse, and when I eventually sighted the grey cliffs of Gris Nez they were only a few hundred yards away. But a sharp right-hand bank took me clear of the cliffs, and then I hugged the coastline down to Boulogne, where I ran into better weather. Although I encountered a couple of hard rainstorms later, I was able to make Amiens comfortably in about two-and-a half-hours flying time.
>
> I shall never forget taxying up to the other machines that Sunday afternoon. The thousands of Frenchmen congregated round the aerodrome at Amiens put me in mind of a Hendon pageant, but the illusion vanished

when the machine came to a standstill, because, much to my astonishment, my passenger stood up and answered the cheers of the crowd with much gusto and saluted the Entente Cordiale by waving aloft another empty bottle of whisky. At that moment my eye caught sight of Major Higgins, my commanding officer. I thought that the fifty-six days No. 1 Field Punishment subsequently meted out to him rather hard luck under the circumstances.[5]

Several other flights from England suffered forced landings. And as the RFC prepared to fly on to Maubeuge, a B.E.8 crashed over the aerodrome at Amiens, killing both crewmen. And yet despite their unreliability, fragility and the modest numbers involved, aircraft would be of vital importance to the outcome of the 1914 campaign.

The aircraft of the RFC had immediately proved their worth during the 1912 army manoeuvres. Lieutenant-General Sir James Grierson, one of the corps commanders involved, was sufficiently taken by the speed and accuracy of the intelligence supplied by aircraft to write: 'The impression left on my mind is that their use has revolutionised the art of war. So long as hostile aircraft are hovering over one's troops all movements are liable to be seen and reported, and therefore the first step in war will be to get rid of the hostile aircraft.'[6]

These would prove prophetic words. Reconnaissance remained aviation's chief function, but the realization of the aircraft's full military potential would not be long in coming. The Italian-Turkish War (1911–12) fought in Libya had been closely observed by the staffs of the major European armies for the innovations made in aerial observation for artillery, aerial photography, the dropping of propaganda leaflets and even bombing. As for Grierson's demand for aircraft to counter the activities of hostile machines, those sent over to France by the RFC remained unarmed but aircrew carried revolvers and rifles to take pot shots at their adversaries. Louis Strange wanted to take things further, however, developing an improvised mounting for his new Lewis machine gun. Once German planes were sighted, he hoped to use it in earnest.

•

When the BEF left for France a personal message was issued to every man from the Secretary of State for War, Lord Kitchener. Both an exhortation and a warning, it reminded the soldier to do his duty, be on his best behavior and resist the temptations of 'wine and women'.

Other, more bellicose messages were delivered by senior officers during the voyage. Lieutenant Henry Slingsby – of the 2nd King's Own Yorkshire Light Infantry (KOYLI), part of the 5th Division's 13th Brigade – was sternly warned by Brigadier-General G. J. Cuthbert of his duty in the approaching hostilities: 'Remember, that no officer or man of the 13th Infantry Brigade is to surrender'.[7] The divisional commander, Major-General Sir Charles Fergusson, was keyed up to fever pitch a few days later when he addressed the battalion. The KOYLI War Diary reported his message that 'there must be no surrendering, and that men must fight to the last, with their fists if their rifles were useless. That he would be found with them in the last ditch.'[8] Within a week, however, Fergusson would be tamely retiring from the battlefield, his division in disarray.

Such rabble-rousing speeches tended to reflect the uncertainties of the officers making them, and as far as the other ranks were concerned, they seldom impressed. Corporal John Lucy of the 2nd Royal Irish Rifles recalled how, on the cross-Channel voyage, his fellow soldiers were lectured by an officer 'who told the men in melodramatic fashion that the Kaiser had a grasping hand outstretched to seize them, but that the hand was a withered hand. This speech had not quite the effect intended, for it was a source of amusement for the troops for many days, during which we heard humorous and dramatic references to withered hands.' These pep talks, Lucy concluded, 'raised only critical or cynical feelings'.[9]

Lucy arrived in France on 14 August, and after his battalion had assembled at Rouen, it joined the remainder of the BEF in the train journey across northern France to the concentration area between Maubeuge and Le Cateau. Here the units of the BEF would form up into the brigades and divisions that would support the French Fifth Army. As the trains advanced eastwards, the troops were greeted by cheering civilians at every stop. Lucy eventually found the attentions exhausting: 'These French civilians were too excitable by far, and rather upsetting. Had we given them all they demanded as souvenirs we should have eventually fought naked at Mons, armed only with flowers and bon-bons.'[10]

Within the concentration area, there was a rest period of a few days as the BEF placed itself on a war footing. Aubrey Herbert, a civilian attached to the Irish Guards, described the relaxed atmosphere of the time: 'The men had fraternised with the people and, to the irritation of the colonel, wore flowers in their hair and caps. There was no drunkenness – in fact the men complained that there was nothing strong enough to make a man drunk.'[11] Troops helped the local women bring in the harvest (their menfolk already away at the front), while attempts were made to toughen up the reservists with route marches. During their free time the men played football while recovering from brutal inoculations against typhus.

———————————————— • ————————————————

The mobilization of the BEF, its voyage over the Channel (without a single casualty) and rail transfer to the concentration area had been swift and efficient, a quiet triumph of staff work. An effective staff system was obviously essential to the proper working of the army, and once in France the high command and its staff became part of the General Headquarters (GHQ) under Field Marshal Sir John French. GHQ was composed of three branches, each divided into a number of sections. The task of supplying the BEF with food, munitions, transport and other equipment was the responsibility of the Quartermaster General's branch (Q), while the Adjutant General's branch (A) dealt with military personnel, which included the movement of troops to the front, disciplinary matters, soldiers' pay, prisoners of war and medical services and casualties.

Both Q and A branches had performed strongly up to this point, and were to do so for the remainder of the campaign. This would not, however, be the case with the third branch, that of the General Staff (G), whose function was to provide direct military support to the Commander-in-Chief. Under the control of the Chief of the General Staff, Lieutenant-General Sir Archibald Murray, G branch was divided into an intelligence section (I), responsible for gleaning information about the enemy, and an operations section (O), whose role was to prepare and deliver the orders for the direction of the BEF in the field.

In continental Europe, the concept of a general staff that initiated military doctrine and directed the deployment and movement of large armies was well established. In Britain, with its background of fighting small colonial wars, this had not been the case, and it was only in 1906 that the General Staff had come into being. Its influence was limited, however, forced to compete with the already established Q and A branches. It also suffered from the belief held by many commanders that staff officers should not have a directing role in the conduct of operations, but should simply convey the wishes of the Commander-in-Chief.

Whatever the feelings of senior officers, the demand for capable staff officers in 1914 was greater than the supply. The shortage was underlined by the situation found in Haig's I Corps – the only properly constituted corps formation in the British Army – when the intelligence officer Colonel John Charteris encountered one of the new staff officers assigned to the corps. In a letter to his wife, Charteris wrote: 'Colonel X, who has recently blossomed into a staff officer, consulted me very confidentially. "You know all about the army – tell me how many battalions are there in a division?"'[12]

Each division in peacetime was allotted two trained staff officers, augmented to six on the outbreak of war. But according to Colonel J. E. Edmonds, the senior staff officer of the 4th Division (and subsequently the Official Historian), those assigned to his division were either incompetent or lacked interest in their appointment. On assuming command of the Cavalry Division, Major-General Edmund Allenby discovered that he had no permanent staff officers at all, and had to quickly improvise a staff from men with limited experience. These failings would rebound on the BEF when it came to grips with the German Army.

During the late 19th century the army had been reorganized on the basis of the Cardwell system, which, with a few exceptions, combined two regular battalions into a single regiment. One battalion was stationed abroad for extended periods, leaving the home battalion to supply a stream of trained reinforcements to the overseas battalion.

The system worked well enough for the maintenance of Britain's colonial garrisons, but the geographically scattered home battalions (invariably understrength) did not provide an effective tool for the exercise of command, even after the development of a six-division BEF in the early years of the 20th century. The large-scale manoeuvres that would have tested senior officers were infrequent. The units of a divisional command were brought together for six weeks of the year, with just four days spent in army manoeuvres against an opposing formation.

Training facilities were limited too, with the army often forced to negotiate with private landowners on an ad hoc basis for areas in which to conduct tactical exercises. Some idea of the difficult circumstances affecting training can be seen in a simple diary entry made by the commander of the 10th Infantry Brigade, Alymer Haldane. He was forced to conduct a battalion exercise on the golf course at Hythe, and helpfully noted: 'Machine-gun fire. To represent this a biscuit tin hammered with a drum stick is good.'[13]

With or without suitable training opportunities, Britain's generals did not inspire great confidence. Apart from their personal strengths and weaknesses, the system tended to encourage a restrictive approach to command. According to Martin Samuels, British military doctrine considered the conduct of war as inherently structured, and 'effectiveness was seen as being achieved through the maintenance of order'.[14] Even if Samuels has over-emphasized the distinctions between British and German operational theory, the British outlook stressed a strict obedience to orders within a tightly controlled operational framework. As a consequence, commanders lacked the flexibility to respond to the unforeseen circumstances that were inevitably thrown up in war.

●

GHQ crossed over to France on 14 August and took up position in the town of Le Cateau, while Field Marshal French and his immediate staff went by train to Paris to meet the French president and war minister, before driving by motor car to the French general headquarters (GQG) at Vitry-le-François near Reims. There, he was introduced to General Joseph Joffre, the French Commander-in-Chief. Fortunately for Anglo-French relations, both men got on well, forming a mutual respect that would prove vital in negotiating the trials of the coming campaign.

From Reims, French travelled northwards on the 17th to the headquarters of Fifth Army at Rethell to rendezvous with its commander, General Charles Lanrezac. This meeting went badly, however. Lanrezac was one of the few French generals who correctly foresaw that the main German thrust would be made against the French left, thus leaving his

France and Belgium 1914

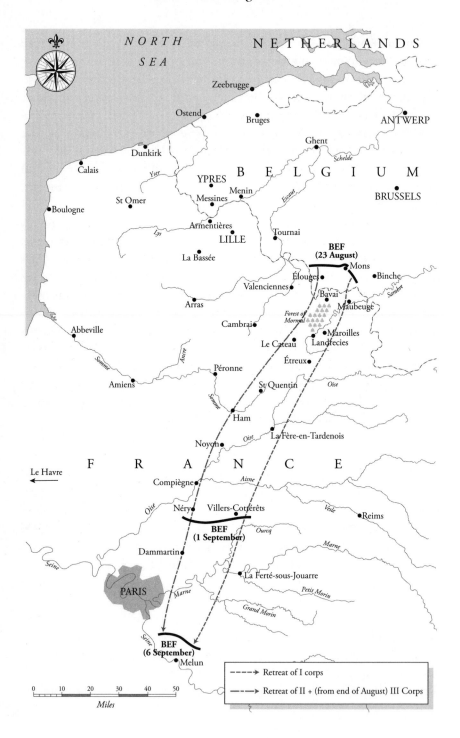

army outnumbered and potentially outflanked. His concern translated into a deepening pessimism, combined with an irritation with the British, based on the unfounded assumption that the BEF had been slow in arriving to support his left flank.

The BEF's commander possessed only schoolboy French, which made the meeting without proper translators present especially fraught. According to the version of the meeting assembled by Lieutenant E. L. Spears (the British liaison officer at Fifth Army), Field Marshal French, struggling with some difficult pronunciation, asked if he thought the Germans would cross the River Meuse at the town of Huy: 'Lanrezac shrugged his shoulders impatiently. "Tell the Marshal," he said curtly, "that in my opinion the Germans have merely gone to the Meuse to fish."'[15] Beyond Lanrezac's sarcasm, the meeting was further undermined by confusion over the deployment of British cavalry and the actual date when the BEF would be fully operational. As a result of these misunderstandings, both armies, although deployed side-by-side, would operate and fight separately.

On leaving Lanrezac's headquarters, French drove to British GHQ at Le Cateau. On arrival he was informed of the fatal heart attack suffered by II Corps commander Lieutenant-General Grierson. French telegraphed London asking for Sir Hubert Plumer to be sent out as Grierson's replacement, but Kitchener spitefully despatched General Sir Horace Smith-Dorrien instead, well aware of the antipathy between the two men. French did, however, receive some good news. On 19 August, the 4th Division, previously held back in England, was released for service in France, and four battalions of infantry originally assigned to act as line-of-communication troops were combined as the 19th Infantry Brigade for front-line use. Buoyed up by this knowledge, French prepared to lead his troops into battle.

CHAPTER THREE

THE MARCH TO MONS

On the evening of 20 August GHQ issued orders for the BEF to march due north, so that by the 23rd it would be holding a line facing north-east between the Belgium village of Lens and the town of Binche. There it would guard the left flank of Lanrezac's Fifth Army, which was also advancing northwards, towards the River Sambre. General Sordet's Cavalry Corps and three divisions of French Territorials would in turn protect the BEF's open left flank, although they had yet to materialize. As to the enemy, news had arrived that troops of General Alexander von Kluck's First Army had entered Brussels, but where the Germans would strike next remained unclear to the Allied high command.

The four brigades of Allenby's Cavalry Division, plus a fifth, independent brigade, led the advance and by the end of the first day had reached Binche and pushed beyond the Condé canal at Mons. The infantry set off in high spirits on the morning of 21 August: the 3rd and 5th Divisions of II Corps marched to the west of Maubeuge, while the 1st and 2nd Divisions of I Corps advanced to the right of II Corps. According to Lance-Corporal A. P. G. Vivian of the 4th Middlesex Regiment, the departure of his battalion resembled more of 'a carnival procession than the grim march of men going to wage war. Flowers and ribbons streamed from the barrels of our rifles, and from every conceivable portion of our uniform, while swarms of giggling and shrieking girls and women weaved in and out our ranks, presenting us with all manner of good things, such as chocolate, fruit and eggs etc.'[1]

Thus far, the BEF – and the French and German armies – had been conducted to war by rail, providing a swift and relatively comfortable transit to the war zone. But once beyond the rail-heads, the infantry were reliant on their own legs, no more mobile than Marlborough's army, which had tramped the same roads two centuries earlier. The strain of the first day's march soon became apparent, the hot weather, the hard, cobble-stoned pavé roads and general unfitness of the reservists all taking their toll.

Harry Beaumont had returned to the 1st Royal West Kents from his job as an insurance agent: 'We were saddled with pack and equipment weighing nearly eighty pounds, and our khaki uniforms, flannel shirts, and thick woollen pants, fit for an Arctic climate, added to our discomfort in the sweltering heat. By midday the temperature reached ninety degrees in the shade! We were soon soaked in perspiration, and all looked almost as if they had been dragged through water!'[2]

Despite the best efforts of the officers, whether carrying rifles and packs or simply encouraging the men, growing numbers began to fall out. A. L. Ransome of the 1st Dorsets recalled the progress of a fellow battalion in the 15th Infantry Brigade: 'I can only describe the battalion in front of us as being in "pear-shaped" formation, with the pear's stalk leading. Its colonel and the adjutant rode at the rear, striving to get the mass of humanity into some semblance of order, but all the time more and more men, reservists, no doubt, dropped out and seated themselves at the road-side.'[3] The brigade commander, Lord Edward Gleichen, was sympathetic to his men's plight:

> Stragglers, I regret to say, were already many – all of them reservists, who had not carried a pack for years. They had every intention of keeping up, of course, but simply could not. I talked to several of them and urged them along, but the answer was always the same – 'Oh, I'll get along all right, sir, after a bit of a rest; but I ain't accustomed to carrying a big weight like this on a hot day', and their scarlet streaming faces certainly bore out their views. To do them justice, they practically all did turn up.[4]

The 52 battalions of infantry struggling through the late August heat towards the Belgium frontier were the chief fighting element of the

BEF, and success would ultimately depend on their battlefield ability. Modest efforts to improve the quality of the infantry had begun in the 1890s, but the overall inadequacies in training, tactics and weapons were brutally exposed in the Boer War. In the aftermath of the war, the reforming process continued with more urgency, but ultimately it was unable to answer the fundamental question of modern warfare: how to develop tactics that would accommodate the recent and revolutionary developments in firepower.

The magazine-fed, bolt-action rifle, which fired a high-velocity bullet using smokeless propellants, had become the standard firearm of the infantryman during the closing years of the 19th century. The modern rifle could fire accurately at large targets up to 1,000 yards, while its flatter trajectory greatly increased the 'killing zone' through which the enemy would have to pass. The new propellants (cordite in the British Army) did not produce the billowing clouds of smoke typical of gunpowder rifles, enabling the rifleman to see his target while not giving away his own position to the enemy. The British Army of 1914 was armed with the excellent .303in. Short, Magazine, Lee-Enfield (SMLE); its high rate of fire produced the devastating barrages that won infantry fire-fights.

A second, fundamental increase in infantry firepower originated in 1884, when the American-born inventor and entrepreneur Hiram Maxim produced the first effective machine gun. The army saw the Maxim's potential, and within ten years it was being used in colonial campaigns in Africa. It was capable of firing around 500 rounds per minute, which gave it the equivalent firepower of just under 30 modern bolt-action rifles.[5] A lighter, improved version was developed by Vickers, and by August 1914, the Vickers – roughly equivalent to 40 rifles – had been issued to the cavalry, although the infantry still relied on the Maxim during 1914.

These advances in firepower gave the defensive enormous advantages over the offensive. Attacking forces moving in close formation would be massacred at long range. To minimize casualties, the attacking troops were forced to spread out, making use of the ground for concealment and protection, with small groups of infantrymen advancing in short rushes, being covered by fire from their comrades. Such tactics made the control of troops by their officers exceptionally difficult, and called for highly trained, self-motivated soldiers who had the nerve and skill to maintain a dispersed advance amidst a storm of steel. Many military commentators believed this to be impossible.

Despite the imbalance between defence and attack, the British Army maintained a determined belief in the inherent superiority of the offensive – a 'cult of the offensive' according to some historians.[6] Military success ultimately depends upon a philosophy of aggressive, offensive action, and, at the tactical level, British commanders were correct in trying to combat the tendency of an advance to stall into a long-range fire-fight with the attackers at a disadvantage. But they lacked an appropriate tactical system to integrate firepower into a war of movement, relying too much on physical courage over tactical finesse.

The focus on the offensive also tended to downgrade attention to a mastery of defensive tactics. 'In order to foster the offensive spirit', wrote the historian of the Cheshire Regiment, 'retirement as an operation of war was ignored during training.'[7] This comment was typical of an overall lack of concern with one of the less exciting branches of military operations. Edward Spiers, writing of the pre-war army, noted that 'some reforms, especially practice in the construction of entrenchments, proved exceedingly tedious in peace time. The poor quality of the entrenching tools, the laborious nature of the task, and the subsequent chore of refilling the trenches, ensured that this was the least relished and least practised of the post [Boer]-war proposals.'[8]

Within the army there was a small group of officers – based around the School of Musketry at Hythe – who demonstrated a fuller understanding of the nature of modern warfare. Major N. R. McMahon, chief instructor at Hythe between 1905 and 1909, urged an increase in the number of the battalion's machine guns from two to six. More radical still, he also called for light machine guns (such as the new Lewis gun) or automatic rifles to be used by attacking troops to provide local fire supremacy in the vital, final phase of the assault.

McMahon and the other progressives were stoutly opposed by the army's reactionary wing, who countered with the argument that increased firepower slowed the tempo of the offensive, which, in turn, undermined the morale and resolve of the soldier. In this they had a point, but their case was totally undermined by a fantastical belief in the primacy of cold steel, despite all evidence to the contrary. An example of this attitude came in the confused series of assertions made by Brigadier-General Launcelot Kiggell – subsequently Commandant at the Staff College, Camberley – during the summation to the 1910 Staff Conference:

> After the Boer War the general opinion was that the result of the battle would depend on fire-arms alone, and that the sword and bayonet were played out. But this idea is erroneous and was proved to be so in the late [Russo-Japanese] war in Manchuria. Every one admits that. Victory is won actually by the bayonet, or by the fear of it, which amounts to the same thing as far as the actual conduct of the attack is concerned. This fact was proved beyond doubt in the late war. I think the whole question rather hangs on that; and if we accept the view that victory is actually won by the bayonet, it settles the point.[9]

Somewhere between the progressives and the reactionaries, and often oscillating between the two poles, were the modest reformers who ultimately held sway in the army, and who included senior officers such as French and Haig. They were well aware of the need for improvement in the army's tactical ability but lacked the vision to comprehend both the problems and the opportunities of the firepower revolution, and, as a consequence, clung to the mental template established in the late-Victorian colonial army of their youth.

Despite the inability of most senior officers to come to terms with new ways of waging war, the decade before 1914 was one of real if limited tactical improvement. This was especially the case with developments in musketry (the tactical use of firearms) carried out by McMahon and his fellow progressives at the School of Musketry, even though they lacked authority to impose their views on the army (hence the rejection of the request for more machine guns).

Marksmanship had been at low ebb during and immediately after the Boer War. At a competition held by the Aldershot Command in 1902, the 12 best marksmen fired 1,210 rounds at targets ranging from 210 to 2,600 yards. Only ten hits were recorded (the results were not published).[10] In the early years of the 20th century much effort was put into improving British marksmanship, ranging from Lord Roberts' efforts to encourage rifle shooting in general to the more specific proposals of the Hythe enthusiasts. McMahon used the rejection of his plea for more automatic weapons as a spur for better musketry. 'There is only one alternative open to us,' he wrote. 'We must train every soldier in our army to become a "human machine gun". Every man must receive intensive training with his rifle until he can fire – with reasonable accuracy – fifteen rounds per minute.'[11]

But McMahon also realized that marksmanship was only a part of the infantry firepower equation. He even spoke out against those obsessed with target shooting, explaining that in field conditions crack shots did little better than soldiers with average shooting skills. The key to success in the infantry fire-fight was to lay down a rapid, intense barrage of fire into a zone that would kill or incapacitate any enemy soldier moving within it. In these conditions, disciplined volume fire was more important than individual accuracy.[12]

As part of the improved tactical training, soldiers fired at realistic targets. C. L. Longley recalled aiming at a 'brown life-sized head and shoulders against a green ground', while Benjamin Clouting of the 4th Dragoon Guards fired at moving, full-sized cavalry targets operated by a pulley.[13] But these imaginative techniques were not universal, and many battalion commanders – who exerted enormous control over training – were content with simple bulls-eye shooting.

Overall, improvements in musketry – and tactics – did make the infantry who took to the field in 1914 far more effective than their predecessors in South Africa, but these advances failed to go far enough in providing a solution to the problem of reducing the terrible vulnerability of troops advancing in the open against a well-entrenched enemy. The best way of protecting attacking troops was through artillery support: smashing in front-line defences and forcing the enemy to keep their heads down and, in so doing, reducing the intensity of their fire. But this was a complex process that demanded training and tactics not yet in place in the British Army.

As was the case with the rifle and machine gun, artillery had also undergone a process of transformation. The introduction of powerful smokeless propellants during the 19th century increased accurate field-gun ranges out to 4,000 yards and more, thus enabling artillery to fire from deep positions at targets beyond the front line, and to maintain a high degree of concealment through the reduction of muzzle smoke.

A further significant advance came with the invention of a hydrostatic buffer and recuperator system that absorbed recoil without any movement of the gun's carriage. This advanced recoil action ensured that the gun was still accurately aligned on target after each shot; there was no need for the crew to manhandle the gun back into position, and this made rapid fire a reality. The new artillery pieces were appropriately known in Britain as Quick Firing (QF). They had a secondary advantage, in that the absence of carriage recoil allowed the gun crew to remain close by their artillery piece at all times, and so could be protected from rifle bullets and shrapnel by the addition of a small steel shield.

The French 75mm field gun, introduced in 1897, was the first of the new QF artillery pieces, producing an extraordinarily high rate of fire of up to 30 rounds per minute. In 1904 the British followed the French lead when the 18-pounder (84mm calibre) field gun entered service, with the smaller and lighter 13-pounder (75mm) assigned to the cavalry. The 18-pounder was an effective field gun, capable of 20 rounds per minute in short bursts and firing an 18½lb shrapnel shell. An infantry division was allotted three brigades of 18-pounders, with each brigade consisting of three six-gun batteries.

During the opening months of the war, British field guns were only supplied with shrapnel shells, and it was not until the battle of Ypres in October that high-explosive shells first arrived at the front line. Although not effective against entrenchments or buildings, accurately fused shrapnel was deadly against troops in the open. An 18-pounder shrapnel shell contained 374 bullets and a small explosive charge. Once the target had been selected, the fuse timer was set to the appropriate distance and primed to burst the explosive charge just above and in front of the chosen spot, causing a hail of bullets to be projected down and forwards on the enemy troops below. Estimating the range correctly involved both skill and luck, and troops on both sides regularly observed shrapnel bursting too high to cause casualties.

The 18-pounder field gun was partnered by the 4.5in. field howitzer, with one brigade of three six-gun batteries allotted to each division. The howitzer entered service in 1910, and as well as shrapnel fired a 35lb high-explosive shell in a high, plunging trajectory that could drop the shell into enemy trenches. The last artillery piece in the BEF's arsenal was the 60-pounder field gun, with a four-gun battery attached to each infantry division. This was the only heavy gun deployed by the British in the first phase of the campaign, and while few in numbers it was an excellent artillery piece, firing a 60lb high-explosive shell in a flat trajectory to a maximum range of 10,300 yards.

The increased rate of fire and extended range of the modern artillery piece opened up new tactical possibilities in both attack and defence. There was the usual struggle between reactionary and progressive elements. The reactionaries failed to grasp the key advantage of modern artillery – that fire could be concentrated while allowing the guns themselves to be dispersed and hidden from enemy view, in what would be called indirect fire. The old guard was still attached to the idea of the guns themselves being concentrated, stretching out in long lines, wheel-to-wheel, and deployed in the front line, firing over open sights directly at the enemy. In the back of their minds was the feeling that there was something cowardly in not deploying the guns amidst the infantry they were there to support.

British artillery was divided into three branches, each with differing approaches to the conduct of operations. The Royal Horse Artillery (RHA) was the most prestigious branch, adopting the dashing approach of the hussar or light dragoon; but, assigned to the cavalry (and armed only with 13-pounders), they were of limited value once major hostilities began. The bulk of the BEF's artillery came under the control of the Royal Field Artillery (RFA), which supported the infantry divisions with their 18-pounders and 4.5in. howitzers. Like the RHA, the RFA highlighted the dashing aspects of their calling at the expense of the technical side. This was the preserve of the decidedly unfashionable Royal Garrison Artillery (RGA), responsible for the long-range heavy artillery that would come to dominate warfare on the Western Front.

Some idea of the artillery's thinking can be seen in this extract from the memoirs of Major-General S. C. M. Archibald, a distinguished artilleryman who was a lieutenant in a battery of 18-pounders in 1914:

When the war broke out early in August 1914 we had almost completed our training season and were pretty smart and efficient, according to our lights. But these lights were somewhat limited. Our gunnery and methods of fire were very simple and elementary. Targets were only engaged by observation, so the battery commander had to get someone where he could see the target. If this was not possible, nothing could be done about it.[14]

Archibald had described one of the enduring problems of indirect fire by observation: if an artillery battery was hidden, then it had to use a forward observer to visually locate the enemy target and guide the battery's fire onto it. The best communication method between observer and battery lay in running out telephone cable between the two, but telephone lines were easily cut, with communication then reliant on runners, semaphore or other forms of visual communication. Only the introduction of wireless would solve the problem, but the necessity of using indirect fire to protect exposed guns from counter-battery fire was essential – as the British were to discover to their cost at Le Cateau.

Archibald also recognized that he and his fellow gunners had little experience of other seemingly arcane but vital aspects of the gunner's craft, such as knowledge of atmospheric conditions, firing by night or map shooting. But his chief criticism was the absence of communication between artillery and infantry: 'There was no liaison between gunners and infantry; in fact it would scarcely be an exaggeration to say that at the beginning of the war, gunners and infantry fought separate wars.'[15] Co-operation between the different arms was the cornerstone of success in battle, and in 1914, for defence and especially attack, this demanded a complete integration of the infantry's rifles and machine guns with the guns of the artillery.

●

At 4 p.m. on 21 September, General Sir Horace Smith-Dorrien arrived in Bavai and took command of II Corps. The next day the BEF crossed into Belgium. Lieutenant G. C. Wynne of the King's Own Yorkshire Light Infantry (KOYLI) was one of many who noticed the change in landscape as they marched over the border:

> During the morning we crossed the Belgium frontier with its small custom-house in a dip of the road and passed from the metalled chaussées of France on to the cobbled roads of Belgium. The difference from the prosperous and neatly kept French farms and the poor ill-conditioned

Belgian cottages was very noticeable. Everything seemed on a poorer scale and dirtier; though perhaps it is scarcely fair to pass judgment on Belgium by one of its uglier parts.[16]

 The BEF had advanced into the Borinage, Belgium's great mining and industrial district, and Wynne described how the view north from the village of Dour was covered 'with mountainous coal-pit slag-heaps and away beyond them to the east could be seen the chimneys of Mons'.[17] The area was criss-crossed with small lanes and light railways, and long, straggling villages that merged into each other. The slag heaps restricted movement and visibility; they would also narrow down the field of fire for the artillery.

 While the infantry continued to march, the cavalry and the Royal Flying Corps (RFC) gathered intelligence. On the afternoon of the 21st an aircraft of the RFC spotted large numbers of German cavalry with infantry and guns south-east of Nivelles, less than 20 miles from Mons. Other reports confirmed the appearance of General von der Marwitz's II Cavalry Corps.

 George Barrow had been co-opted by Major-General Allenby at the outbreak of war to act as the senior intelligence officer in the Cavalry Division. As the division pushed into Belgium, Barrow was assailed by rumours of an impending German onslaught. He drove into Mons on the 21st in an attempt to confirm the truth of these numerous but still vague reports:

With the consent of the French authorities, I took possession of the railway telephone office. Here I sat all day and far into the night ringing up all possible and impossible places in Belgium not known to be in German hands. Replies took the following forms: 'No signs of enemy activity, but rumours they are in A---'. 'Germans are five miles distant on road to B---'. 'Have just received message from C--- that enemy close to town. Germans are on outskirts of town; we are closing down.' A German voice or failure to get contact told that the enemy had already arrived.

 It was easy from these replies to get a fairly accurate picture of the German line of advance. Allenby sent this information on to GHQ. It showed the German right extended much farther west than had been suspected. But GHQ preferred to rely on its own agents and more orthodox intelligence methods. It replied: 'The information which you have acquired and conveyed to the Commander-in-Chief appears to be somewhat exaggerated. It is probable that only mounted troops supported by Jägers are in your immediate neighbourhood.' Events showed that the information was far from exaggerated.[18]

On 21 August the French Fifth Army's advance was abruptly halted by Bülow's Second Army, and by nightfall the French had been thrown back across the Sambre River. Lanrezac's fear of being overwhelmed by superior numbers was reinforced by reports of Hausen's Third Army advancing towards his right flank. On the 22nd Lanrezac ordered a general retreat without informing Field Marshal French, an unfortunate omission that was to have lasting consequences. But on that day, the RFC flew 12 reconnaissance missions that clearly demonstrated the presence of substantial German forces bearing down on the BEF. These aerial reports were backed up by the experiences of the Cavalry Division, which fought a series of sharp engagements with the German cavalry screen advancing from the north.

The 4th Royal Dragoon Guards were the victors in the skirmish north of Mons, guaranteeing them a place in history in the first encounter between the BEF and the German Army. Elsewhere, the 6th Dragoon Guards crossed over the Condé canal to the west of Mons and discovered German cavalry lurking in the woods to the north of the canal. According to the regimental history, 'Several successful mounted attacks against German cuirassiers were carried out by A Squadron, before the regiment withdrew across the two bridges [over the canal] at St Albert.'[19]

To the east of Mons, the independent 5th Cavalry Brigade advanced towards the small town of Binche, acting as the flank guard for the BEF's right wing. Further east still was the French Fifth Army, but no meaningful contact had been made with any French units. Among the brigade's three regiments were the Royal Scots Greys, although their famous grey horses had been dyed a khaki-brown shade for reasons of security.[20]

On their landing in France the Greys had taken on Paul Maze, a bilingual French artist, as a semi-official interpreter. On the morning of the 22nd, Maze reported to regimental headquarters, deployed on a small rise beyond Binche and overlooking a valley where two dismounted squadrons of the Greys had taken up a forward defensive line. Maze trained a telescope on a railway embankment just over a mile away and saw 'a number of little grey figures scrambling down on to the flat. Moving along the railway line more and more were appearing and beyond, from a slight rise in the ground, others were coming up.'[21]

The transformation from peace to war was as swift as it was dramatic: two French cavalrymen were seen escaping from the enemy lines like hunted animals; scouts from the Greys told their CO that they had been attacked by German lancers; and from across the valley a line of gun flashes broadcast the enemy attack with shells exploding around the headquarters. Meanwhile, the two forward companies of the Greys fought off a German attack, claiming at least 30 casualties for the loss of one officer wounded before retiring.

The commander of the nearby 3rd Cavalry Brigade, Brigadier-General Hubert Gough, could see the fight going on around Binche, and he brought up his 16th Lancers and two batteries of Royal Horse Artillery (RHA) in support. The German artillery fire was heavy, if not particularly accurate, and at 11.15 a.m. Gough ordered the guns of E Battery into action; in so doing they fired the first British artillery shells of the war.

To Gough's annoyance, the 13-pounder guns lacked the range to hit their targets.[22] But the battery's gun flashes did not go unnoticed. In a significant portent of the future, Bombardier Saville Crowsley recorded this incident in his diary: 'We had not been long in action before a German aeroplane came hovering over our position, dropped a time fuse, giving the range to our guns, and returned to its own lines. Then came our first experience of being under shell fire as their first round fell in the ground 15 yards from me.'[23] Gough sensibly withdrew the battery to a safer position.

During the afternoon of the 22nd the cavalry of both the 3rd and 5th Brigades moved back to protect Haig's I Corps. The 3rd Brigade then joined the other cavalry brigades advancing westwards to take up position on the left flank of the BEF. The British cavalry commanders were encouraged that their regiments had stood this first test of battle, in part a consequence of the post-Boer War reforms to the cavalry.

During the war in South Africa mounted infantry had often demonstrated a combat edge over conventional cavalry, and calls were made for the entire cavalry arm to be converted in this manner. This was anathema to the influential cavalry lobby, horrified that the 'cavalry spirit' – where man and horse operated in close and sympathetic harmony – would be lost, replaced, in their view, by a foot soldier astride an old nag. The debate between the proponents of mounted infantry – who included the army reformer Lord Roberts – and the cavalry school – with Sir John French in the lead – continued until 1914, and although the cavalry school won the day it incorporated ideas from its opponents.

The enthusiasm of the diehards for lance, sword and the charge was tempered by a serious attempt to come to grips with dismounted action and the effective application of firepower. The new .303in. SMLE rifle was introduced with great attention paid to gaining good musketry skills. In the 14th Hussars, for example, 71 per cent of its troopers had gained their marksman badge in 1908, far in advance of many infantry battalions (by way of comparison, marksman percentages for the 10th Infantry Brigade in 1912 were: 1st Royal Irish Fusiliers, 17.5 per cent; 2nd Seaforth Highlanders, 15.2 per cent; 2nd KRRC, 25.7 per cent; 2nd Royal Dublin Fusiliers, 8.2 per cent).[24] The cavalry also enjoyed the advantage of being equipped with the lighter, more efficient Vickers machine gun.

The Boer War had underlined the importance of good animal care, and the quality of horsemastership demonstrated by the British cavalry was superior to that of the French or Germans. And given the essential fragility of the horse at war, this enabled British cavalry regiments to operate in the field for longer periods.

The intelligence provided by the cavalry (and RFC) on the 21st and 22nd should have rung alarm bells in the minds of Field Marshal Sir John French and GHQ. The bulk of the German First Army – more than twice the size of the BEF – was pressing forward with terrifying haste, holding the potential to overwhelm the British on both flanks. Added to German numerical superiority was the knowledge that its army was considered the finest in Europe.

CHAPTER FOUR

THE KAISER'S ARMY

Prussia's overwhelming success against Austria in 1866 and then over France in 1870 confirmed German military pre-eminence in Europe, and in the years that followed the Imperial German Army set the standard against which others were measured. But Germany's ineptitude in matters of foreign policy led to the formation of a hostile Franco-Russian alliance in the 1890s. This demanded a new focus to German military strategy, which acknowledged that the combined French and Russian forces possessed a substantial material superiority that could not be ignored.

The eventual German strategic response was to rely on its geographical advantage of operating on interior lines, and to use its extensive rail network to strike first against France and then to redeploy its armies eastward against Russia. The strategy was undoubtedly a gamble, but its planners reassured themselves with their belief in the superiority of the German Army's organization and tactics.

Central to the German approach to waging war was *Auftragstaktik*, which roughly translated means 'a mission-based command'. This concept gained momentum during the 19th century, as German armies became too large and dispersed for a single commander to control in detail. Rather than issue a specific set of orders to a subordinate, the commander provided a directive or goal to be achieved. The subordinate was expected to display initiative and was given latitude in how the mission was to be carried out, but central to its success was the subordinate's fundamental knowledge of the commander's intent, which was made possible by the establishment of a commonly accepted military doctrine.

This form of command depended on a dynamic relationship between commander and subordinate, with each aware of the other's actions. *Auftragstaktik* acted as a model for what might be achieved and inevitably did not always work perfectly in actuality, but it was superior to the passive and restrictive nature of the British way of command.

The German Great General Staff, which dated back to the Napoleonic Wars, was at the heart of the German command system. It was an elite organization that secured the services of able and ambitious officers, with a close relationship between positions on the staff and command in the field. The rather facile distinction – often made in the British Army – between staff officers (over-privileged) and regimental officers (lacking in intelligence) would have been scorned by members of the German General Staff.

Within each large German formation the commander was supported by his chief of staff. He acted as the junior partner in the command relationship, but his advice was to be ignored at the commander's peril. This concept of dual command was rejected by most armies, but according to one German commentator, 'the relationship between the commander and his chief of staff is expected to conform to that prevailing in a happy marriage. The two men are expected to form a unity rather than two distinct personalities, supplementing each other, composing any differences that might arise without distinguishing the share which each of them contributes to the common good.'[1]

A further reason for the exalted position of the chief of staff was a throwback to the aristocratic system of senior commanders being drawn from Germany's noble houses, so that deficiencies in military expertise were rectified by the presence of the professionals from the General Staff. By and large, the system of dual command worked well. The Kaiser's son, Crown Prince Wilhelm, was given command of Fifth Army, although it came under the direction of the army chief of staff, Major-General Konstantin Schmidt von Knobelsdorf.

●

On the eve of war the German peacetime field army stood at 782,344 soldiers, which on mobilization increased to 2,100,000.[2] Men called to the colours came from those recently discharged from military service; they were still in good physical condition and were familiar with the latest weapons and tactics. And ties with their parent unit remained strong, as one British observer noted: 'A German squadron, battery or company officer will recognize his command after mobilization whereas our officers will not.'[3]

Germany's system of conscription stated that all males were liable to military service for two years on reaching the age of 20. Each year produced a cohort of 600,000 men, but around half were turned away. This allowed the army to select the more promising recruits but, on the other hand, it failed to provide sufficient numbers of regular troops to realistically carry out the plans of the General Staff for the successful conduct of a two-front war.[4]

Set against a population of 65 million in 1914, the German Army was surprisingly small, especially when compared with that of its main rival, France (39 million), whose field army stood at around 700,000 (excluding colonial troops).[5] That the German Army had failed to expand to meet the demands of a two-front war was a product of several factors: a fear that expanding the size of officer corps would dilute its aristocratic character; the restrictions on funding from the German government (also paying for a massive programme of naval expansion); and a general belief in quality over quantity.

This inability to match numbers to operational requirements led to the anomalous situation where second-line formations were required to take their place alongside regulars at the outbreak of war. This would have disastrous consequences for the Germans when forced to deploy reserve divisions en masse against the Allies at Ypres in October 1914.

Two years of military service was considered sufficient to produce a well-trained soldier, although the German Army worked on the principle of each man being combat-ready at a basic level by the end of the first year. The recruit was instructed in the two essentials of a successful infantryman: to march long distances, and to achieve a high level of competence in the use of his rifle. He was armed with the 7.92mm Mauser, a bolt-action rifle with a five-round magazine. It was comparable to the British Lee-Enfield, being slightly more accurate but with a slightly slower rate of fire. German infantry training was rigorous and took into account the realities of modern warfare. And despite Allied claims to the contrary, the German soldier was not an automaton driven on by his officers.

A foolish myth propagated in the British Official History, and repeated in a succession of memoirs and histories, was that the Germans were so overwhelmed by British rifle fire that they literally confused it with that of machine guns.[6] It should hardly need saying that the steady chugging sound of a belt-fed Maxim or Vickers machine gun (from a single source) bore no resemblance to the dispersed, uneven crackle of bolt-action rifle fire. Numerous contemporary accounts confirm this distinction; medical officer Arthur Martin compared the sound of the 'typewriter Maxim' against the 'phut of a Mauser bullet'.[7]

There is also a lack of documentary evidence to suggest that such claims were made at all. German troops were often impressed by the discipline, accuracy and intensity of British rifle fire.[8] In a British report on the battle of the Aisne, one German prisoner apparently said of the British infantry, 'that every man must be equipped with a machine gun, so hot was the fire'. But this was intended as a flattering metaphor, and no more than that.[9]

Nor did German infantrymen advance firing from the hip, as has often been claimed. Again, the idea in itself is nonsensical, a counter-intuitive practice that would be seen as bizarre to a well-trained infantryman of any army. Terence Zuber reasonably suggests that this fallacy came from a British miss-sighting of German troops advancing with their rifles at the trail, that is, held in one hand to the side of the soldier's body.[10]

Within the German Army, special attention was paid to the development of Non-Commissioned Officers (NCOs), selected from the ranks or from special NCO training schools where promising adolescents looking for a military career were fast-tracked in military and leadership skills. The NCO was expected to demonstrate initiative and, in keeping with the concept of *Auftragstaktik*, was given an opportunity to make his own decisions in the light of operational requirements. The NCO enjoyed a high status within the army, and on successful completion of his time with his regiment was guaranteed a job within the civil service.

The army corps was the largest permanent formation in the German Army, and each of the original 25 active corps was assigned a specific area – usually corresponding to a historic region – from where it drew its recruits. Thus each corps had its own regional character, providing an emotional attachment for the troops of that formation. As an example, Kluck's First Army possessed a strong Prussian feel, with II Corps based in Pomerania and III Corps drawing upon Brandenburgers.

Each corps comprised two infantry divisions, along with specialist troops that included a battalion of Jäger light infantry, pioneers, a squadron of aircraft and four batteries of 15cm heavy howitzers. The German division was broadly similar in size, organization and equipment to that of its British equivalent, each fielding 12 infantry battalions and an artillery component of 70-plus guns.

Germany's field artillery was organized on a divisional basis, with each division deploying two regiments (a total of 72 guns) that were subdivided into two sections each of three six-gun batteries. There were two kinds of artillery piece: a 7.7cm field gun and a 10.5cm light howitzer. Both guns were capable of firing either shrapnel or high explosive (plus a not very successful composite shrapnel/high-explosive shell). The howitzer was a modern weapon, and its shell's high trajectory would become increasingly useful as trench warfare developed. The older field gun, however, compared less well with the French 75mm field gun and the British 18-pounder.

Where German artillery excelled was in its mobile heavy field pieces, notably the 15cm (5.9in.) and 21cm (8in.) heavy howitzers, the latter organized at army level. They had a fearsome psychological effect against troops in the open and were capable of ripping apart trenches and other field fortifications. The British and French had neglected heavy artillery, preferring the fast-firing light and medium guns of open warfare. Both nations would be forced to repair this omission, raiding their arsenals for obsolescent guns to fill the gap until new models could be manufactured.

As in other nations, the cavalry enjoyed an exhalted social position within the German Army. Massed cavalry charges had been a traditional feature of the German autumn manoeuvres, their prime function seemingly to please the Kaiser. But these colourful displays obscured the reality of German cavalry deployment in 1914, with horsemen relegated to less exalted but more useful reconnaissance duties.

The German mounted arm was divided into divisional cavalry, with a cavalry regiment assigned to each infantry division, and strategic cavalry, organized as independent cavalry divisions or corps. The strategic cavalry formations combined the twin functions of reconnaissance, providing intelligence of enemy positions and movement, and screening, protecting the main army by repelling the enemy's own reconnaissance patrols. Ten cavalry divisions were assigned to the West, but as they were evenly deployed along the German line there were insufficient numbers on the open German right flank where horsemen would be most useful. They were also poorly handled by senior commanders during the 1914 campaign, so that Kluck remained largely in the dark as to the whereabouts of French and British forces.

All cavalry units were equipped with lances, hence their blanket description by the Allies as 'uhlans' (lancers). They were additionally armed with swords and carbines, the latter weapon inferior in range and accuracy to the Lee-Enfield rifles carried by their mounted British opponents. As a consequence, German cavalrymen were not expected to engage in sustained fire-fights but, instead, retire on their supporting infantry when under attack. In the strategic formations, a cavalry division was equipped with a machine gun company and a large battalion of Jäger light infantry. As well as the standard four infantry companies, the Jäger battalion had a bicycle company and its own six-gun machine gun company, which, along with extra ammunition transports, gave it a total strength of around 1,500 men.

That the Jäger battalions fielded six machine guns was evidence of the army's commitment to this new weapon. The Germans had been slow in adopting the machine gun, believing it too cumbersome and too likely to jam for front-line deployment. But their successful use by the Japanese Army in Manchuria – where swathes of Russians were mown down by Japanese bullets – changed attitudes, as did a reduction in the weapon's weight and an improvement in reliability. Utilizing the Maxim recoil action, the MG-08 was still a cumbersome weapon, and mounted on a sled it required three or four men to manhandle it over rough ground. Its advantages, however, more than compensated for any shortcomings: not only did it have a high rate of fire (500 rounds per minute) but the machine-gun commander could immediately concentrate fire on a given point in the enemy's line when required.

In contrast to the British, who assigned two machine guns per infantry battalion, the Germans brigaded their weapons into a six-gun company for each (three-battalion) regiment. In 1912 a move was made to increase the number of machine guns to six per battalion, and although only partially achieved by August 1914 'most active regiments,' according to Samuels, 'went to war with two six-gun companies'.[11] By 1914 machine guns were well integrated into tactical doctrine, both for offensive and defensive operations, with an emphasis on concentrated and aggressive front-line action.

Of even greater significance than the machine gun for the future conduct of war was another new technological development: aviation.[12] Baron Ferdinand von Zeppelin had pioneered rigid airships, building the first of his distinctive cigar-shaped craft that would bear his name in 1900. Prompted by public enthusiasm, the army bought two Zeppelins in 1909 to supplement the non-rigid blimps already in service. Little interest was shown in aircraft, until German observers at the Reims air week of 1909 became aware of advances made by the French Army.

The Taube monoplane – with its distinctive bird-like wings, more hawk than dove – entered German service in 1911, and would become the most numerous aircraft type during the 1914 campaign. Aircraft were faster and more manoeuvrable than airships, and could operate in fairly bad weather. The Germans still persevered with the Zeppelin, because it could communicate directly with the ground by radio–telegraph and its range of 280 miles was far greater than that of any aircraft. And its strong, internal aluminium frame provided a means for carrying bombs and machine guns. In 1914, five Zeppelins were deployed in the West, but Z–9, based in Düsseldorf and assigned to overfly Belgium in support of Kluck's First Army, was grounded during August because of turbulent atmospheric conditions.[13] This deprived the Germans of the long-range intelligence that might have located the presence of the BEF, then marching to take up position alongside the French Fifth Army.

A further reconnaissance failing was revealed in the operational deployment of German aircraft; while they had a flying time of up to five hours and a maximum range of 125 miles, they were typically restricted to shorter ranges – between 35 and 60 miles – replicating cavalry reconnaissance patrols.[14] As a consequence, aerial intelligence was confined to the tactical rather than strategic sphere. But the Germans were in the forefront of air-artillery co-operation. From the outset of hostilities, the soldiers of the BEF would see aircraft circling over them, letting off flares and dropping streamers for German gunners to locate their positions.

●

As in all armies, the constituent elements of the German Army varied in quality, but, crucially, the Germans were better in welding these components into an effective whole. The 1888 Regulations formed the bedrock of German tactical practice and demonstrated a prescient understanding of how the power of the defence could only be overcome by attackers gaining a localized fire superiority through the co-ordination of rifle and artillery fire (and subsequently that of machine guns).

The 1888 Regulations were amended in 1906 and 1911, with a greater emphasis given to encouraging the offensive spirit, whatever the cost. This was a retrograde step but it reflected the understandable fears of senior officers that their troops would buckle under the strains of modern combat. There was always a discontinuity between the training manuals' idealized proposals and what regimental officers and NCOs could or would carry out. The new regulations therefore attempted to make tactical movements easier to carry out.[15] Even on manoeuvres the natural fallibility of ordinary soldiers was evident, so that, for example, infantry would be seen bunching together at critical moments or attacks would be rushed forward without the necessary artillery support.

In the ultimate challenge of combat itself, German troops would also sometimes fail to maintain the standards set by the army regulations. During the initial assault on the Belgian city of Liège on 5 August, General Otto von Emmich launched a clumsy attack on Fort Barchon that was repulsed with heavy loss. The engagement, described by a Belgian officer, did not reflect well on German tactical ability: 'They made no attempt at deploying, but came on line after line, almost shoulder to shoulder, until as we shot them down, the fallen were heaped on top of each other in an awful barricade of dead and wounded that threatened to mask our guns.'[16]

The assault by the German 4th Cavalry Division on Halen on 11–12 August was also poorly handled, with whole regiments mounting vainglorious charges against well-prepared Belgian positions and suffering heavily as a consequence.[17] And at least one of the attacks made against British positions along the Condé canal at Mons on 23 August was poorly planned and executed.[18] But in the main, the Germany Army demonstrated a high level of competence in the tactical and operational spheres.

In the realm of grand strategy, however, Germany was to demonstrate fundamental weaknesses that would ultimately bring about its downfall. Despite the growing influence of the German parliament (*Reichstag*), ultimate power in Germany still resided in a highly militarized aristocratic elite with the unstable and bellicose Kaiser Wilhelm at its head. Both Wilhelm and the leaders of the German Army and Navy had a poor grasp of international affairs but felt no hesitation in making ill-conceived interventions in foreign policy – both before and during the war.

Within the General Staff, its renowned technical ability was undermined by a cynical naivety towards the wider world. When drawing up plans for an assault against France, the Chief of the General Staff, Count Alfred von Schlieffen, openly contemplated a breach of Belgian neutrality, working on the assumption that the French would have already done so.[19] He even harboured the possibility that Belgium might ally itself with Germany as a consequence of the French actions. His successor, Helmuth von Moltke, and the General Staff were astonished to learn that the invasion of Belgium had produced a strongly negative response in Britain. 'In its presumptions as to British intentions,' writes Hew Strachan, 'the German General Staff showed how it projected its own strategic outlook, its cavalier approach to the question of neutrality, on to its opponents.'[20]

As to the attack in the West, the debate over German strategic planning remains controversial. After the war, German generals, eager to avoid responsibility for the failure to secure victory in 1914, heaped blame on the deceased Moltke on the basis that he had 'tampered' with a plan developed by Schlieffen. Recent research has revealed that the 'Schlieffen Plan' – written in 1905 at the end of Schlieffen's tenure of command – was not a fixed set of operational orders but a memorandum (*Denkschrift*), a discussion document that was also an oblique request to the War Ministry for an increase in the size of the army.[21]

Moltke's 1914 strategy was more flexible than the 'Schlieffen Plan' suggested. He did place the main weight of German forces on the right (northern) flank, with the intention of driving through Belgium to outflank the French, but, rightly or wrongly, he also hoped to exploit weaknesses in the French offensive into Lorraine, with German counter-attacks being launched in the central part of the line depending on circumstances. And, deep in the psyche of all German General Staff officers, was the golden prospect of repeating Hannibal's great victory over the Romans at Cannae, with both flanks encircling the enemy forces to bring about their annihilation. As a consequence, the left (southern) flank of the German line, while expected to defend in the first instance, was always more than a holding screen. But Moltke's central problem remained constant: he lacked sufficient manpower to guarantee success against Russia and a resurgent France, soon to be be joined by Belgium and then Britain. This dilemma was never satisfactorily resolved.

In the hours before war was declared, Germany attempted to browbeat the Belgians into letting its armies march through their country, but the refusal led to the German invasion. Small and poorly equipped, the Belgian Army could not halt the German juggernaut, but after the loss of Liège and Brussels it retreated back to the fortress of Antwerp to continue to fight. General von Kluck's First Army marched through Brussels on 20 August, and while the bulk of his army swung southward to begin its envelopment of the French left wing, he was obliged to divert forces to contain the Belgians in Antwerp. On the 21st, Bülow's Second Army smashed into Lanrezac's Fifth Army, throwing it back across the Sambre. If Bülow could lock Fifth Army in battle, it would allow Kluck's forces to drive around Fifth Army's left flank and rear to destroy it in detail. But, unknown to the Germans, the BEF now lay between Kluck's First Army and the French.

CHAPTER FIVE

ENCOUNTER AT MONS

After his march through Brussels on 20 August, General von Kluck was greatly vexed by the order subordinating his forces to General von Bülow's Second Army. As well as being forced to advance directly south from Brussels to maintain position alongside Second Army, Kluck temporarily lost control of the three divisions of General von der Marwitz's II Cavalry Corps. Kluck had hoped to advance on a more westerly course, using Marwitz's cavalry to protect his open right flank and at the same time track down the BEF.

Kluck had been misinformed by the German Supreme Command that the British would most likely land at Calais, Dunkirk and Ostend, and that their lines of supply and communication would run directly from these three ports. As a consequence, Kluck believed the British to be to the west of his line of advance – and not, as they actually were, directly in front of him to the south. The further he pushed south the more concerned he became about a British presence on his right flank. Even on the morning of 23 August, reports of enemy troops detraining at Tournai led Kluck to halt First Army for two hours in anticipation of wheeling west to engage what might be the BEF. And, having regained control of Marwitz's Corps, he sent it on an exhausting march towards Tournai, a fruitless mission as the enemy was discovered to be no more than a brigade of French reservists retiring on Lille.

The First Army orders for the 23rd anticipated a straightforward day's marching through and around Mons. It was only when German patrols were repeatedly fired upon by British troops that Kluck realized he had stumbled upon the BEF.

While German cavalry and aircraft had been unable to locate the BEF before the morning of the 23rd, during the previous two days British intelligence had assembled a worryingly accurate picture of German strength – even if this information went largely unheeded by the Commander-in-Chief. Colonel George Macdonogh, the senior intelligence officer at GHQ, had attempted to alert Field Marshal French of the danger to the BEF's exposed left flank, but infected by Major-General Henry Wilson's contagious optimism, French blithely discounted Macdonogh's warnings and insisted the advance continue.

On the morning of the 22nd French had encountered Lieutenant Edward Spears, the British liaison officer with the French Fifth Army. Spears brought disquieting news that Fifth Army had been attacked by the German Second Army the previous day. French remained unconcerned, however, and only in the evening when Spears returned to GHQ did the first seeds of doubt enter French's mind. Spears explained that matters were worse than he had first feared, that the Fifth Army advance had been repulsed, leaving the BEF in a position 9 miles ahead of the French line, with a gap of several miles extending between the two armies. The BEF was dangerously exposed, with both flanks now vulnerable to German assault.[1]

French convened a meeting with his staff, informing them that as a precautionary measure the advance for the following day would be postponed. After the meeting, a French officer from Fifth Army arrived at GHQ asking the BEF to launch an attack against the flank of the German Second Army. This was a patently ridiculous request, potentially exposing the flank and rear of the BEF to German attack. French refused but said he would hold his ground around Mons on 23 August.

The British position was in no sense a defensive one; it was merely where the BEF had halted after their day's march on the 22nd. It would have been wiser to have withdrawn a few miles further south, where the ground was better suited to holding the line, but French remained unconvinced of the size of the force approaching the BEF. Nor did he wish to be seen to be letting his ally down through a precipitate withdrawal.

Haig's I Corps was echeloned in a diagonal line from the village of Harmignies to Grand Reng, and would take a minimal part in the forthcoming encounter. The battle would be fought in the area allotted to Smith-Dorrien's II Corps, which comprised the town of Mons and a line along the Condé Canal, which ran directly west from Mons. The canal projected northwards around Mons and the village of Nimy, creating a salient that became the forward part of the British line. Behind Mons were a number of small hills, the most notable being the thickly wooded Bois la Haut and Hill 93, both of which provided good observation to the north and east of the town.

The canal itself was about 20 yards wide, and while not fordable there were 18 crossing points along the stretch held by the British. The land on both sides of the canal was intersected by a myriad of artificial watercourses that made cross-country movement difficult, although the chief concern of the British remained the profusion of slag heaps on the southern side that severely restricted the artillery's field of fire. Of this area the Official History was moved to write in disapproving tones:

> The space occupied by the II Corps in particular, within the quadrangle Mons–Frameries–Dour–Boussu, is practically one huge unsightly village, traversed by a vast number of devious cobbled roads which lead from no particular starting-point to no particular destination, and broken by pit-heads and colossal slag-heaps, often over a hundred feet high. It is, in fact, a close and blind country, such as no army had yet been called upon to fight in against a civilised enemy in a great campaign.[2]

French met his corps and divisional commanders at 5.30 a.m. on the 23rd to inform them of his decision to temporarily halt the BEF at Mons. Orders were issued to Smith-Dorrien to strengthen his forward line and prepare the bridges over the canal for demolition. As the meeting concluded the first German patrols were edging forward towards Mons. French, however, was not overly concerned at the German threat, a belief confirmed by his decision to leave his headquarters and motor over to Valenciennes. There he would inspect the newly constituted 19th Infantry Brigade, due to take up position on the left of II Corps. French would not return until the afternoon, effectively leaving the BEF leaderless during the opening stages of the engagement.

Smith-Dorrien deployed his 5th Division on the left, along the Condé Canal from the bridge at Le Petit Crepin to Jemappes, while his 3rd Division, on the right, continued the defensive line along the canal to Mons and then around the Nimy salient to the road to Harmignies, where it met up with Haig's I Corps. Smith-Dorrien realized this line was far from ideal and began to prepare a better position to the south in case he was hard-pressed by the Germans. The Nimy salient was especially vulnerable, and it was this area that would come under the initial and most intense German attack.

•

Three German army corps from Kluck's First Army would be involved in the battle. First into action, against the Nimy salient and the British right, was IX Corps, followed by III Corps's attack on the British centre, with IV Corps arriving in the late afternoon to advance on the British left.

The whole line taken by the British II Corps was stretched dangerously thin, and nowhere was this more the case than in the Nimy salient, with just the 4th Royal Fusiliers and 4th Middlesex holding an extended line that was open to artillery and machine-gun fire from three sides. Lieutenant Kinglake Tower of the Royal Fusiliers was inspecting his outpost line at around 8 a.m. when he saw one of his sentries bring down a German cavalryman who had emerged from woods 300 yards distant. A second German patrol was also ambushed, and a wounded officer taken to the rear.

Like so many other soldiers on that day, Tower was taken by the strange unreality of the transition from peace to war, especially as the local people seemed largely oblivious to what was going on around them. 'By this time the sun was getting quite hot', he wrote. 'A gorgeous morning and the church bells were ringing for service and the Belgian peasants could be seen walking quietly to church. What a contrast and it seemed hardly believable that we were at war and that a few men had just been killed only a few yards away.'[3] But with the Germans so obviously close, Tower tried to gather more precise details of their numbers and line of advance:

I stopped at the little level crossing where there was an old Belgian station master and his daughter, and I asked them to telephone up the line and try and find out if there were many German troops about. The reply came back from the next station: 'German cavalry, infantry and guns have been passing here continuously for the last three hours and are still doing so.' With this news I hurried across the canal and sent it to headquarters.[4]

On the German side, the commander of IX Corps swiftly deployed his field batteries, concentrating fire on the salient shortly before 9 a.m. The men of the 4th Middlesex were in a difficult position; the two forward companies were out of touch with the rest of the battalion and hopelessly outnumbered. Although B Company was able to fall back to the battalion under a mass of shrapnel and high explosive, D Company suffered heavy casualties. The collapse of the British forward line allowed the Germans a relatively easy passage over the canal.

Captain T. S. Wollocombe, 4th Middlesex adjutant stationed at battalion headquarters, noticed the novel and unpleasant effect of shell fire on their nerves: 'Men were getting a bit jumpy, not being used to such firing, so we [the officers] couldn't afford to do much ducking (although it is difficult not to do it instinctively) or it would have made them worse.'[5]

German pressure mounted, and at around 1 p.m. a platoon from A Company, under the command of a sergeant, was spotted retiring without orders. Lieutenant-Colonel C. P. A. Hull, the battalion CO, was furious, threatening to have the sergeant shot. Wollocombe helped intercept the retreating men and 'got them back to the line by the track in front of us. They did not seem to mind coming back in the least. The CO asked no questions then, but the sergeant was left missing after the action and so nothing more was said about it.'[6]

Shortly before this incident, Wollocombe had received a message from the 8th Brigade headquarters: '"You will decide when bridges and boats within your zone should be destroyed – acknowledge." I acknowledged in the ordinary way. It was too late. The enemy were across or crossing.'[7] That this message had been sent (just before 1 p.m.) – with the Middlesex Regiment fighting for its life – reflected the lack of grip that was typical of British command. It was only when the 4th Middlesex had lost the fight for the salient that the brigade reserve – the

2nd Royal Irish Regiment – was sent forward to provide assistance. By then, however, German fire was so heavy that the Irish were pinned down, unable to help their beleaguered Middlesex comrades.

The 4th Royal Fusiliers – commanded by Lieutenant-Colonel McMahon, the former chief instructor of the School of Musketry – were also hard-pressed. Lieutenant Tower was in the front line:

> The Germans still continued to advance, the more we shot the more appeared until the whole country in front of us was alive with them running like little ants. Guns had now been brought up and the deafening crashes of the shrapnel shells bursting on top of us added to the continuous roar of rifle fire. Heavy shells were falling in the town of Mons about a mile behind us, and I remember seeing a church tower collapse and fall into the street. We were, however, too busy to look behind us, for the enemy were just getting closer and closer to us in front and had now began to bring massed machine gun fire to bear on our parapets on the canal bank.[8]

As the British struggled to hold the salient, the line along the Condé Canal had also come under attack: an artillery bombardment at 10.30 a.m., followed 30 minutes later by an infantry assault. Three battalions from the British 9th Brigade – deployed immediately to the west of Mons – were unable to counter the progress made by the German 6th Division. The German infantry, supported by their artillery, pushed forward in short bounds, making steady progress. The defenders were reliant on rifles and machine guns, the British gunners unable to provide useful assistance. By 2.30 p.m. the Germans had advanced to within 200 yards of the canal near Jemappes, held by the 1st Royal Scots Fusiliers.

Although GHQ had issued an order for the canal crossings to be prepared for demolition, this had been poorly carried out. In some instances there had been insufficient time to lay charges, in others the charges were incorrectly laid or lacked the appropriate detonators. Officers and men of the Royal Engineers worked gallantly under fire in an attempt to blow the bridges – winning many medals for their bravery – but the simple truth was that far too many crossings remained intact.

At Jemappes only one of the three bridges had been destroyed. Intense German fire forced the Scots Fusiliers – and the 1st Northumberland Fusiliers immediately to the west – to withdraw, allowing the Germans to cross the canal. More German troops followed, and by 4 p.m. a sizeable force was pushing south to high ground above Jemappes.

Further west along the canal, the 13th Brigade defended the line on either side of St Ghislain. Rather than hold just the canal line, the two forward battalions – the 1st Royal West Kents and 2nd King's Own Scottish Borderers (KOSB) – occupied strongpoints on the northern side and stood their ground as the Germans advanced. This had the advantage of breaking up the German attack, which was further impeded by the dykes and osier beds that were especially profuse in this area.

The British also benefitted from direct artillery support from the 120th Battery, its 18-pounder guns wheeled into the front line around St Ghislain. Deploying guns so far forward was always a risky business and during the day the battery suffered casualties (and the loss of two guns during the withdrawal). But this was a position that provided a good field of fire, and the gunners were joined by the brigade's full complement of eight machine guns. Together, they did much to stall the German advance.[9]

Further to rear, the four 60-pounders of Major Christopher de Sausmarez's 108th Heavy Battery searched out targets behind the German front line. There was a great cheer, when the battery hit 'a German ammunition wagon at 5,600 yards, firing an H.E. (Lyddite) shell'.[10]

The German attack against St Ghislain was made by the 12th Infantry Regiment (known as the 'Brandenburg Grenadiers' in most British sources), and was poorly planned and executed, the troops rushing forward without gaining fire superiority. Harry Beaumont of the 1st Royal West Kents described his part in the action:

We advanced over the bridge at St Ghislain, and took up position in a glass factory on the opposite side of the canal. Its walls were quickly loopholed. Here, concealed from the enemy's view, and covered from his shell-fire, we came into action for the first time. The country in front of our position was flat, and dotted with numerous circular fenced-in copses, a common feature of that part of Belgium. The Germans, moving between them, made easy targets, and we opened fire. Their losses that afternoon must have been tremendous.[11]

Just what these losses were has been a matter of some debate. One enthusiastic claim suggested 3,000 total casualties, but this is surely fanciful, as this figure comprised the entire strength of the regiment.[12] A more sensible, if low number, was just over 600 men killed, wounded and missing.[13]

Further west along the canal, part of the 2nd KOSB and 1st East Surreys faced the assault of the German 52nd Infantry Regiment. Both British battalions had companies on the northern side of the canal but were unable to halt the Germans' progress. The forward line of the KOSB fell back in reasonable order, and on seeing this retirement at around 6 p.m., the CO of the East Surreys ordered his C Company, north of the canal, to similarly retire. But C Company's position was divided by a high railway embankment running north to south; the troops of the western side failed to receive the order and were surrounded by Germans. On realizing the danger the remainder of C Company made a desperate bayonet charge to break through the enemy ring but most were cut down or captured.

The East Surreys' A Company had been held back in reserve, and it was now rushed forward to reinforce the main defensive line along the canal. Lieutenant George Roupell, a platoon commander in A Company, recalled seeing the Germans coming through a wood about 200 yards from his position:

> Our men had a good firing position and a clear target at short range but in spite of this a number of them were firing high. I could only tell this from seeing the branches fall from the trees about the German heads but I found it hard to control the fire as there was so much noise. Eventually I drew my sword and walked along the line beating the men on the backside and, as I got their attention, telling them to fire low; so much for all our beautiful fire orders taught in peace time! The Germans made several attempts to penetrate from the wood but each attempt was met by rapid fire, and those of the enemy not hit retired back into the wood out of sight.[14]

The 2nd King's Own Yorkshire Light Infantry (KOYLI) had moved up from its reserve position at Boussu to a line just south of the canal, ready to support the KOSB if required. Lieutenant G. C. Wynne of the KOYLI sheltered in the swampy ground a hundred yards from the canal, and spent most of the afternoon awaiting further orders:

> Wounded of the Scottish Borderers began to come or were carried through the orchard and thence across a field we were in and through a wood

behind into Boussu. Five unfortunate white cows in the field across the road were constantly being hit and careered madly about the field, each hit showing itself most gruesomely upon them. Two succumbed eventually but the others managed to cross a deep dyke and get away.[15]

Shortly after 6 p.m. the KOYLI were finally ordered forward to take up positions along the canal and cover the retirement of the KOSB. The men were soaked, wading through the dykes to reach the canal, but once there they opened fire on the Germans, who made no attempt to cross the canal.

Immediately to the left of the East Surreys, at the most westerly point in the British front line, were the 1st Duke of Cornwall's Light Infantry (DCLI) and the 1st Middlesex, the latter battalion from the independent 19th Infantry Brigade that had marched to the line from Valenciennes. Their position was vulnerable, but the two divisions of the German IV Corps only reached the canal late in the afternoon. After some light skirmishing, the British withdrew as darkness fell. The Germans were content to hold their position on the canal and wait until morning to resume their advance.

●

The desultory nature of the fighting on the far left of the British line came in marked contrast to the desperate struggle for the Nimy salient. By mid-afternoon, the guns of the German 18th Infantry Division, ringing the salient, were fully ranged-in and as many as 26 machine guns had been brought up to pour fire onto the wavering line held by the three British battalions.[16] The position held by the 4th Middlesex was in serious danger of being overrun, and shortly after 3 p.m., the Middlesex – along with the Royal Irish Regiment – fell back, eventually to form a new line to the south of Mons. Disengaging from a fire-fight with enemy infantry less than 200 yards away is always a difficult business, and although the Official History wrote that the retreat was 'conducted methodically and in good order',[17] it was something of an undignified scramble as the British soldiers turned and ran for cover, successfully re-forming below the southern slopes of Bois la Haut.

The 4th Royal Fusiliers – to the left of the Middlesex in the Nimy salient – were in a similar situation. Reinforcements under the command

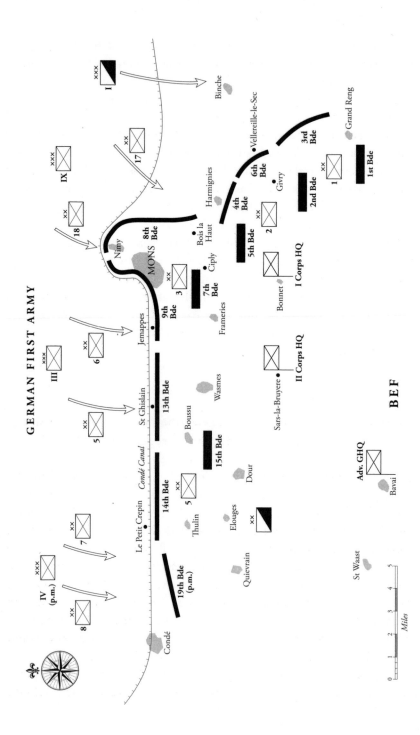

of Captain W. A. C. Bowden-Smith were despatched to shore up the front line, but, according to Lieutenant Tower, most were hit by enemy fire as they ran forward:

> I had a shot which took off my hat and another through my sleeve and two bits of shrapnel in my puttees but untouched. Captain Bowden-Smith was hit with shrapnel in the stomach and lay at my feet in fearful agony. One could do nothing for the wounded, and now the enemy had got around our right flank – the Middlesex Regiment retired without letting us know. We were now being shot at from all sides and the position was hopeless.[18]

Ordered to retire, Tower collected what men he could immediately find – just six fusiliers – and prepared to fall back on Mons:

> I first went and saw Bowden-Smith who was slowly dying and did what I could to make him comfortable. We dashed off under a hail of fire, and I don't know how on earth we ever got away as only one man of my six was hit. I don't think I've had a narrower escape or even a more frightful day and I felt absolutely done in. Never shall I forget August 23rd 1914. We had a baptism of fire with a vengeance and the few that remained of our company were left dazed and disconsolate. We had inflicted heavy losses but at what cost. Nearly the whole company 250 strong had gone, four officers had been killed and one naturally felt their loss very keenly.[19]

Once beyond the town of Mons, the 4th Fusiliers retired behind the 1st Lincolns, who were manning a new defensive line. The losses suffered by the Royal Fusiliers were not as great as Tower feared; once the battalion had re-formed its total casualties amounted to around 150 men – not especially high given the hard pounding it had received.[20]

The attack on II Corps' right wing – held by the 1st Gordon Highlanders and 2nd Royal Scots, reinforced by the 2nd Royal Irish Rifles – did not properly develop until the afternoon. As well as a main line of trenches, the Gordons had sufficient time to prepare a line of dummy trenches to their rear as a decoy for the German guns. This was also one of the sections of the line where the British infantry received artillery support, from the 40th Brigade RFA deployed on and around the Bois la Haut; its three 18-pounder batteries were heavily engaged throughout the day. The demand for ammunition was constant, and during the early afternoon Captain C.A.L. Brownlow of the brigade's ammunition column escorted four ammunition wagons to the gunners of the 23rd Battery. On the road to the Bois he encountered traffic travelling the other way:

> Coming down this road there were three horse ambulances crammed with wounded men, dusty and torn and swathed in blood-soaked bandages and looking straight before them with staring eyes. Around the ambulances were a disheveled crowd of limping men, for whom no room could be found. And as this company of suffering humanity moved slowly by they left behind them on the white and dusty Belgian road a scarlet trail of English blood.[21]

Malcolm Hay, an officer in D Company of the Gordon Highlanders, had spent an expectant morning preparing for action. When the Germans finally emerged from nearby woods, the combination of artillery, machine-gun and rifle fire held them in place throughout the day. A final assault was made in the early evening:

> The German attack now began to press on both flanks – on the left perhaps with less vigour, but on the right an ever-increasing intensity of rifle fire seemed to come almost from behind our trenches; but on neither left nor right could anything be seen of the fighting. The ceaseless tapping of our two machine-guns was anxious hearing during that long afternoon, and in the confusion of bursting shells the sound of busy rifles seemed to be echoing on all sides.
>
> A long line of the now familiar grey coats advanced slowly about ten yards from the wood and lay down in the beetroot field. Two or three lines of supports issued forth from the wood, and the first line pushed close up to the white house; but as long as we could see to shoot, and while our shells were sprinkling the fields with shrapnel, the enemy failed to reach their objective and suffered heavy casualties. After the sun had set the vigour of the fight was past, and in the twilight a few shells were exchanged from wood to wood, although machine-guns still drummed and rifles cracked, keeping the enemy from further advance.[22]

The Royal Scots and Royal Irish Rifles – deployed to the right of the Gordon Highlanders – were also able to hold their ground, altogether inflicting 381 casualties on the German 75th Infantry Regiment.[23]

While II Corps was closely engaged in battle, Haig's I Corps remained largely immobile. At 3 p.m. Major-General Hubert Hamilton, commander of the hard-pressed 3rd Division, asked for assistance from I Corps. Haig's response was to send two battalions from the 4th (Guards) Brigade to take over Hill 93 from the Royal Scots and Irish Rifles. Later in the day, Haig despatched three battalions from his 5th Brigade to cover a potential gap between the British 3rd and 5th Divisions.

Elsewhere, the only other action instigated by I Corps came from the 18-pounders of the 34th Brigade RFA, which had a reasonable line of fire towards the Germans advancing on II Corps' right wing. The 70th Battery was on the far right of the brigade's position behind the small rise at Vellereille-le-Sec, with two two-gun sections pushed forward. Lieutenant Alan Durand commanded one of the sections, which began to fire on German infantry targets at 2,300 yards' range. But the four semi-concealed guns of the 70th Battery – whose muzzle flashes were clearly visible – came under counter-battery fire at around 4 p.m. from German howitzers whose position around Binche outflanked the British from the east. Durand described the engagement in a letter home:

> We immediately opened fire on them, I believe with good effect. They didn't get our range for some time, about 20 minutes. But then they gave us hell. Each time we opened fire they gave us two or three rounds of gunfire, as they had eight guns to our four. We had a warm time. I was with no. 4 gun. They silenced us two or three times, but the Major [battery commander Major Stanley-Clarke at the forward observation post] sent down more orders and we started off again. At once, of course, they let us have it, and after a short time we had to stop a bit.[24]

In this short passage, Durand described the dilemma facing a battery commander under fire: should he allow his gunners to retreat to safety (albeit temporarily) and accept 'defeat' in the counter-battery duel or insist his men stand by their guns regardless of casualties? If the fire was considered overwhelming then a temporary withdrawal was an accepted practice, but this inevitably handed the tactical initiative to the enemy, and any commander had to draw a fine line between prudence and what might subsequently be construed as cowardice. In this instance, Major Stanley-Clarke allowed his gunners to retire, but only when the enemy fire was at its most fierce.

Durand, for his part, had to force some of his crew members to man their guns, with a sergeant fearfully crouching under the gun shield 'where he could hardly carry out his duties' and then claiming the gun had been knocked out when it was still serviceable. The fire on the 70th Battery was certainly heavy; the historian of the Royal Artillery recorded how 'the Germans put three guns out of action with splinters through the outer buffer cases' – thus revealing a weakness of the 18-pounder under battlefield conditions.[25] The 34th Brigade RFA suffered 27 wounded, and two officers and three men killed (all from the 70th Battery). Among the wounded were Durand and the reluctant NCO gunner.[26]

●

The onset of darkness provided Smith-Dorrien's II Corps with the opportunity of safely withdrawing to a new defensive position on higher ground a couple of miles to the south of Mons and the Condé Canal. The order to retire reached the units at different times, a consequence of the general confusion of battle and the lack of trained staff officers within the BEF. Whereas the 9th Brigade – under severe German pressure – had been ordered to withdraw from the mid-afternoon onward, the battalions on both left and right flanks did not receive their orders until the evening and some only retired in the early hours of the 24th. But all British units were successfully extricated from the Mons position.

British losses were relatively light, at a little over 1,600 killed, wounded and missing (only 40 to I Corps, the rest to II Corps). And these were concentrated among a few units; the hardest hit were the 4th Middlesex (over 400 casualties) and 2nd Royal Irish (over 300). No official German casualty list was issued,[27] which generated a wide range of conjectural figures – ranging from 2,000 to 10,000 – although the British Official History proposed the guarded, if rather unhelpful, 'the losses must have been heavy'.[28]

In one sense, the debate over German casualty figures has been a red herring. Even the highest quoted figure of 10,000 would have been too low to have delayed Kluck's First Army, and what had become clear by the evening of the 23rd was that the Germans had breached II Corps' defences, forcing it to retire or be overwhelmed. But this debate has become inextricably bound up with a genuinely important attempt to assess how well the respective sides had fought in this first Anglo-German encounter.

The first-hand accounts of the period regularly described enemy troops falling to the ground when under fire, with the implication that they had become casualties. But, in reality, they were going to ground to take cover, no doubt suffering some losses in the process. This basic misperception almost inevitably acted to inflate enemy casualty figures on both sides.

The Official History naturally drew most heavily on British narratives, but it also consulted a number of German histories to support the argument that the Germans had suffered heavily. A key source was the dramatic memoir of novelist Walther Bloem, a company officer in the 12th Infantry Regiment which had suffered heavy casualties.[29] Bloem emphasized the shooting prowess of the British infantry, and his book was subsequently published in Britain with an approving foreword by the Official Historian, Sir James Edmonds.[30] That the 12th Infantry Regiment had suffered heavy casualties without achieving its objective was not disputed, but the controversial point remained: how representative or otherwise was this of the overall German battlefield performance at Mons – and beyond?

While Edmonds made no specific claim for the generality of Bloem's account of his regiment's misfortunes, the Official History's enthusiastic account of the BEF at Mons no doubt encouraged subsequent British writers to leap to this conclusion. John Terraine, the influential British historian of the Great War, used Bloem's narrative to casually announce, 'It was the same story everywhere.'[31] But Terence Zuber has strongly refuted this explanation, insisting that 'the experience of IR 12 was the exception'.[32]

Zuber's book, *The Mons Myth*, makes extensive use of German regimental histories that underline the well-organized nature of the German advance. For their part, the British Official History and British regimental histories took a partisan view of the battle. This, in turn, influenced later writers of both personal memoirs and histories to see the battle in terms of accurate British rifle fire inflicting carnage amongst clumsily led German infantry – apparently firing from the hip and ignorant of the distinction between rifles and machine guns!

Looking at British accounts written shortly after the battle – and consequently less influenced, if at all, by other narratives – no clear-cut view emerges, although the caricatured version of German assault tactics found in so many of the later regimental and popular histories is notably absent. Lieutenant Malcolm Hay wrote a detailed, level-headed memoir of his experiences at Mons and Le Cateau (published in 1916). His account of German tactics at Mons refuted those recently published in the British press:

> Various descriptions of the battle of Mons speak of the Germans advancing like grey clouds covering the earth, of 'massed formations' moving across the open to within close range of our trenches, to be decimated by 'murderous fire'.
>
> On every extended battle line incidents will occur affording opportunities for picturesque writing, but in the attack and defence of an open position in the days of pre-trench war, excepting always the noise of bursting shells, the hum of bullets and the absence of umpires, the whole affair is a passable imitation of a field-day in peace time.[33]

In an attempt to summarize the respective German and British tactical skills at Mons, it can be seen that success went to those units that fought the best all-arms battle. For the most part, the Germans conducted an effective co-ordinated attack, with their infantry supported by artillery and machine guns. It was no surprise that they broke through those parts of the British line which lacked artillery support and where they could concentrate their own superior firepower, as in the Nimy salient or along the canal around Jemappes. By the same token, the Germans were repulsed or held in those sectors where they could not bring their superior firepower to bear and where the British infantry enjoyed a good level of assistance from their gunners – as was the case with Hay's Gordon Highlanders on the far right of II Corps.

•

For the simple reason that Mons was the first battle fought by the British in World War I, it was accorded a greater importance than it strictly deserved. More than half of the BEF effectively stood idle during the battle, and even in II Corps only a few infantry battalions were heavily engaged. For the units that had played only a minor role in the encounter, the retirement order came as a surprise; they assumed the fight would resume the next day in the positions they held.

This was also an assumption shared by the British Commander-in-Chief, who on his return to GHQ in the early afternoon of the 23rd continued to believe the enemy forces facing the BEF need not be a cause for alarm. Orders were even prepared for a continuation of the British advance on the following day, ignoring a further intelligence report at 6 p.m. from Colonel Macdonogh stressing the danger faced by the BEF. It took the arrival of a subsequent message from General Joffre – that the BEF was opposed by three enemy army corps – to moderate French's enthusiasm. Even then French felt sufficiently confident to send II Corps the following order at 8.40 p.m.: 'I will stand the attack [by the Germans] on the ground now occupied by the troops. You will therefore strengthen your position by every possible means during the night.'[34]

But at midnight, French received a bombshell from Lieutenant Spears. He informed French that Fifth Army was in full retreat, a move that left the BEF isolated and facing the imminent prospect of destruction. In his biography of French, Richard Holmes described the Field Marshal's reaction:

> The news of Lanrezac's decision stunned French. He had done his best, whatever his personal feelings, to give loyal support to Lanrezac, who now intended to retire without so much as a by-your-leave. The incident did more than confirm Sir John in his hatred of Lanrezac. It convinced him that the French were basically untrustworthy as allies, and sowed seeds of distrust which, from time to time, bore bitter fruit.[35]

The scales had fallen from French's eyes, the carefree optimism of the previous days replaced in an instant by a fearful pessimism. A general strategic withdrawal of the whole BEF was now a priority, and orders to that effect were issued at 1 a.m. on the 24th. The great retreat was underway.

PART TWO

THE GREAT RETREAT

CHAPTER SIX

DISENGAGEMENT

Following French's decision to order a retreat, his chief of staff, Lieutenant-General Sir Archibald Murray, summoned the senior staff officers of I and II Corps and the Cavalry Division to GHQ at Le Cateau. At the 1 a.m. meeting on 24 August he vaguely informed them that the BEF was to retire in a southerly direction. Murray failed to provide proper march orders – apart from an instruction for Haig's I Corps to cover the retirement of Smith-Dorrien's II Corps – leaving the corps staffs to work out the details of the retirement among themselves.

Lack of sleep and the exhausting tension of the last few days were having their effect on Murray. He was not alone in feeling the strain. Lieutenant-General Haig noticed signs of tiredness among many senior officers. At a meeting with Major-General Hubert Hamilton (3rd Division) on the 23rd, Haig reported that he 'seemed to me quite worn out with fatigue',[1] and while visiting Major-General Charles Monro (2nd Division) in the early hours of the following morning, '[I] marked his map, as he and his staff officer (Colonel Gordon) were very sleepy'.[2] A short while later Haig drove to the headquarters of the 6th Infantry Brigade: 'I saw General Davies [and some of his staff]; all very tired and sleepy.'[3] And yet this was only the beginning of the retreat.

At the end of his meeting with Murray, Brigadier-General George Forestier-Walker, the chief of staff of II Corps, was forced to drive 35 miles back to his headquarters, thereby delaying the transmission of the retreat order to the 3rd and 5th Divisions of his corps. Brigadier-General J. E. 'Johnnie' Gough, I Corps' chief of staff, was more fortunate, having a direct telegraph link with his own headquarters, so that by 2 a.m. Haig was aware of the new situation.

On receiving the message from Gough, Haig immediately disregarded the order to cover II Corps. His corps was not in the correct position to protect Smith-Dorrien's force, and quite reasonably he was concerned that his own troops might be enveloped if he delayed his withdrawal. While Gough was returning from GHQ, Haig motored to the headquarters of his subordinate commanders to explain the details of the retreat. His energy and thoroughness came in marked contrast to the sluggish approach to command too often characteristic of his colleagues. Haig assembled a rearguard of the 5th Cavalry Brigade and supporting artillery; his two divisions marched away as dawn broke.

Haig's vigorous response to the retreat order was made practicable by motor transport, which he singled out as enabling him to 'give personal orders to all the chief commanders in the space of an hour. Written orders reached them later, but the movement [in retreat] was started on certain lines in a way which would have been impossible before the days of the motor.'[4] Despite reliability problems, cars and motorcycles swiftly proved their worth in the personal transmission of messages and orders, and earned the praise of other senior officers. And yet they were an insufficient means of controlling the vast numbers of troops spread over the wide areas that had become commonplace by 1914.

To command effectively, generals required a mobile, reliable and secure real-time means of communication.[5] This would eventually be supplied by radio, but in 1914, wireless telegraphy sets – able to transmit and receive radio messages – were still in their infancy. GHQ and the Cavalry Division had been issued with radios, but they were cumbersome and far from reliable, and as a consequence were seldom used by ground forces on the move. The civilian telephone system in France and Belgium was extensively used by the Allies, but the network of telephone lines was relatively sparse and rarely of use for the control of troops on the battlefield.

At the tactical level, the BEF had its own telephone lines that could be laid by trained signallers from one headquarters to another. But this system had obvious limitations during the mobile operations typical of the opening stages of the 1914 campaign. Telephone lines were also easily cut, especially during artillery bombardments, and had to be supplemented by traditional optical methods that included semaphore flags and Morse lanterns. And, when all else failed, there was the despatch rider, whether motorized or still reliant on bicycle, horse or foot. Whatever the system, however, the technological barriers to efficient communication were never fully lifted, making the exercise of command all the more difficult.

•

The retreat of II Corps was always going to be a difficult task, with the Germans pressed hard against the British positions and ready to renew the assault at first light on the 24th. Smith-Dorrien ordered his 5th Division to hold the line and protect the withdrawal of the 3rd Division. The 5th Division would then break contact, covered in turn by Allenby's Cavalry Division (which exercised temporary command over the 19th Infantry Brigade).

The German plan for 24 August was to pin down the British, while launching an enveloping move to the west to crush them against the fortifications at Maubeuge. General von Kluck still erroneously believed the BEF's lines of communication ran due west, and that, if in difficulties, it would attempt to retreat in that direction.

The German attack against the British line south of Mons opened with a general bombardment before dawn, followed at 5.15 a.m. by an infantry advance. As planned, the British 3rd Division began to fall back, its 8th Brigade, on the right, coming under light artillery fire before marching away safely in a south-westerly direction. The other two brigades were caught in an infantry fire-fight. The 9th Infantry Brigade held the village of Frameries against the German 6th Division, and after inflicting heavy casualties on the enemy adroitly withdrew from the village, which was entered unopposed by the Germans at around 10 a.m.

The 3rd Battalion of the German 20th Infantry Regiment, which had led the assault on Frameries, lost 500 men and officers.[6] Captain Brandis voiced his appreciation of British tactical skill: 'Up to all the tricks of the trade from their experiences of small wars, the English veterans brilliantly understood how to slip off at the right moment.'[7]

The 7th Brigade defended the line around Ciply, but eventually found its position outflanked. Well-directed German machine-gun fire from the slag heaps around Frameries inflicted heavy losses on the 2nd South Lancashire Regiment, which after losing as many as 300 men fell back with the rest of the brigade without further hindrance from the Germans. As the British troops retreated, they were joined by an army of refugees. Almost all British accounts of this period described the unfortunate multitude, invariably with a sense of compassion for their fate and sometimes with feelings of guilt at their abandonment.

The main weight of the German attack now fell upon Major-General Sir Charles Fergusson's 5th Division. The German guns opened up before dawn, and once there was sufficient light, aircraft were sent up to locate British positions. Captain Arthur Osburn, the MO attached to the 2nd Cavalry Brigade, was tending the wounded from the previous day's fighting when he looked up to see Taube aircraft, 'sending out smoke signals as to our position; within 30 seconds their gunners were sending shrapnel over us in bursts'.[8] Having moved to a new position, he recalled how it was swiftly rediscovered and 'promptly marked by the German planes, and we were plastered with shrapnel – prompt and accurate enough but bursting much too high; the bullets rattling off our boots harmlessly'.[9]

A few miles to the east, around the village of Wasmes, Brigadier-General Edward Gleichen had also come under enemy fire while reorganizing the defences of the 1st Dorsets, a battalion in his 15th Infantry Brigade:

> I was standing with [Lieutenant-Colonel L. J.] Bols and a few of his officers when a shrapnel burst with a tremendous crack close over our heads, bringing down branches and leaves in showers. Yet not a man or horse was hit. The shrapnel bullets whizzed along the pavement in all directions, right among our feet, like hail it seemed; yet the only result was a lot of bad language from Saunders, who had got a nasty jar on the heel from one of the bullets: but it did not even cut the leather.[10]

Accounts of German shrapnel bursting at too great a height were common during the 1914 campaign. If a salvo of shrapnel shells burst at the correct height – ideally just over 30 feet above and before the target – the result could be devastating against troops in the open, but in practice this was a hard technique to master: the estimation of the target's range had to be almost perfect if the fuse's timer was to set off the charge at the correct height and distance. The British gunners prided themselves on their ability to burst shrapnel low – almost 'on the graze' – although German reports suggested British shrapnel shells similarly tended to burst at too great a height.[11]

Even if Brigadier-General Gleichen was not unduly worried by the enemy's shrapnel, then his troops and those of 13th Brigade were now in difficulty. The departure of the 3rd Division had exposed the right flank of the 5th Division, a situation made more serious by the withdrawal of the 5th Brigade, which, loaned from I Corps, had helped bridge the gap between the two divisions of II Corps. The Dorsets, 1st Bedfords and 2nd Duke of Wellington's Regiment were holding the front line, and were in danger of being overwhelmed when the order for a general retreat was given at about 11 a.m. Extricating these forward units under heavy artillery and small-arms fire proved difficult, and while the Dorsets and Bedfords eventually got away, the Duke of Wellington's failed to receive the retreat order; they were driven from their position a little after midday, losing nearly 400 men in the process.

As the 5th Division began to disengage from the fight, Fergusson became aware that his withdrawal was not being covered by Allenby's Cavalry Division. The British cavalry – with the 19th Infantry Brigade in tow – had begun to retire without first ascertaining the true situation of the 5th Division, an unfortunate but not unusual example of the poor liaison within the BEF. As a consequence, Fergusson was forced to ask Allenby for help, who duly obliged by sending back the 2nd and 3rd Cavalry Brigades to reoccupy positions held earlier in the morning. In the meantime, Fergusson despatched the 1st Norfolks and 1st Cheshires (with the 119th Battery) to act as a temporary rearguard by holding the high ground to the west of Élouges.

The infantry rearguard – under the command of Lieutenant-Colonel C. R. Ballard, the Norfolks' CO – took up a defensive line to the west of Élouges around midday, with the Cheshires on the left and Norfolks and the 119th Battery on the right. The cavalry also arrived, taking up positions to the left of the infantry, with the 9th Lancers of Brigadier-General de Lisle's 2nd Cavalry Brigade in the lead. It was at this point that the artillery of the German IV Corps began to fire on the British positions. The German assault was led by 8th Division infantry, advancing through and to the west of the village of Quievrain, supported by most of its divisional artillery.

Seeing the enemy in the far distance, de Lisle rode over to Lieutenant-Colonel David Campbell, CO of the 9th Lancers, and instructed him, in the words of the Official History, 'to deliver, if necessary, a mounted attack northwards in order to take the German advance in the flank'.[12] Apart from the fact that the Lancers would be advancing against the German front (and not flank) it was the sort of ambiguous order that had the potential for trouble, soon realized in this instance. Campbell – an enthusiastic polo player and amateur jockey (he had won the Grand National in 1896) – seemingly interpreted his instructions in an old-fashioned cavalry manner, leading his regiment forward at the gallop in the general direction of the enemy, more than a mile away. Two nearby squadrons of the 4th Dragoon Guards also joined the charge, although no formal order seemed to have been issued to them.

The charge has been much written about, with one recent history describing it as an 'epic moment'.[13] The only thing epic about it was its folly. Even in Napoleonic times, for cavalry to attack formed infantry was to invite disaster but to do so against modern artillery, machine guns and rifles was sheer lunacy, the lancers and dragoon guards charging into a mass of exploding shrapnel. Lieutenant Roger Chance of the 4th Dragoon Guards described his part in the action:

> All I can do is follow my leader, who forms troop in squadron columns and is off at the gallop, swords pointed. We span the unmetalled road, which runs straight, un-fenced, through a stubble field dotted with corn stooks. A cloud of dust has risen ahead, pierced by the flash of shell bursts. If there is a hail of bullets, I am not aware of it, as with [Sergeant] Talbot glimpsed alongside, the men thundering after us.[14]

Chance's sergeant was hit and went down in a 'crashing somersault, to be ridden over, dead or alive'. As others tumbled to the ground it looked to be a scene of carnage. Among the wounded was Major Tom Bridges; suffering from concussion and a broken jaw he narrowly escaped capture by the Germans.

In the event, the British cavalry got off relatively lightly. The charge did not end in the mouths of the Germans guns, but, more prosaically, was halted by a simple barbed-wire fence. Captain Francis Grenfell of the 9th Lancers summed it up: 'We simply galloped about like rabbits in front of a line of guns.'[15] In order to escape the German fire, the mob of horsemen careered to the right, along the line of the fence, before retiring behind the infantry screen of the Norfolks.

The cavalry's losses amounted to just 169 men killed, wounded and missing, but its consequences were serious, scattering the 2nd Cavalry Brigade into disparate sub-units that were without command or much useful function for several days.[16] This moment of madness further weakened Allenby's control over the semi-independent brigades of the Cavalry Division, diminishing its ability to protect II Corps' withdrawal. Trying to make the best of it, the Official History made the anodyne claim that the 'advance of the 2nd Cavalry Brigade seems to have produced some moral effect in delaying the German attack',[17] while the chief culprit, de Lisle, had the brazen nerve to applaud the 'true cavalry spirit of the 9th Lancers in daring to charge unbroken infantry in order to save neighbouring troops'.[18]

The charge may have delayed the advance of a few units of the German 8th Division by a few minutes at most, but it was an unnecessary distraction for the infantry rearguard formed by the Norfolks and Cheshires. This was certainly the view of Lieutenant Matterson of the Cheshire Regiment, who along with 'his brother officers all wondered why the charge had been made, and felt that had the [Cavalry] Brigade been retained in hand it would have been able to extricate them when the time came for them to withdraw'.[19] This simple comment revealed de Lisle's assertion for the nonsense it was.

Although L Battery RHA and the machine guns of the 3rd Cavalry Brigade provided useful fire support, Ballard's infantry rearguard was left in an increasingly isolated position. Following the arrival of lead units of the German IV Corps' 7th Division, advancing against the Norfolks' right flank, a swift withdrawal was the only option to avoid envelopment. Ballard's troops had done well, forcing the marching German troops into an encounter deployment, but their numbers were insufficient. As a consequence, the Germans were simply bypassing the British rearguard.

At 2.30 p.m. Ballard ordered a general retreat. The advance of the German 7th Division nearly overwhelmed the 119th Battery, but under heavy fire its guns were manhandled to safety under the leadership of the battery commander, Major Alexander, helped by a group of 9th Lancers led by Captain Grenfell – both officers receiving VCs for their efforts. While the bulk of the Norfolks retired largely intact, the Cheshires were cut off.

In one of the confusions typical of the great retreat, Lieutenant-Colonel D. C. Boger of the Cheshires had apparently been told to fight to the end, despite this obviously being merely a delaying action. Three messages were subsequently sent to the Cheshires to retire, but none arrived. They fought on towards the end of the afternoon, and only when their position was completely surrounded did they accept the German request to surrender. Brigadier-General Gleichen rated the Cheshires as the best shots under his command, and subsequently wrote: 'The Germans were astonished at their rifle fire, and owned to very heavy losses. They asked whether we trained our men to fire at the enemy's balls, as most of their men were hit thereabouts.'[20]

A few men from the Cheshires broke through the German cordon and joined the reserve company; the following day 'only two officers and two hundred men answered their names at St Waast'.[21] The Norfolk casualties were 250 officers and men, including 100 of their wounded left behind at Élouges.

In the series of running engagements that marked the BEF's withdrawal on 24 August, the British suffered approximately 2,600 casualties, heavier than those experienced at Mons the previous day.[22] But the BEF had shaken free from Kluck's grip, and the British columns continued to march south.

*

During the advance to Mons the supply of food and munitions to the BEF had been relatively straightforward, coming under the overall control of the Quartermaster General's Branch, with Major-General Sir William Robertson at its head. Robertson was the only man in the British Army to rise through the ranks from private to field marshal, maintaining a rough-hewn image, complete with dropped aitches.

But he was one of the few senior commanders who believed that the main weight of the German offensive might well be made across Belgium and into northern France. Such an eventuality would render the BEF's supply chain from Le Havre and Boulogne through to the advanced base at Amiens distinctly vulnerable. Even before the first shots were fired, Robertson consulted Major-General F. S. Robb (Inspector-General of Communications) on 22 August to plan a transfer of the lines of communication to the safer Atlantic port of St Nazaire. Two days later the first stage of the plan was put into effect.

Of more immediate importance was the physical maintenance of the BEF as it withdrew from Mons. Distributing supplies from the railheads to the retreating units – whose position at any one time was seldom known – taxed Robertson's abilities to the full:

> I could only guess as to the place where they might be, send their food to it, and a further supply to other probable places, in the hope that if the first consignment did not reach them the second would. The expedient was also adopted of dumping supplies – flitches of bacon, sides of beef, cheese, boxes of biscuits – alongside the roads so that the troops might help themselves as they passed. Much of the food thus deposited had to be left where it was put but on the whole the object of ensuring that plenty of food should be obtainable when and where wanted was fairly well achieved.[23]

Inevitably some of these roadside dumps fell into German hands, but they were essential in maintaining the fighting capability of the retreating British troops. The 1st East Surreys began their march at 2 a.m. on the 24th, and the tired and hungry men were pleased to discover the presence of one of these improvised supply dumps. According to Lieutenant George Roupell, 'a small party was sent on ahead to divide up the rations, and the column was rationed without halting. As each man went by he was given two biscuits, a tin of bully beef, and every second man, a pot of jam.'[24]

Complicating matters was the loss of greatcoats and packs. Although some battalions resolutely held on to their personal equipment, others had either thrown them away or been ordered to discard them. The great heat of the final days of August, the lack of fitness among the reservists and the necessity for speed in getting away from Mons, influenced many commanding officers to ditch all unnecessary encumbrances. Corporal John Lucy of the 2nd Royal Irish Rifles was exasperated by the order:

> The men of the regiment hated the idea of abandoning their packs and greatcoats. That alarmed them. They could imagine this gear being discovered by the enemy, and the German exultation at having us on the run. Besides, although the pack was heavy, we preferred it. It kept us upright, and balanced the heavily laden ammunition pouches in front. Gloomily the troops salved their mess tins, the only article allowed to be taken from the cast-away packs.[25]

Corporal Lucy, like so many other soldiers in the BEF, was disconcerted to be retreating from the enemy. 'Marching away like this was distasteful,' he grumbled. 'In fact, it was not soldiering.'[26]

General von Kluck's First Army had made only limited progress on 24 August – thanks mainly to the rearguard actions of II Corps – but he hoped to continue with his enveloping manoeuvre on the 25th. In addition to the three army corps engaged at Mons (III, IV and IX), Kluck was anticipating the imminent arrival of reinforcements: II Corps and IV Reserve Corps and, significantly, Marwitz's II Cavalry Corps, the latter to provide him with the vital mobile element he had previously lacked. If these powerful formations could hold and then outflank the BEF, victory would be his. But Kluck's plans were almost immediately compromised by an error in German aerial reconnaissance.

Early on the morning of the 25th a report from the German III Corps' aviation section suggested that the BEF was retiring on the fortress of Maubeuge. The tensions within First Army staff were clearly evident: on the basis of this scrap of intelligence, the axis of the German advance was suddenly transformed from a southerly march to that of the south-east. III Corps and half of IV Corps turned away from the pursuit of the British II Corps towards the Sambre River and Maubeuge. Marwitz's Cavalry Corps also shifted its line of advance in the general direction of Le Cateau. Subsequent reports correctly revealed the BEF to be still retreating directly to the south, but attempts to re-direct the German formations arrived too late, with the result that for most of the 25th only the German IV Corps' 8th Division was actively pursuing Smith-

Dorrien's men. The consequences of this mistake would be far reaching, the Germans short of sufficient troops to trap and overwhelm the British.

●

On the evening of 24 August, Sir John French had ordered both corps to resume the retreat in the early hours of the 25th and to take up a defensive position either side of Le Cateau. A densely wooded area, the Forest of Mormal, forced the two corps to separate, II Corps marching to the west and I Corps to the east of the forest. This division of forces was far from ideal, but it was assumed that they would reunite by the end of the day's march around Le Cateau, which lay directly to the south of the forest.

During the 25th, the two divisions of I Corps continued the withdrawal, although as a result of confusion at GHQ, they were slow in beginning the day's march. As a consequence, the head of the 2nd Division halted at Landrecies in the late afternoon, roughly 7 miles short of the previously agreed position to the east of Le Cateau. For Haig's troops it had been a fairly uneventful day, but this was soon about to change as a result of the German First Army's change of direction. The staffs of both British GHQ and I Corps had failed to reconnoiter the Forest of Mormal, which was less impenetrable than first assumed. Following Kluck's order, the German 6th Division pushed through the forest towards Aulney; lead elements of the 5th Division emerged from the forest at Maroilles, while IV Corps' 7th Division skirted the forest to the south, ready to cross the Sambre at Landrecies.

At Maroilles and Landrecies, as light began to fade, German advance guards clashed with the British 2nd Division. Although these encounters were little more than skirmishes, they caused a degree of panic that worked its way up the chain of command. Haig had suffered a severe bout of diarrhoea and was not at his best when he crossed from his temporary headquarters at Le Grand Fayt to take personal command of the 4th (Guards) Brigade's defence of Landrecies. A confused fire-fight went on into the night; casualties were light and the sporadic fighting eventually died down – as it did further north at Maroilles. The main effect of the action was on the normally imperturbable Haig. According to Haig's aide-de-camp (ADC), John Charteris, 'he was quite jolted out of his usual placidity. He said, "If we are caught, by God we'll sell our lives dearly."'[27]

The alarm spread to I Corps HQ at Le Grand Fayt. In the words of one officer, 'some mounted men galloped in, saying they had been fired on and that the Germans were approaching! For a short time panic reigned: regiments lined each side of the road and fired on nothing in particular; one field gun even went as far as to fire a round; transport became inextricably blocked trying to turn round.'[28]

At 11.30 p.m. Haig and his staff returned from Landrecies to Le Grand Fayt. Haig was deeply troubled, fearing the skirmishes to be the opening phase of a German enveloping action. Haig apparently told his staff that 'the Guards Brigade were in a tight corner. He also said that, as far as he could see, the British Expeditionary Force was surrounded and liable to be completely annihilated.'[29]

At 12.30 a.m. on the 26th Haig issued orders for his corps to resume the march towards Guise, and not attempt to take up position alongside II Corps at Le Cateau (adhering to an earlier directive from GHQ to continue the retreat). He then phoned GHQ – which had retired from Le Cateau to St Quentin – at 1.35 a.m., claiming to be under 'heavy attack'. This news thoroughly alarmed French and Wilson, so much so that French contacted II Corps at 3.50 a.m. asking for support for I Corps. Much to French's irritation, Smith-Dorrien refused, explaining that he was too hard-pressed to spare any troops. Indeed, it was II Corps that faced the greatest danger from the advancing Germans.

During 24 August, the British 3rd and 5th Divisions of II Corps had successfully opened up a gap between themselves and the Germans, but the distance was dangerously small. Captain C. A. L. Brownlow recalled how 'one felt the presence of the enemy, who in their tens of thousands lay like an evil tide but a few miles to the northward.'[30]

For II Corps, the 25th would be a day of hard marching, the sweltering heat relieved only by a drenching rainstorm in the late afternoon. Most battalions marched at least 25 miles, which stretched them to the limit. Lieutenant G. C. Wynne wrote of the progress of the King's Own Yorkshire Light Infantry: 'We all trudged along in an atmosphere of blasphemous silence.'[31]

The progress of II Corps was hampered by the passage of Sordet's Cavalry Corps, moving east to west across the British line of march. For the khaki-clad soldiers of the BEF the sight of the French cavalry – with blue tunics and red breeches – was seldom forgotten, especially the cuirassiers, who, with their steel breastplates and helmets with streaming horsehair plumes, looked positively Napoleonic. Many observers found the sight inspiring, but others were less impressed, Captain H. B. Owens dismissing them as 'people at a pantomime'.[32]

A more serious, semi-permanent impediment for the retreating BEF came from the unabating tide of refugees fleeing the Germans. For the British troops, the sight of the desperate civilians was especially painful, as Captain Brownlow recalled: 'These poor people who we had come to protect and save and who but a couple of days before had welcomed us as deliverers, now looked at us askance with reproachable eyes. The bitterest incident of all was when, passing through a little village, we trod underfoot a strip of cloth which had hung in greeting across the street and which bore the words: "Welcome to our saviours, the British!"'[33]

While the BEF was retiring from Mons, the RFC continued to provide GHQ with valuable intelligence of German movements, and the position of retreating British units. Lieutenant Louis Strange was up in the air early on 25 August:

We soon realised that great events were taking place. We were under fire; shells bursting in unexpected places and we constantly saw troops on the move. We made a number of reconnaissances, and when I dropped low, it came as a shock to me to sight the grey-green uniforms of German forces in localities which had been held by our own men the day before. The Germans blazed away whenever they saw me, but my machine took no damage. Up in the air I constantly saw fierce fights going on in isolated places when I looked down on one side, while a mile away on the other were transport, troops, and guns all mixed up in the commencement of the historic retreat.[34]

The long day's march on the 25th had been exhausting, and there was confusion among units as they neared Le Cateau. This was especially true of the Cavalry Division, whose regiments were increasingly scattered and unable to put in place an effective screen to protect II Corps. The brigade was the largest permanent cavalry formation in the British cavalry, and the brigade commanders tended to pursue a fairly independent line, despite their incorporation as a division. The 2nd Brigade had been dispersed at Élouges, while Brigadier-General Gough's

3rd Cavalry Brigade had severed contact with divisional HQ and was operating on its own.[35]

The BEF had been pushed hard, but so too had the men of Kluck's First Army. Throughout the day, reports from the RFC indicated the presence of long columns of infantry marching from the north and the appearance of cavalry units pressing forward from the north-west. By the evening of the 25th it began to look as if the Germans were catching the British. There were several skirmishes between German cavalry and the British rearguard, although the Germans did not press hard, preferring only to maintain contact with the British.

Some of the pressure on II Corps was relieved by the arrival of Major-General Thomas Snow's 4th Division. The division had been transported to Le Cateau and neighbouring rail stations late on the evening of the 24th, although many of its supporting arms had been delayed in the process. While at full strength in infantry and field artillery, the division did not have its cavalry and cyclists, heavy battery of 60-pounders, field engineers, signals company, ammunition column and field ambulances. Consequently, the division had no long-range artillery, lacked an effective reconnaissance and communication facility and would be unable to evacuate wounded from the battlefield. And, as with much of the rest of the BEF, it had insufficient entrenching tools.

The field defences established by the 4th Division around the village of Solesmes – a choke point through which much of II Corps would be forced to travel – earned the criticism of General Snow himself: 'I rode around the troops who were supposed to be entrenched. In spite of what the troops had learned in the Boer War, in spite of what they had been taught, all they had done was to make a few scratchings of the nature of what was called a shelter pit, of no use whatever against any sort of fire.'[36] Worse was to follow:

> During the morning I ordered up a part of the 12th Brigade to extend my left towards Quievy. I was much horrified when I went to visit them to find that they had piled arms in an open space on a slope facing the direction of the enemy and had taken off their accoutrements and hung them up on the piles of rifles. Had artillery fire been opened there would have been a disaster. I was very angry and such a thing never happened again.[37]

Unfortunately for Snow and the 12th Brigade, this casual behaviour in the face of the enemy was, in fact, to be repeated just 24 hours later, with disastrous results for at least one battalion.

As night fell, the 4th Division – plus several cavalry regiments and two battalions of the 7th Infantry Brigade – were still in position around the village of Solesmes. They prevented any potential last-minute push by the German vanguard to catch II Corps, but in so doing they had to retire to their positions in darkness, with only the distant light of villages set alight by the Germans to guide them.

Consideration had been given by GHQ to making a stand at Le Cateau – civilians had been engaged to dig trenches on the high ground to the west of the town – but the instruction from GHQ at 9 p.m. on the 25th was that the retreat would continue. Accordingly, II Corps' operational order called for the troops to be ready to march at 7 a.m. the following morning.

CHAPTER SEVEN

LE CATEAU: THE DECISION TO FIGHT

The exhausted troops of II Corps arrived at the Le Cateau position during the late afternoon and evening of 25 August. Le Cateau itself became a vast traffic jam, as cavalry, artillery, transport wagons and infantry jostled through its narrow streets. Arthur Osburn, with the remnants of the 4th Dragoon Guards, 250-men strong, took two-and-a-half hours to pass through the town, the regiment becoming further fragmented in the process.

Captain James Jack, an acting staff officer in the recently formed 19th Infantry Brigade, followed the 5th Division into Le Cateau, having been sent ahead of the brigade to organize accommodation:

Between 7 and 11 p.m. the soaked and hungry battalions stagger into the square where they are met by their quartermasters and me as usual. It is heartrending to witness the exhaustion of all ranks after their march of almost 23 miles in steam-heat and heavily loaded, besides going into action about Romeries and Huassy in support of the cavalry. The men have scarcely been off their feet for three days besides having had no more than snatches of sleep or scraps of food because of transport delays through road-blocks. The last battalion to report, the Welch Fusiliers, drop down on the cobbled square saying they can go no further.[1]

A few miles further west, the 3rd Division took up a line between Caudry and Troisvilles. Most of the division had managed to establish a position in the late afternoon, but rearguard units were slow to arrive. The 3rd Worcestershire Regiment reached Caudry shortly before midnight, although, according to the regimental history, 'when the troops marched in they were somewhat astonished to see shops still lighted and people sitting at the little tables of the cafes.'[2] It was several hours later before the last of the rearguard, the 2nd Royal Irish Rifles, were able to lay down their weapons and enjoy a few hours' sleep.

That the gap between the Germans and the struggling infantry of II Corps seemed to be closing was an obvious worry for General Smith-Dorrien, but it was the situation facing Major-General Allenby's Cavalry Division that brought on the crisis. It was not until after 11 p.m. on the 25th that Allenby was first informed of Field Marshal French's order for the continuation of the retreat. Allenby was painfully aware that he now had insufficient forces – just the 4th Cavalry Brigade under his direct control – to cover the retreat on the 26th. The situation was made worse with the news that the Germans had just occupied the high ground around Viesly, only a few miles north of the British position.

Allenby rode over to II Corps' headquarters at Bertry. In what must have been an extremely difficult meeting, he admitted to Smith-Dorrien that he could not provide an effective rearguard, and that unless II Corps and the 4th Division resumed the march before dawn he believed the 'enemy would be upon them before they could start.'[3] To make matters worse, Smith-Dorrien had received reports that Haig's I Corps was in trouble and that a worrying gap had developed between the two formations. The 3rd Division headquarters was nearby, and at 2 a.m. Smith-Dorrien summoned Major-General Hamilton for an assessment on the state of readiness of his troops. Hamilton's reply confirmed his worst suspicions, as the Official History recorded: 'Many units of the division were still coming in, and [Hamilton] did not think he could get them formed up for retreat before 9 a.m.'[4]

Smith-Dorrien was in an impossible position. French had made it clear that the retreat was to continue but, in the II Corps commander's view, supported by senior colleagues, such a retreat might well end in disaster. Visions of German artillery tearing holes through the retreating infantry columns, with regiments of uhlans charging the survivors, may well have raced through Smith-Dorrien's mind. Asking for Allenby's support – readily given – he made the momentous decision to stand and fight. He took comfort in the Field Service Regulations that not only permitted a subordinate commander to depart 'from the letter of his [superior's] order' in changed circumstances, but demanded that he do so.[5]

Smith-Dorrien hoped to force the German First Army to deploy into battle formation, deliver it a sharp blow and then retire at an opportune moment, most probably at nightfall. As II Corps headquarters at Bertry lacked a telephone line, a message outlining the decision to fight on the 26th was sent by motor car to GHQ at St Quentin at 3.30 a.m. (arriving there some 90 minutes later). Meanwhile, a staff officer was sent to Major-General Snow, requesting him to come under II Corps orders, although the message only reached 4th Division headquarters at around 5 a.m. Smith-Dorrien hurried over to give the new orders to the 5th Division commander, Major-General Fergusson. Relaying this information to the other subordinate commanders – at brigade and battalion level – was inevitably more difficult, especially as their locations were not always known.

Whether the decision to fight at Le Cateau was right or wrong became a matter of fierce debate, eventually descending into an acrimonious post-war dispute between Smith-Dorrien and French and their respective supporters. Even with the benefit of hindsight it is hard to come to a conclusive decision either way. But what was clear was the dismay caused at GHQ.

When Field Marshal French was woken at 5 a.m. with the news of II Corps' order to fight, he immediately despatched a return message that reluctantly accepted Smith-Dorrien's decision. But on reflection he changed his mind and ordered Wilson to establish phone contact with Smith-Dorrien to demand II Corps continue the retreat. But when Wilson got through to Smith-Dorrien (at Bertry station) it was too late; the battle was already underway. French had refused to wake the exhausted Murray when the news first arrived, but after the chief of staff awoke and was informed of the situation, he apparently fainted in shock.

The Battle of Le Cateau, 26 August 1914

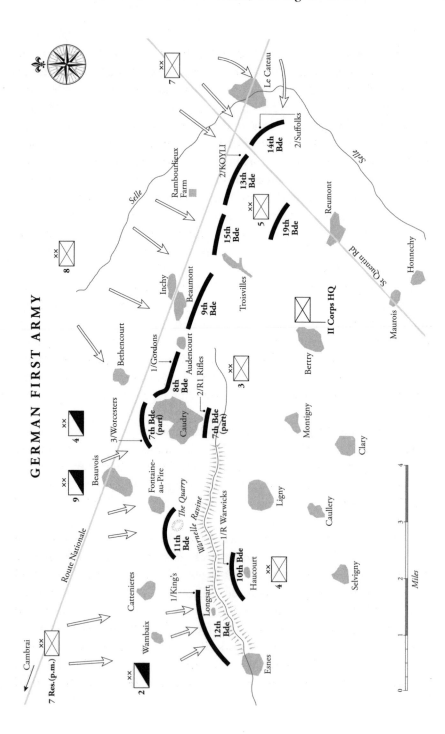

French, Murray and Wilson at GHQ were isolated from what was actually happening to the long columns marching south, relying on snippets of intelligence and rumour that tended to confirm existing prejudices and exacerbate growing doubts. On the night of the 25th/26th the earlier cry for help from the supposedly unflappable Haig caused deep consternation, but, in GHQ's eyes, the decision of Smith-Dorrien to take on the might of the German First Army presaged almost certain annihilation.

Another unfortunate consequence of Smith-Dorrien's last-minute decision to halt the retreat and prepare for battle was to further confuse an already confused situation among the troops of his new command, now comprising II Corps, the 4th Division, the 19th Infantry Brigade and part of the Cavalry Division. Some units believed they were to adopt the original GHQ plan for the BEF to defend the line on both sides of Le Cateau; others had instructions to continue the retreat.

•

The battle of Le Cateau would be fought over the rolling downland of northern France, similar in appearance to the army's newly acquired training grounds on Salisbury Plain, and a far cry from the mining villages and slag heaps of Mons. In his study of the battle, Major A. F. Becke described the topography of the battlefield:

> At the time of the action the district was covered principally with corn-fields, but the corn was nearly all cut and stood in the fields in stooks; whilst scattered over the open but undulating landscape were patches of beet and clover fields. The only restriction to the free movement of all arms was an occasional wire fence. Most of the roads were sunken where they crossed the spurs, the cuttings being shallow trenches varying from three feet to six feet in depth; in other words they were ready for occupation by troops acting on the defensive wherever they happened to face in the required direction.[6]

Both sides would make good use of these sunken roads during the battle. The open landscape allowed good fields of fire in most directions, although the numerous valleys provided concealment for advancing troops, dead ground that the Germans were to exploit to the full. The weakness of the British position was further undermined by the fact that it had been adopted in haste, with little attention given to establishing a defensive line until the retreat orders were cancelled by Smith-Dorrien. As a consequence, large sections of what would become the British front line were dangerously sited on forward slopes, only too visible to German artillery and machine guns.

The three British divisions were deployed in a slightly convex line, the 4th Division on the left, 3rd Division in the centre and 5th Division on the right. The 19th Infantry Brigade acted as Smith-Dorrien's immediate reserve, with the cavalry deployed further to the rear, playing little if any part in the action. Given the superior size of the German First Army, Smith-Dorrien faced a real possibility of being overwhelmed on both flanks.

On the British left were several units of French Territorials, soon to be reinforced by the arrival of Sordet's Cavalry Corps; between them they proved sufficient to prevent any German outflanking move against the British 4th Division. A more serious situation had developed on the British right, however, with the 5th Division anchored on high ground just south of the town of Le Cateau. Immediately to the right of the British position lay the valley of the River Selle with a spur of high ground rising to the east. In the original GHQ plan this position was to have been covered by I Corps, now very absent. The 1st Duke of Cornwall's Light Infantry (DCLI) and a half-battalion (two companies) of 1st East Surreys had been sent to the east of Le Cateau to link up with I Corps. But they were never expected to act as a flank guard and Smith-Dorien's right remained up in the air. If the Germans secured the spur and advanced up the Selle valley, the entire British position would be fatally compromised.

As potentially the most vulnerable section of the British line, it was vital that the 5th Division conduct a determined and well thought-through plan of battle, but the deployment orders issued by the division's senior officers would have dreadful consequences.

During the night of the 25th/26th the units of the 5th Division remained uncertain over their orders. The weary men of the 2nd King's Own Yorkshire Light Infantry (KOYLI) had arrived at Le Cateau in the afternoon believing they would fight the following day, cheered by talk of the arrival of vast numbers of French troops. During the evening the men were given their first hot meal in 60 hours and settled down for the night.

Lieutenant G. C. Wynne was woken at 2.30 a.m.: 'The colonel called out the officers and told us that another long retirement was to be made by the division and from orders just received, the 13th Brigade would act as a rearguard and the KOYLI were to act as the rear battalion. We were to occupy some trenches nearby, astride the St Quentin road and hold the enemy's advance till 11 a.m. when we ourselves should retire.'[7]

Wynne recorded a general slump in the battalion's morale at the news of the continuation of the retreat. Wynne and his fellow officers were gloomily discussing the prospects of the coming day's forced march, when at about 5.30 a.m., 'A signaller came up with a message from the colonel to say that there would be no retirement, followed shortly by another message from Divisional Headquarters that all ammunition, food and water were to be kept in the firing line.'[8]

For the infantry in the forward positions, the news that they would soon be in combat produced a last-minute round of digging to construct some sort of defensive line to face the Germans. Equipped only with their own entrenching tools – 'grubbers' – little could be achieved before the first German shells came screaming over their position.

The shallow kneeling or shelter trenches dug by the two front-line battalions – the 2nd KOYLI and 2nd Suffolks – were 2 or 3 feet deep, providing the crouching soldier with basic protection. There was insufficient time to connect the front-line trenches into a continuous line, so companies and platoons had limited contact with each other. The trenches were also sited in full view of the advancing Germans and dangerously isolated from the supporting British troops on and behind the crest of the slope.

When Smith-Dorrien had issued his stand-and-fight order he intended it as part of a delaying action, a means to gain time and distance from his pursuers. In the transmission of the order from II Corps to 5th Division headquarters the bald and admittedly ambiguous 'no retirement' had effectively been transformed into a 'no retirement whatsoever' order.

The KOYLI and the Suffolks were instructed by staff officers and by their respective brigadiers that they must hold firm whatever the cost. Brigadier-General Cuthbert of the 13th Brigade sent a hand-written note to the KOYLI CO stating that 'there will no retirement for the fighting troops'.[9] According to the Suffolks' regimental history, Brigadier-General Rolt of the 14th Brigade told his men, 'You understand, there is to be no thought of retirement.'[10] But in this regimental history, Smith-Dorrien wrote a highly unusual foreword to the specific chapter on Le Cateau, disclaiming responsibility: 'Some one, not I, ordered that on no account were the Suffolks to retire.'[11]

In the light of Smith-Dorrien's denial, the direct order to the 13th and 14th Brigades would almost certainly have come from Major-General Fergusson, possibly fearful that the previous order for a withdrawal at 11 a.m. might affect his troops' resolve. The no retirement order was also issued to the artillery assigned to the two infantry brigades. Brigadier-General John Headlam, Commander Royal Artillery (CRA) – the division's senior artillery officer – adopted the order with a reckless determination.

A field artillery brigade had been attached to each of the 5th Division's infantry brigades. On the far right of the line, the 15th Brigade RFA (Lieutenant-Colonel C. F. Stevens) was assigned to the 14th Infantry Brigade, and the 28th Brigade RFA (Lieutenant-Colonel E. C. Cameron) supported the 13th Infantry Brigade in the centre.

As was usual in the Royal Artillery, the battery commanders began to establish their gun lines as they thought best, at some distance from the front line and making use of hollows in the terrain to hide the guns and their give-away muzzle flashes.

Headlam put a stop to this.[12] He immediately sent the six howitzers of Major Jones's 37th Battery to an exposed site directly behind the Suffolks' line, and then ordered Stevens to deploy his three batteries (11th, 52nd, 80th) alongside Jones's battery. The battery commanders were appalled. They reluctantly obeyed orders, however, although Major Henning (11th Battery) briefly withdrew his guns to a better site 400 yards to the rear, until instructed by Stevens to return to his original position. The battery commanders were emphatically instructed that, if necessary, they were to fight to the last; there would be no retirement without written orders and the men would stand by their guns whatever the enemy fire. When told of this, Major Nutt (52nd Battery) ran back from his forward observation post to the gun line to explain the enormity of the situation to his officers and men.

The vulnerability of the batteries in Cameron's 28th Brigade RFA (122nd, 123rd, 124th) was perhaps greater still. The three batteries were deployed between the forward trench line and the reserves of the KOYLI. The battery commanders and other officers were similarly dismayed by this forward deployment. Major Kinsman (124th Battery) pointed out that 'the position was an impossible one – a death trap'.[13] Lieutenant Lutyens (122nd Battery) wrote: 'We realised from the start, of course, that our gun positions couldn't be worse.'[14] The KOYLI were also unhappy with the artillery deployment, the regimental history circumspectly pointing out that the presence of the guns and their attendant limbers and horse teams, 'complicated matters' and 'severed communications between portions of the KOYLI battalion'.[15]

Why Headlam made this error of judgment – condemning both his gunners and the nearby infantry to certain ruin – remains a mystery. Contrary to some suggestions, he was not an old-school reactionary unable to cope with the recent advances in artillery technology. If anything he was a mainstream progressive, who in the lead up to the war had called for the establishment of a permanent school of gunnery on Salisbury Plain, encouraged more realistic peacetime training and, ironically, advocated advances in telephone technology to improve the artillery's indirect-fire capability.[16]

It is possible that Headlam felt the need to ensure that his gunners provide a more visible presence to the front-line troops than had been the case at Mons, where despite the difficulties in finding good fields of fire in the industrial terrain, the artillery response had been generally lethargic. And like all senior officers he was under enormous stress, a stress that may have led him to fall back on old ways where courage was believed to count for more than tactical acumen. The artillery historian Shelford Bidwell described the sort of emotional response that lay behind Headlam's decision: 'Quaint as it may seem now, many officers considered it to be ignoble to flinch from fire, however deadly, or to seek safety behind cover. It was the duty of gunners to support the infantry, and this meant to share their dangers and sacrifices, *and be seen to share them.*'[17]

The final 5th Division infantry-artillery brigade pairing – Brigadier-General Gleichen's 15th Infantry Brigade and the 27th Brigade RFA (Lieutenant-Colonel W. H. Onslow) – was deployed on the left, covering a slightly wider front than the other two brigades but under less German pressure. The 'no retirement' order had not been issued, and infantry and gunners were able to conduct operations with a suitable degree of latitude.

Major-General Hubert Hamilton's 3rd Division – holding the centre of the line – experienced few of the deployment problems of the 5th Division. The absence of an early morning German attack also gave its infantry more time to dig-in and generally prepare for battle.

Major-General Thomas Snow's 4th Division, on the British left, had spent a wretched night withdrawing from its rearguard positions around Solesmes, some units remaining in place until 9 p.m. with many getting lost in the darkness. Unsurprisingly, there was a great deal of muddle and delay, so much so that some battalions were only moving into position at around 5 a.m., just as the lead elements of Marwitz's II Cavalry Corps struck the division. In a mode of self-criticism almost unique among senior officers, Major-General Snow upbraided his own complacency during the night march: 'What I did not realise, and what I ought to have known, was that the Germans were so close on my heels; another instance of want of imagination.'[18]

•

The German First Army was certainly pressing hard on the British. Kluck could rightly applaud the extraordinary marching prowess of his infantry but his reconnaissance – cavalry and aviation – and intelligence services repeatedly let him down; he still had little idea of the strength and intentions of the British forces he was soon to attack. The 7th and 8th Divisions of his IV Corps were pushing towards the centre and right of Smith-Dorrien's line, while his II Cavalry Corps was closing in on the British left. Although the German cavalry were effective in pinning down Snow's 4th Division, their involvement in the battle was a strategic mistake. As the only mobile arm attached to First Army, the cavalry's prime function should have been to envelop the BEF by striking at its rear further to the south, and not engage in a dismounted, frontal fire-fight.

As the battle opened on the morning of 26 August, the forces deployed on both sides were broadly even, and it was with these troops that the battle would be decided. But towards the end of the day – with the battle virtually over – the Germans would begin to gain a significant material advantage, as advance troops of IV Reserve Corps arrived on the battlefield to support the cavalry attacking the British left, while

III Corps advanced towards the open British right flank, ready for action if the battle continued into the following day.

It was against the 4th Division that the first shots of the battle were fired. Lieutenant-General von der Marwitz's II Cavalry Corps comprised the 2nd, 4th and 9th Cavalry Divisions, a seemingly formidable force to pit against a single infantry division. In terms of firepower, however, the Cavalry Corps was at a disadvantage, its 36 field guns amounting to half those in the British division's inventory, with 18 machine guns against 24. And the German cavalry were armed with carbines that compared poorly with the British infantry's Lee Enfields. The Cavalry Corps did have a special advantage, however, in the attachment of five 'over-sized' Jäger light infantry battalions, each fielding a company of six machine guns.

Major-General Snow received Smith-Dorrien's order to stand and fight at 5 a.m. – just as the German cavalry divisions were about to launch their attack. The 4th Division's front line stretched eastwards from Esnes to Fontaine-au-Pire, with 12th Brigade on the left and 11th Brigade on the right. A low valley ran behind these two brigades – the grandly named Warnelle Ravine – and on the far side was the divisional headquarters at Haucourt, with the 10th Brigade held in reserve nearby.

The upheaval created by the 4th Division's nocturnal withdrawal would affect the division throughout the day, exacerbated by the difficulty of its headquarters in communicating with the brigades and battalions. Colonel J. E. Edmonds, the division's senior staff officer, was forced to improvise: 'Having no signals company, headquarters could only keep touch of the battle by using our own eyes and employing mounted orderlies and officers.'[19] When the headquarters was established outside Haucourt, a divisional flag was hoisted from the blue third of a French tricolour found in the town hall.

Despite such efforts, command and control was irretrievably weakened, with senior officers too often reduced to the role of spectators. During the night, Brigadier-General Haldane had effectively lost command of half of his 10th Brigade; although close by, he was unable to regain contact with the 1st Royal Warwickshire Regiment and the 2nd Royal Dublin Fusiliers, who were without any higher command throughout the battle and for several days afterwards.

Both of the 4th Division's two forward brigades (11th and 12th) came under attack before 6 a.m. The 12th Brigade was soon in difficulties.

Seemingly unaware of the close proximity of the Germans, the brigade had made little effort to establish an outpost line. The right-hand battalion – the 1st King's Own (Royal Lancasters) – was still in column with its arms stacked when it was ambushed by massed machine-gun fire from Jägers and dismounted cavalry. The initial barrage of German machine-gun fire killed the CO and produced instant chaos as the men scrambled to retrieve their rifles and return fire. German artillery joined in the attack, blasting the remnants of the battalion backwards to the safety of the dead ground of the Warnelle Ravine.

On the other side of the ravine, Captain Harold Hart of the Warwickshires witnessed the debacle: 'As we looked northward, a terrible sight was to be seen; down the Cattenieres road poured the remnants of a battalion, the 1st King's Own, while two of their wagons, the horses dead, lay on the side of the road.'[20] The Warwicks' CO, Lieutenant-Colonel J. F. Elkington, made a snap decision to support the King's Own. Lieutenant Bernard Montgomery of C Company described the ensuing action in his memoirs:

> Our battalion was deployed in two lines; my company and one other were forward, with the remaining companies out of sight some hundred yards to the rear. The CO galloped up to us forward companies and shouted to us to attack the enemy on the forward hill at once. This was the only order; there was no reconnaissance, no plan, no covering fire.[21]

Of his own part in the attack, Montgomery had this to say:

> Waving my sword I ran forward in front of my platoon, but unfortunately I had only gone six paces when I tripped over my scabbard, the sword fell from my hand (I hadn't wound that sword strap round my wrist in the approved fashion!) and I fell flat on my face on very hard ground. By the time I had picked myself up and rushed after my men I found that most of them had been killed.[22]

Hart was in a reserve position but he immediately went forward and was ordered by Elkington to join the attack: 'The leading company had got a flying start, and had got well up the hill before those in the rear had got more than two-thirds of the way up and were already being driven back under artillery, machine gun and rifle fire.'[23]

The Warwickshires fell back to their original position, joined by soldiers from the King's Own. Nothing had been gained by Elkington's rash action, and although the casualties were relatively light – just under 50 killed and wounded – the battalion, as the regimental history dolefully noted, 'was now split up and out of touch with what was going on around it'.[24]

The Jägers and cavalry now began to concentrate on the three remaining battalions of the 12th Brigade. The German fire – especially from their machine guns – was considered sufficiently heavy and accurate for the brigade commander, Brigadier-General H. M. Wilson, to retire to a new position across the Warnelle Ravine. Major-General Snow found himself an exasperated onlooker: 'The left part of the position was given up about 9 a.m. and the 12th Brigade fell back on Haucourt with its left about Esnes. I never quite understood the necessity of this retirement, except that the brigade had been shaken at the outset.'[25]

During the withdrawal of the 4th Division on the night of the 25th/26th, the artillery had been ahead of the infantry. When the order to fight had been issued the infantry turned around to face the enemy, leaving the guns well behind them. In this opening phase of the battle, artillery support was necessarily limited, but once the batteries were back in position the division became a more effective force. C. L. Brereton, an officer in the 68th Battery (14th Brigade, RFA), described his unit's deployment as the 12th Brigade fell back across the Warnelle Ravine:

> Infantry were coming hurriedly down the slopes towards us and through us. Most of them looked exhausted, and it was evident that they had been badly cut up. Wounded were being tended by the side of the road, but it was obvious there were no ambulances, and practically no medical arrangements. We eventually got into action just S. E. of Haucourt, and registered to the ridge in front and to a few other points. The ground was very heavy and horses already rather exhausted. Enemy's infantry soon poured over the crest, but we engaged them with great success and they retired back over the crest.[26]

The precipitate withdrawal of the 12th Brigade – now mixed up with the 10th Brigade on the south side of the ravine – did at least produce a strong defensive line, which, with the firepower of two artillery brigades, prevented any further German progress against the British left flank.

The 11th Brigade, deployed on the right of the 4th Division's sector, put up a determined fight. They were also attacked by a combination of Jägers and dismounted cavalrymen, supported by an impressive tally of 24 machine guns (against the eight of the 11th Brigade). Initial contact was made as early as 4 a.m. and by 6 a.m. fighting was widespread, with the Germans trying to work around the British flanks, whose centre was based on several gravel pits marked on the map as 'The Quarry'. The 1st Battalion Rifle Brigade, on the brigade's right, defended its position against the 3rd Jäger Battalion. Jäger lieutenant Claus-Just von Lattorf wrote admiringly of his fellow light-infantrymen opponents:

> Not for nothing were the elite British troops that opposed us called 'Rifles Brigade' [sic]. They were battle-hardened professional soldiers, who had fought on every continent. They were a tough, callous lot, who maintained an extraordinary calm, even when wounded. Their marksmanship and fieldcraft on favourable terrain was of such a high order that even for Jägers it was extraordinarily difficult to draw a bead on them.[27]

The Germans had some success in bringing enfilade fire to bear on the left of the 11th Brigade, forcing some of the British to withdraw to a railway embankment to the south-west of The Quarry. But as the morning developed the fighting lessened in intensity, both sides short of ammunition. The Germans were also aware that the vanguard of their IV Reserve Corps was near at hand.

•

In the centre of the British line – held by the 3rd Division – the German assault did not develop fully until late morning. Captain Brownlow's ammunition column – serving the division's 40th Brigade RFA – was continuing its southerly withdrawal when a staff officer intercepted it and ordered it to turn around and advance to the sound of the guns. Brownlow recalled trotting over the crest of a rise by the village of Clary and seeing the whole battlefield spread out before him:

> Though the infantry were invisible, I could see our artillery, who presented a grand spectacle. On the southern slopes of the ridge, some fully and some

partially concealed from the enemy, our batteries stretched in an irregular line from right to left. The guns and wagons and detachments stood dark and distinct, though diminished through distance to minute weapons and tiny figures. Every gun was firing, and countless flashes of light scintillated against the gold and green sweep of the country. The whole of the scene was flecked with the white and yellow smoke clouds of enemy shrapnel and high explosive, the nearer of which appeared to be tongued with cruel yellow flames. I could see the bursting shells smashing and crumping the villages, sweeping the batteries with a hail of death and searching the valleys and hidden approaches. And all the while the thunder of the guns rolled and reverberated in deep-toned waves of sound which spread and spread in ever-growing circles.[28]

The panoramic view described by Brownlow – of an army fighting in the open – would have been a recognizable sight to any 19th-century soldier but was soon to be a thing of the past. Le Cateau would be the last such battle fought by the British Army before the advent of trench warfare.

Brownlow's artilleryman's eye also caught the need for the concealment of the guns. In the 3rd Division's sector most of the early fighting consisted of a series of artillery duels, and those batteries exposed to enemy view suffered accordingly. This was the experience of Lieutenant S. C. M. Archibald's 6th Battery (40th Brigade RFA), deployed behind Audencourt, in the centre of the 3rd Division line. Following standard practice, the battery commander (Major Brooke) went to the Observation Post (OP) 200–300 yards forward of the battery, now hidden behind a low crest that ran parallel with the gun line. The six-horse gun team retired to the rear to the safety of the wagon line with its reserves of ammunition (every gun or howitzer was assigned two ammunition wagons, each with a six-horse team).

Almost immediately the battery was ordered to switch its firing line 45 degrees to the east, leaving the left-hand side of the battery only semi-covered. As the gunners began to fire on the advancing German infantry they came under fire from a German battery. 'The Bosches,' Archibald wrote, 'evidently thought we were being rather a nuisance for soon they turned another battery on to us, and we began to take casualties. Most of the men stood up to the shelling admirably though one or two of the younger ones needed a bit of encouragement and in one case, firm treatment.'[29]

To make matters more difficult, the ammunition wagons were unable to come up to the battery, and with ammunition running low the 18-pounder shells had to be transferred by hand over open ground. Archibald continued his account:

> By this time we had about 3 killed and 12 wounded, not a great number but enough, combined with the difficulties of ammunition supply, to slow down our rate of fire. Brooke had now been joined at the O.P. by the Colonel and the CRA, and I was given the order to withdraw the [gun-crew] detachments to cover, into the sunken road at the right rear of the position. There we waited for some time while rifle bullets kept cracking and whining over, and we were able to pay attention to some of the wounded and get the worst ones off to a dressing station.[30]

The counter-battery duels would continue until the British artillery was eventually ordered to withdraw.

•

The 8th and 9th Infantry Brigades, holding the centre and right of the 3rd Division line, resisted the enemy attacks made in the late morning. A German officer of the 153rd Regiment, while praising the professionalism of his own troops' advance against the British 8th Brigade, also wrote: 'The intense infantry fire from the main British positions, carefully concealed in the sugar-beet fields, which even at 500m could hardly be detected with the naked eye, finally slowed the advance.'[31]

The 1st Gordon Highlanders were among the well-hidden troops facing the 153rd Regiment. Within their ranks, Lieutenant Malcolm Hay noticed how the artillery duel eventually went in favour of the Germans, who were greatly aided by aircraft flying over British trenches and artillery positions to indicate their presence to German gunners. Hay also saw the first signs of the German infantry advance in the early afternoon:

> My glasses showed they were extended to not more than two paces, keeping a very bad line, evidently very weary and marching in the hot sun in manifold

disgust. The command, 'Five rounds rapid at the stubble field 900 yards,' produced a cinematographic picture in my field-glasses. The Germans hopped into cover like rabbits. Some threw themselves flat behind the corn stooks, and when the firing ceased got up and bolted back to the wood. Two or three who had appeared to fling themselves down, remained motionless.[32]

After this surprise, the German infantry swiftly adopted correct training-ground tactics, with artillery in support, as Hay described:

> The enemy, having discovered that we could be dangerous even at 900 yards, then successfully crossed the stubble field in two short rushes without losing a man, and reinforced their men who were advancing through the beetroot fields on our right.
>
> They were advancing in short rushes across pastureland which provided no cover whatever, and they offered a clearly visible target even when lying down. Although our men were nearly all first-class shots, they did not often hit the target. This was owing to the unpleasant fact that the German gunners kept up a steady stream of shrapnel, which burst just in front of our trenches and broke over the top like a wave. Shooting at the advancing enemy had to be timed by the bursting shell.[33]

Despite the accurate fire from the German guns, the Gordons slowed the enemy advance, so that their infantry took more than an hour to reach the main Cambrai–Le Cateau road, some 400 yards from the closest British trench. 'Here they were able to concentrate in great numbers,' Hay continued, 'as the road runs along an embankment behind which nothing but artillery could reach them. This was the situation on our front at about three o'clock in the afternoon.'[34]

The Germans seemed content to hold their position and await reinforcements, although they maintained a heavy fire on the British line. At 4 p.m. Hay was hit in the head by a German machine-gun bullet, but through the good care of his comrades and subsequently by French medical staff, he survived.

The 7th Brigade, assigned to defend the town of Caudry on the 3rd Division's left had a more difficult time. Caudry acted as a promontory in the British line, and from the outset was heavily shelled. While shrapnel shells did little more than break tiles on house roofs, the high-explosive shells of the German artillery smashed through the buildings. The fire from a battery of 15cm heavy howitzers – whose black smoke gave them the various nicknames of coal-boxes, black marias or Jack Johnsons – was directed on Caudry. Corporal John Lucy of the 2nd Royal Irish Rifles was woken by the crash of German artillery:

> Enemy shells began to slash into the streets, and a rumble of falling masonry was heard between the reverberating reports of the explosions. It sounded exactly like thunder, blinding flashes followed by the rumble of collapsing houses. The townspeople grew afraid and panicked about. They ran into houses, carefully locking their doors, and at the next roar of shells they opened their doors again, and so kept rushing out and in like rabbits, and sometimes grouping for a moment or two in the streets in little staring crowds.[35]

The initial dispositions of the 7th Brigade had the 3rd Worcestershires holding a line of trenches to the north-west of Caudry, the 2nd South Lancashires directly to the north and the 1st Wiltshires to the north-east, with the Irish Rifles in reserve to the south of the town. But as so often occurred in the British deployment there was widespread bewilderment, units retiring without orders and then being sent back into line. Brigadier-General McCracken seemed to have had little or no control over his brigade. Captain H. F. Stacke, the regimental historian of the Worcestershires, offered this explanation for the breakdown in discipline:

> No very definite orders as to the length of their resistance reached the front line. All ranks knew that a general retreat was in progress. Moved by that knowledge, rather than pressure of the enemy, various units of the defending troops fell back from the northern to the southern end of the town. In so doing several units became disordered and there were many stragglers. Lt. A. C. Johnston of the Regiment, attached to the 7th Brigade Staff, rallied stragglers of all units in the main square of the town, organized them into a fighting force and then led them to a new position on a spur to the westward.[36]

Lieutenant Johnston took a less understanding view of the soldiers' behaviour: 'There were a lot of men making their way back in a disgraceful manner, even NCOs. I managed, however, to stop them quite easily and to get them back into the firing line without trouble. It makes one sad and anxious for the future to see Englishmen behave like this, and the fire was not really heavy nor the losses great.'[37]

Johnston led these troops to join the other defenders manning the northern perimeter of Caudry, where, if nothing else, they escaped the high-explosive bombardment of the town itself. Companies from both the Royal Irish Regiment and Royal Irish Rifles were sent through the town to reinforce the line, although, in fact, the dismounted German cavalrymen firing at the British positions lacked the resources to mount an attack and merely maintained a steady pressure with rifles and machine guns.

At around 1.40 p.m. the German artillery fire increased in intensity, leading the forward elements of the 7th Brigade to evacuate Caudry. On seeing the unauthorized withdrawal, General Hamilton ordered the brigade to retake the town, which had now been occupied by the Germans. Hamilton also ordered Lieutenant-Colonel Bird of the Irish Rifles to take command of the brigade, as a shell blast had apparently stunned Brigadier-General McCracken. A counter-attack spearheaded by the Worcestershires and Irish Rifles retook Caudry, except for the northern edge, which remained in German hands. Bird continued to hold his position despite receiving various instructions to retire, until Hamilton gave him a direct order to do so.

Even allowing for the feeble performance of elements of the 7th Brigade in Caudry, the troops of the 3rd Division were comfortably holding the line. But their fate, along with the rest of Smith-Dorrien's force, depended on what was happening to the 5th Division in and around Le Cateau on the right flank. It was here that the battle would be decided.

CHAPTER EIGHT

LE CATEAU: THE DEFEAT

The 19th Infantry Brigade had spent the night in Le Cateau, but before dawn broke on the 26th preparations were underway to redeploy the four battalions to act as a reserve behind the British front line. As the brigade assembled in the town square at around 6 a.m., a sudden cry of alarm signalled an attack by German cavalry. They were easily repulsed, but as the last of the British infantry marched westward out of Le Cateau along the Cambrai road, so advance troops of the German 72nd Infantry Regiment took over the town.

The sudden arrival of the Germans in Le Cateau caught the 1st Duke of Cornwall's Light Infantry (DCLI) and the two companies of 1st East Surreys by surprise. Having bivouacked for the night immediately to the east of Le Cateau, the British troops – unaware that the retreat order had been cancelled – were preparing to rejoin II Corps to the west of the town when they came under German small-arms fire. They were driven from their positions. After a failed counter-attack on Le Cateau, intermingled companies and platoons of the two battalions withdrew in various directions. Some retired due east and eventually ended up with Haig's I Corps, although the majority fell back in a southerly direction alongside the Selle valley to rejoin II Corps later in the day. As a consequence, however, the 14th Infantry Brigade had lost the use of a battalion and a half as it prepared to hold the vital high ground south-west of Le Cateau.

While the DCLI and East Surreys were retreating they encountered Gough's 3rd Cavalry Brigade. Although a few guns of the brigade's horse artillery gave some help to the hard-pressed right-flank of II Corps, Gough made no attempt to liaise with Smith-Dorrien or his commanders to provide any real assistance to the 5th Division. After the war, Gough insouciantly explained away his lack of initiative: 'The position I held was … important to the right flank of II Corps, but unfortunately, owing to my entire ignorance of the situation, I did not hold it as long as I might have done.'[1]

•

The German 72nd Infantry Regiment – temporarily detached from the 8th Division – waited for the arrival of the 7th Division, whose 66th and 26th Infantry Regiments would spearhead the attack on the British positions around Le Cateau. The German batteries swiftly unlimbered to support the infantry advance, which, as the light improved, came under British artillery fire. Major Nutt of the 52nd Battery noted that his guns, 'opened fire on columns about 6.15 a.m., range about 5,000 yards, they soon deployed and disappeared into dead ground'.[2] Although the German guns were hidden behind the forward slopes, gun flashes were visible and these were fired upon, Nutt claiming to have silenced one battery.

Lieutenant Roderick MacLeod of the 80th Battery recalled that when 'the mist lifted the high ground on the opposite side of the valley beyond the embankment was seen to be crowded with Germans. We opened with battery fire at 4,000 yards, gradually reducing the range as the Germans advanced. They suffered severely.'[3] During their approach march towards Le Cateau the German infantry columns had proved vulnerable, but having come under fire they deployed into skirmishing lines, making good use of the available dead ground. Ominously, it did not take long for the German gunners to get the range of the British batteries of the 15th Brigade RFA. MacLeod endured the bombardment:

More and more German batteries came into action, a big concentration being at Rambourlieux farm which was now visible on our left flank and from which they enfiladed our position. Our wagon lines were also hit. Some German aeroplanes flew over us, and when vertically above let drop what looked like streamers of silver paper. This was evidently a method of giving the Germans the range to our guns, for shortly afterwards their fire on our batteries, after a couple of ranging rounds, became much more accurate and heavy, and we all began to suffer several casualties, though many shrapnel bullets were kept off by our gun shields with a rattling noise. I was proud of the steadiness of my men. They might have been on a gun drill parade.[4]

MacLeod was under the impression that the German guns outnumbered those of the British by four to one. Given the intensity of fire raining down on the British, this was understandable but, overall, the numbers were broadly even; the difference came through superior German concentration of fire, the exposed nature of the British batteries and the German gunners' ability to fire a large volume of high explosive, not least the 95lb shells from their 15cm howitzers. The German gunners hidden behind Rambourlieux farm were surprised and delighted at seeing the British artillery out in the open, one commander apparently 'beside himself with joy'.[5]

The British guns also came under German rifle and machine-gun fire; their size made them easy long-range targets. Lieutenant Schacht, the commander of the machine-gun company of the 26th Regiment, recorded how he 'could see a battery which, according to our doctrine, was located too far forward, in amongst the line of infantrymen'.[6] Schacht then successfully turned his machine guns on the battery at a range in excess of 1,500 yards.

The three batteries of 28th Brigade RFA almost immediately became targets for German sharpshooters on the Montay spur to their front. The 123rd and 124th Batteries were highly visible, with the latter only realizing it was facing the 'wrong way' when it came under German artillery fire (the gunners were forced to manhandle the guns around during the German bombardment). The 122nd Battery was less exposed, and one of its officers, Lieutenant Lionel Lutyens, described how the crews 'kept up as steady and as smart a rate of fire as if they were on parade, right up to the last moment, and the other two batteries kept on firing in spite of terrible casualties'.[7]

In addition to the gun crews suffering heavy losses, the senior officers at their forward observation posts were also being hit. Colonel Stevens, the 15th Brigade RFA commander, was forward with Major Jones (37th Battery), stationed alongside the Suffolks' machine-gun detachment, and though both men were repeatedly wounded early on in the battle they remained at their posts. Nutt was shot through the throat at 11.50 a.m., but he continued to whisper orders to his gunners; a suggestion that the battery should retire was categorically rebuffed.

The heavy German fire had also cut the telephone wires connecting the guns to the battery commanders; signallers waving flags were then used, but as they progressively became casualties so the batteries were forced to rely on a chain of orderlies to lie out in the open and shout out instructions.

As a result of the increasing losses to enemy fire and, in some batteries, shortages of ammunition, the rate of fire of the British guns slackened. By 12.20 p.m., in Nutt's 52nd Battery, only one gun was firing, and then 'at long intervals'.[8] All the while, the crews and forward infantry were being blasted by shrapnel and high explosive. An officer in the 18th Hussars – on the far side of the Selle valley – wrote how 'the whole spur was churned up by German shells, and earth was thrown about as if by a succession of mines'.[9]

Another observer of the destruction of the two artillery brigades was the British divisional artillery commander himself, Brigadier-General John Headlam: 'The Germans had brought up their heavy howitzers, and, what was worse, had somehow located the position of our guns for they commenced registering them scientifically. It was terrible to watch the heavy salvoes creeping nearer and nearer, and to see the reply getting fainter and fainter until it all but died away – and then to see the concentrated fire methodically turned on the next battery.'[10] That Headlam had expressly ordered the guns forward – allowing the Germans to 'somehow locate' them through the simple expedient of eyesight – seemed to have been forgotten.

Fortunately for the main 5th Division position, the two batteries held back continued to function effectively. The 61st (Howitzer) Battery was completely hidden from German view, and maintained a constant fire until ordered to withdraw. The four 60-pounders of the 108th Battery were also concealed in a dip although, according to battery commander Major de Sausmarez, they were unable to find good counter-battery targets until around midday:

> The light had now improved and the guns, which from near the township of Croix had been doing so much damage, were at last discovered as well as some on a position closer in. The guns at Croix appeared to cease firing soon after the battery had found their range, whilst those closer in began to sweep and search for the [108th] Battery, whose position, however, was so well concealed that they never brought really effective fire to bear on it.[11]

The 27th Brigade RFA – supporting the 15th Infantry Brigade on the division's left – was not the focus of the main German attack, but in marked contrast to much of the division's artillery, its guns were well concealed, and in the words of brigade adjutant Captain Josslyn Ramsden, fired all day, 'practically without being touched, so well had their position been chosen'.[12]

•

Although the British guns were the Germans' prime target during the morning, the close proximity of artillery to infantry ensured that 'overs' caused casualties among the infantry. At around 7 a.m. the positions held by the 2nd Suffolk Regiment and the 2nd KOYLI were first hit by German artillery fire. Lieutenant Wynne of the KOYLI described the initial phase of the attack, with German shells flying over and amidst his position:

> The bombardment continued throughout the morning and apart from an occasional shot, my platoon lay among the turnips with nothing to do but watch the destruction and wait for its own. A rise in the ground prevented our seeing what was happening at or in front of the trenches on our left facing the Cambrai Road, but about 11 o'clock heavy firing from them and a constant rush of bullets over and about us showed that the infantry attack had begun.[13]

The Suffolks faced the brunt of the initial attack. As the German infantry pushed forward, they were ably supported by the massed fire of their machine guns. The German 26th Infantry Regiment, advancing on the Suffolks and the 15th Brigade RFA, deployed two machine-gun companies, 12 machine guns in all against the two guns of their immediate opponents.[14] Understandably, the Suffolks began to waver. The 2nd Manchesters and 2nd Argyll and Sutherland Highlanders were rushed forward to reinforce the Suffolks' position, but most were shot down or repulsed, leaving only a small number to reach the relative safety of the front-line trenches.

As the morning progressed the continuing German bombardment began to chip away at the morale of the 5th Division. Not long after 10.30 a.m., Major Sausmarez, his 108th Battery towards the rear of the division, revealed his concern: 'Our infantry began to leave the trenches, and the enemy were following them up with shell fire. One line retired slowly past the battery's observing station, there were no officers with it.'[15]

In battle, unauthorized withdrawals were quite common. Thus, for example, a wounded man might be cared for by several solicitous comrades as they escorted him back to a first aid post, or, if there were no officers present, men might simply fall back to a safer line. Experienced officers were well aware of this tendency and either through encouragement or threat (or both) would rally the retiring troops and send them back into combat, usually with few problems. The key was to act swiftly to prevent such withdrawals gaining an unstoppable momentum. By midday, however, the 5th Division was at a tipping point. Sausmarez recalled that now, 'successive waves of infantry were leaving the trenches'.[16]

Major-General Fergusson was also aware of the problem, and at 1.20 p.m. he had signalled Smith-Dorrien at II Corps HQ to say that unless he received reinforcements he would be forced to retire. Fergusson's fears were compounded by the knowledge that any German advance along the Selle valley – which seemed imminent – would place his whole command in jeopardy. Smith-Dorrien's earlier stated intention of a planned withdrawal under cover of darkness was dashed. At 1.40 p.m. a further message arrived from Fergusson, saying his 'troops were beginning to dribble away under their severe punishment'.[17]

Smith-Dorrien agreed to Fergusson's request but was now faced with the difficult process of withdrawing his forces while fully engaged with the enemy. The II Corps chief of staff, Brigadier-General G. T. Forestier-Walker, issued orders for the 5th Division to retire first, to be followed in order by the 3rd and 4th Divisions.

Headlam, belatedly aware of the desperate position of his forward artillery, sent orders for a general withdrawal. His brigade major was despatched to supervise the extraction of the 15th Brigade RFA, while Headlam rode forward to instruct the 28th Brigade RFA to retire, giving permission for the crews to take cover in the sunken road.

Although the sunken road gave protection to the crews, it prevented the horse teams from crossing over to limber up the guns on the far side. As a result, Headlam ordered the teams back, and at some point after 2 p.m. instructed the gunners to disable and then abandon their guns – an order reluctantly obeyed. But the six teams of the 122nd Battery, under Captain A. P. Jones, had already galloped forward, and as they cleared the crest of the slope they encountered a hurricane of machine-gun and artillery fire. Jones, eight drivers and 20 horses were killed almost immediately. The Official History vividly recorded the attempted rescue: 'It was an extraordinary sight: a short wild scene of galloping and falling horses, and then four guns standing derelict, a few limbers lying about, one on the skyline with its pole vertical, and dead men and dead horses everywhere.'[18]

Lieutenant Lutyens recalled how Major Sanders, the 122nd Battery commander, 'had stood upright in the road the whole time, and was the last to leave'.[19] Two guns from the battery were saved, but the other 16 guns of the 28th Brigade RFA were left behind. Lutyens was among the last to gallop away: 'We were bent over our horses' necks all the way down the road, as bullets were still flying pretty thick. We turned off after a few hundreds of yards, up the bank and away to the wagon position. I soon caught [Lieutenant] Peel up, and together we collected what was left of the battery.'[20]

The recall of the 15th Brigade RFA, along with the 37th (Howitzer) Battery, was made difficult by a shortage of horses, limbers and drivers, the wagon lines to the rear having already suffered from German artillery fire. Major Henning of the 11th Battery made the decision to withdraw himself, without reference to higher authority, and although all the officers and many of the men were wounded, five guns were successfully withdrawn (although another was lost later in the retirement).[21] In the other batteries, the surviving crews were surprised to see the arrival of the horse teams, as no formal written order had been issued for them to retire. Colonel Stevens and Majors Jones and Nutt at the forward observation posts refused to withdraw and were subsequently captured.

The 80th Battery had two guns in operation when it came under renewed German fire, wounding the battery commander Major Birley and Lieutenant Roderick MacLeod, the latter hit in the head and arm by shrapnel bullets. While incapacitated, MacLeod witnessed the attempt to rescue the guns: 'At about 2.30 p.m. I saw all the brigade teams racing up at the gallop from the wagon lines led by Major Tailyour, the brigade major, and by Captain Higgon. It was a magnificent sight. Now and again a man or horse or whole team would go down from the fire directed at them. Balaclava all over again!'[22]

MacLeod's comparison with the Charge of the Light Brigade was certainly apt, for as the French observer of the charge, General Bosquet, noted at the time, it may have been magnificent but it was not war – certainly not how war should be waged in 1914. Almost miraculously, five guns were recovered, with some of the wounded, including MacLeod, loaded onto limbers and withdrawn to safety. Of the 24 guns in the 15th Brigade RFA position, ten were lost.

As the artillery retreated they were joined by the infantry of the 5th Division, except for the Suffolks and KOYLI who were now hotly engaged. They were trapped in their trenches on the forward slope of the Le Cateau position; any withdrawal would be made in full sight of the enemy, who possessed an increasingly powerful armoury of weapons to bring to bear on the two battalions. Between 1 and 2 p.m. the Germans had paused to regroup and redeploy their machine guns in new forward positions, and at around 2.30 p.m. they resumed their attack in earnest. The Suffolks – along with men of the Argyll and Sutherland Highlanders and Manchesters – were overcome in the German charge.

The Germans had also brought up troops and machine guns to line the main Le Cateau–Cambrai road, directly in front of the KOYLI. For the first time that day, Wynne – on the right of the battalion – was able to fire directly at the enemy:

The infantry and machine-gun fire from the German lines as they began to advance increased at every moment. The noise was so great around that even by the loudest shouting, I could only give fire orders to the two or three men nearest me. However, though a drizzling shower was relieving a monotony of a dull, grey day, the air was clear and the men could see their obvious target with their naked eye as well as I could see through field glasses. Having passed along the range (900 yards to the German infantry on the slope opposite) I had to leave the rest to them, and they pumped out the bullets with visible pleasure and enjoyment.[23]

At a little after 3 p.m. Wynne witnessed the end of the Suffolks. Preceded by muffled cheering and shouting, just audible over the sound of battle, Wynne and his men saw a mass of German soldiers appear on the low ridge separating them from the Suffolks. They and other British troops immediately opened fire on the 'apparently meaningless mass' but looking through his field glasses Wynne saw khaki uniforms among the field grey: 'The Suffolk Regiment's position just over the sky-line had been rushed with the bayonet, and the charge had continued over the sky-line and a short way down the slope facing us. The fire on our side of the ridge was evidently too much for them and the mass quickly swayed back like a great wave behind the sky-line again.'[24] A few minutes later, 'well-extended lines of German infantry advanced from where the mass had just disappeared. They advanced by sectional rushes down the front slope for about fifty yards, gradually forming a long line extending the length of the ridge, and immediately opened a heavy rifle on us in reply to our own.'[25]

On the KOYLI's left the situation was equally serious: the withdrawal of the King's Own Scottish Borderers had allowed the Germans to take up new forward positions on a slight rise so that the men of the KOYLI were now being fired on from three sides by vastly superior forces. Major C. E. Heathcote, the commander of A Company on the left, was in a reserve position during the start of the engagement, and out of contact with the CO, Lieutenant-Colonel R. C. Bond, he had never received the 'no retirement' order. Unable to communicate with the other companies Heathcote eventually decided to take his men out of the line; they 'retired at a steady double under heavy shrapnel fire, suffering a good many casualties'.[26]

In the KOYLI centre, the troops fought on but ammunition was running low and the Germans closing in. Colonel Bond described the battalion's final moments, which included Major C. A. L. Yate's VC-winning last charge, widely lauded at the time but rendered a little less glorious in Bond's sober report: 'At about 4.20 p.m. the final rush came. In B Company, Major Yate gave the order to meet it with a charge, but the number of men near him able to support it was so small that his desperate call met with practically no response. Major Yate himself, with other officers of his company, was overpowered and disarmed.'[27]

On the KOYLI's right, Wynne was knocked down by a shrapnel blast, and getting up he looked through his glasses to see white flags appearing in the trenches to his left and 'men lying down and taking no further part in the proceedings'.[28] The once constant noise of battle began to fade and Wynne turned to see a line of German infantry, bayonets fixed, advancing on his left flank only yards away. He considered his position hopeless: 'I was completely beaten in the day's game and as befits the conquered I must accept defeat and the consequences with as good grace as I was able.'[29] He stood up with his men and surrendered to soldiers from the 26th Infantry Regiment.

According to the regimental history, KOYLI casualties totalled 600 officers and men, of whom over half were captured. The Suffolks lost more heavily still, suffering around 720 casualties. But the rearguard action had bought vital time for the retreat of the remainder of the 5th Division. The German 26th and 66th Infantry Regiments had focused their attack against these two battalions, and according to Terence Zuber, were 'in no condition to conduct a pursuit. They had lost significant numbers of leaders and the two regiments were mixed up and scattered all over the battlefield.'[30]

The Germans failed – or were unable – to follow up their advantage elsewhere against the British 5th Division when it was at its most vulnerable. Cyril Helm, the MO of what remained of the KOYLI, described the retreat from an advanced dressing station at Maurois: 'The road was now in a most indescribable state of confusion; infantry, cavalry, guns, limbers, wagons, ambulances, staff cars and every conceivable form of vehicle, all going as hard as they could and all mixed up together. Things were not improved by the fact that the Germans were starting to shell the village.'[31]

The Germans' advance along the Selle valley, which had the potential to outflank the British position, was not pressed with any urgency, German efforts held by an ad hoc mixture of British infantry units and two batteries of horse artillery. A strong German cavalry presence was markedly absent when it could have been most useful.

•

The centre of the British line, comprising the 3rd Division and the 15th Infantry Brigade (from the 5th Division), was not in close contact with the enemy at the time when the withdrawal order was sent out in the early afternoon. The retirement should have been relatively trouble-free but was marred by poor staff work and weak leadership.

On the right-centre, the 15th and 9th Infantry Brigades – well-supported by their artillery – had held all German attacks during the day, and withdrew in good order around 3.30 p.m. Two two-gun artillery sections had been pushed forward among the front-line trenches – providing useful, close fire support – but could not be withdrawn and were subsequently disabled and abandoned. Casualties were minimal, and of these it would seem most were caused by German artillery as the troops retired from their trenches.

The experience of the 8th Infantry Brigade – under the command of the all-but anonymous Brigadier-General B. J. C. Doran – holding the centre of the line, was rather different, however. Orders to retire were sent out to the battalions between 3.30 and 4 p.m. The 1st Gordon Highlanders and two companies of the 2nd Royal Irish Regiment, with some men from the 2nd Royal Scots – who held the main defensive line between Audencourt and Caudry – received verbal retirement orders from two separate staff officers. A few troops acted directly on the shouted orders, but the senior officers decided to hold their position until confirmation came through in writing. As this written confirmation did not arrive, they remained in their trenches throughout the evening. A better staff system would have ensured that the orders (verbal or written) were acted upon, although the senior officers in the Gordons showed an unfortunate lack of initiative in failing to find out what was going on around them – even allowing for the noise of battle and the limited visual range of men in trenches, where eye level is at ground level.

The remainder of the brigade – the Royal Scots, part of the Royal Irish Regiment and 4th Middlesex in reserve – began its withdrawal, those troops in the forward trenches coming under artillery fire. It was then that a large group of the retiring infantry began to panic, initiating a headlong rush that dragged in other troops. Lieutenant T. S. Wollocombe, of the 4th Middlesex, put the panic down to poor staff work: 'The order to retire was given in such a way as to cause alarm. The whole division [sic] left the position at once and ran through the village [Audencourt] which was being heavily shelled. This was a rather sad ending to a glorious day, but it was not the men's fault at all as the order was given in such a rotten way.'[32]

The incident, perhaps understandably not mentioned in the regimental histories of those involved, nor indeed the Official History, caused surprise and dismay to its many witnesses. Lieutenant Tower of the 4th Royal Fusiliers wrote: 'The scene on the road baffles any description I can give of it. It was a veritable rout, men horses, guns, refugees and wagons struggling along in disorder to get away at any costs.'[33] In his diary, Captain Johnston of the 3rd Worcestershires similarly recalled that 'it was an awful sight, a perfect rabble of men of all ranks and corps abandoning their equipment and in some cases their rifles in order to get into safety in rear'.[34]

Corporal John Lucy of the 2nd Irish Rifles, withdrawing from Caudry with the battalion ammunition carts, encountered the broken troops some distance behind the front line:

Down the road I went, and saw a dreadful spectacle. Wagons, guns, and men were breaking in helter-skelter on to the road from the captured lines on the right, enemy shells pursuing them. One regiment had partly panicked. The traffic became chaotic. The drivers in rear under the cracking shells whipped up their horses regardless of the rules of the road. Cries of urgency rose on all sides. Infantrymen mounted every vehicle in sight, while others ran alongside. Some of their wounded were slung on the gun limbers.

A staff officer, his face hot with the shame of it, diverted the fleeing men into a side street in the first village we came to, shouting frantically at them: 'For God's sake men, be British soldiers.'

They swept my carts with them in the confusion, and I halted my convoy opposite to them while they were being marshaled with difficulty by the staff officer. The sight of these soldiers from a regular battalion, stampeding, grumbling, and looking about while they were being reformed was an unforgettable and disgraceful scene. The staff officer, noticing that my section did not belong to that lot, ordered me on. The movement of my convoy to rejoin the main road was the last straw, and the sign of *sauve qui peut* to men already in flight. Those farthest down the line from the officer broke away, murmuring, and the whole lot, following suit, streamed off again in an undisciplined mob, leaving the chagrined officer alone and impotent.[35]

Once beyond the reach of the German guns – with exhaustion gaining the upper hand over the imperative for flight – the men came to a halt. They then joined other retreating units, to be directed by staff officers along the various roads chosen for the withdrawal.

The final formation in the British centre – the 7th Infantry Brigade under the temporary command of Lieutenant-Colonel W. D. Bird – held its position south of Caudry until shortly after 5 p.m. when it withdrew in good order, untroubled by German fire.

●

On the British left, the 11th Infantry Brigade, holding The Quarry, found itself increasingly exposed, especially as the early retreat of the 12th Brigade on its left was followed by the withdrawal of the 7th Brigade from Caudry on its right. The Germans resupplied ammunition to the forward troops of the Cavalry Corps, and from approximately midday onwards batteries of artillery from IV Reserve Corps began to arrive and deploy on the battlefield. At a time shortly after 2 p.m., as German fire intensified, Brigadier-General A. G. Hunter-Weston decided to bring his 11th Brigade back across the Warnelle ravine to a less vulnerable position around Ligny.

The dead ground at the bottom of the ravine provided the retreating troops with good cover, but as they emerged on the far side they were caught by the German guns. The regimental historian of the 1st East Lancashires described the withdrawal:

The actual order for the retirement was given verbally to the assembled troops by the brigade commander, and in this difficult position was misunderstood, so that the Brigade moved off practically in mass, contrary to the intention of the brigade commander. The approach of the Brigade into the open in this dense formation, as it commenced to climb the long slope towards Ligny, totally devoid of cover, was the signal for a perfect storm of shrapnel and machine-gun fire from the Germans, causing considerable loss. Companies and platoons became hopelessly disorganised.[36]

Once in Ligny the troops began to dig trenches around the town perimeter. Hunter-Weston had ordered his withdrawal just in time, for shortly after 3 p.m. the advanced guard of the German 7th Reserve Division reached the le Cateau-Cambrai road. Captain Alfred Wirth – on the division's staff – recalled coming under shrapnel fire as he advanced towards Wambaix, and witnessing medical staff helping the wounded: 'they belonged to the 36th Infantry Regiment [7th Reserve Division] which was heavily engaged, and had received its baptism of fire. Heavy rifle fire continued to our front, fresh infantry were sent up into the fight, and we gained ground slowly. By now it was getting dark and the British had retreated from the battlefield.'[37]

General Smith-Dorrien's instruction for a general withdrawal was late in arriving to the 4th Division, and was only transmitted to the brigade commanders at around 5 p.m. But greater problems were to develop with the transmission of the orders to individual units, now completely mixed up. Colonel Edmonds of the divisional staff encountered the 2nd Royal Dublin Fusiliers under the nominal command of Lieutenant-Colonel Arthur Mainwaring, and was disconcerted to find himself button-holed by the battalion's second-in-command: '[He] said to me that he wished I could get the CO away – he was a stout man out of health – as he was demoralizing everybody.'[38] The strain of the fighting had taken its toll on Mainwaring, which was to have unfortunate consequences the following day.

The 4th Division had not been informed that the battle was a delaying action, a source of understandable irritation to Major-General Snow: 'The worst mistake [of II Corps HQ] was not telling me that the retreat was inevitable. Had I known that fact earlier I should have been able to have had the line of retreat reconnoitered, and given more thought as to how the retirement was carried out.'[39] But the damage had been done, and confusion reigned supreme, as Snow accepted: 'A very large portion of my division, including two brigadiers, was separated from the Division and rejoined me in driblets during the next two or three days.'[40]

The 10th Brigade was allotted the role of rearguard, but Brigadier-General Haldane only had control over half his command. He withdrew with the 2nd Seaforth Highlanders and the 1st Royal Irish Fusiliers, unaware of the fate of the Dublin Fusiliers and the 1st Royal Warwickshires. The latter two battalions were so jumbled up that when their commanding officers withdrew, substantial numbers were left behind. Captain Wheeler and a group of Dublin Fusiliers were among the abandoned. They were eventually told to 'get away as best they could. No orders having been issued as to the direction of the next position to be taken up, parties withdrew in every direction, each selecting the route that appeared advisable.'[41]

Another officer left behind was Captain Hart of the Warwickshires. He recalled how he and his men waited until dusk, until the senior officer present, Major A. J. Poole, realized 'that everyone else had gone. At this time, strung along the road for about 600 yards from the edge of Haucourt were about 300 of 1st Royal Warwickshires, about the same number of Royal Dublin Fusiliers, some 40 of the King's Own and a few of the Royal Irish Fusiliers – some 600–700 in all.'[42]

Major Poole, having been ordered to hold his position, dutifully did so until it was patently obvious that they had been left behind. Among Poole's group was Lieutenant Montgomery: 'About 10 p.m. we suddenly realised that we were alone & we could hear the Germans advancing in large numbers. So we hastily formed up and retired.'[43] Poole successfully led his men away, although the Dublin Fusiliers lost touch in the dark, and as daylight broke were caught by the Germans and suffered heavy casualties.

Among the others left behind in the withdrawal was the mixed group from the 8th Brigade consisting of the Gordon Highlanders, along with soldiers from the Royal Irish Regiment and Royal Scots, still holding their trenches between Audencourt and Caudry. In a scene of ultimately tragic farce, the otherwise second-in-command of the battalion, Colonel W. E. Gordon VC, insisted on taking overall command – his brevet rank gave him army superiority of what was now a mixed force – from the Gordons' regular CO, Lieutenant-Colonel F. H. Neish.

Having seen off all German attacks during the day the battalion group passively waited in its trenches, while, it would seem, arguments took place over seniority and whether a retreat could be made without written orders.[44] It was only at 12.30 a.m. on the 27th, with the Germans all around them, that the Highlanders began to withdraw.

The column marched southwards to Montigny and then turned westwards towards Bertry, but at about 2 a.m., just before reaching the town, they were fired on by German troops. The British column recoiled and in the confusion of darkness ended up retiring in the direction of Clary. Fully alerted, the Germans closed on the column, and after a short fire-fight overwhelmed the British; 700 prisoners were taken, 500 of them from the Gordon Highlanders.

By the early hours of 27 August, the Germans had taken control of the Le Cateau battlefield, but lacked the resources to follow up their victory during the hours of darkness. In scenes of confusion, the main bulk of the British force continued to march away during the night and into the next day. The question remained: had the battered British troops put enough distance between themselves and the Germans, who would renew the pursuit in the morning?

CHAPTER NINE

FAILURES OF COMMAND

During the night of 25/26 August the Germans consolidated their position on the Le Cateau battlefield, rounding up British stragglers and preparing for the coming day's operations. But at just the moment when Kluck's forces needed to move swiftly to pursue their beaten foe they displayed neither energy nor focus. IV Corps had admittedly been heavily engaged in the day's fighting and needed time to reorganize. III Corps, however, had begun to arrive on the battlefield at Honnechy as night fell, and with hard marching could have caught a part of the retreating British. But both German corps advanced only a few miles south on the 27th, because the German commander thought the BEF to be elsewhere.

Central to Kluck's thinking was his persistent belief that the British would retreat due west towards Calais and Boulogne. Accordingly, he despatched his mobile forces – Marwitz's Cavalry Corps – in that direction, supported by the recently arrived II Corps. Both of these formations would engage General d'Amade's Cavalry Corps and the Territorial divisions of General Sordet, but they would find no sign of the BEF.

The BEF, of course, continued its southerly line of retreat, holding position on the left flank of the French Fifth Army. Such was Kluck's confusion that his army's progress throughout the Allied retreat might be seen to resemble that of a drunken boxer, staggering on a zigzag course with fists flailing, occasionally catching an opponent with a glancing blow but failing to deliver the knock-out punch that would decide the contest.

General Smith-Dorrien and his command had had a lucky escape. Yet on 27 August this hardly seemed the case. The British, driven from the battlefield, had suffered 7,812 casualties, with 38 guns lost.[1] Because of the disorderly nature of the retreat, losses in the immediate aftermath of the battle appeared higher; some retreating groups and individuals rejoined their regiments more than two weeks later. Enemy casualties were considerably fewer, totalling around 2,900 and indicative of the sound tactics employed by the German Army throughout the battle.[2]

The prime cause of the British defeat at Le Cateau was poor leadership. These failings occurred at all levels, but were most significant at the top. And yet accounts of the battle of Le Cateau from senior British officers – including those by Smith-Dorrien, Fergusson, Headlam and Haldane – adopted a strangely passive voice to suggest that they had played little or no active part in the battle, that British misfortunes were a consequence of external events rather than their own decisions.[3] With this in mind, the notion that the Germans had a vastly superior numerical advantage when the battle was being fought was avidly seized upon.

Major A. F. Becke's semi-official account of Le Cateau (albeit written while the war was still in progress) asserted that as well as the German II Cavalry Corps 'no less than four Corps of the I German Army [had] been engaged at Le Cateau'.[4] Possibly taking its lead from Becke's work, the Official History – and the accompanying map of the battlefield – implied that the German III Corps and IV Reserve Corps had taken part in the battle, whereas, in fact, IV Corps only marched onto the battlefield as the British 4th Division was withdrawing, while III Corps arrived well after the British retreat.

More egregious still was the prominence given to descriptions of isolated heroic acts as being of consequence to the outcome of the battle; used, in fact, as an attempt to cover for weak leadership. To take one instance: in his memoirs, Smith-Dorrien mentioned the chaos of the

5th Division's retreat from its front-line positions, and with a masterly non sequiter concluded: 'Thanks, however, to the determined action of Major Yate of the Yorkshire Light Infantry, who sacrificed himself and his men in holding the Germans off, the troops of the 5th Division got back on the road.'[5] While there could be no denying the determined action mounted by the KOYLI, and its contribution to delaying the German advance, we know from Colonel Bond's own report of the engagement that Yate's 'charge' had no effect at all on the course of the British defence.

•

News of the British defeat caused profound dismay at GHQ that, at times, bordered on panic. Field Marshal French believed II Corps to be ruined, his already poor relationship with Smith-Dorrien further damaged by the latter's decision to disobey his orders and fight at Le Cateau. On the night of the 26th, Smith-Dorrien motored to GHQ at St Quentin to make his report to French, only to find that, unknown to him, the headquarters had moved 35 miles south to Noyon. On finally arriving at GHQ at 2 a.m., Smith-Dorrien engaged in a fractious interview with French before returning to St Quentin as dawn was breaking.

At GHQ, Lieutenant-General Murray, the Chief of the General Staff, had been overcome by stress, leaving Wilson in charge of staff matters. Managing the difficult feat of being cheerfully despondent, Wilson sent out a general order at 8 p.m. on the 27th to discard all ammunition and baggage not directly required by the BEF, so that more wagons would become available to transport exhausted soldiers. Although carried out by some units of the 4th Division, the two corps commanders wisely ignored what was a well-meant but defeatist and unnecessary instruction. Smith-Dorrien was particularly perturbed, noting in his diary: 'I am at a loss to know why this order has been issued and conclude the Headquarters know something we do not. I am afraid the order has had a bad effect on some of the officers, whose nerves have been shattered by the heavy fighting and want of sleep.'

The strain was particularly evident among senior staff officers, who spent both day and night planning and preparing orders. Smith-Dorrien, also under enormous strain, accepted that 'some of the staffs of brigades and divisions are quite worn out and almost unequal to working out orders.' [6]

On the 26th, Colonel John Vaughan, the chief of staff of the Cavalry Division, had collapsed, followed on the 30th by Colonel J. E. Edmonds of the 4th Division. Colonel F. R. F. Boileau, senior staff officer to the 3rd Division, suffered a complete breakdown. Seemingly overcome by the defeat at Le Cateau, he 'went off his head' on the afternoon of the 27th.[7] A less than sympathetic Captain H. B. Owens, MO to the 3rd Cavalry Brigade, attended the tragic outcome: 'Arrived in Ham at about 4 p.m. Had to see a staff officer who had just shot himself in the head with a revolver in a motor car. He was still living.'[8] Boileau died shortly afterwards; Smith-Dorrien diplomatically described his death as a result of being 'very seriously wounded'.[9]

●

The great mass of British troops heading away from the Le Cateau battlefield experienced all the wretched emotions of defeat. Lieutenant George Roupell of the 1st East Surreys recalled 'a feeling of intense depression to think that the British Army should be in full flight'.[10] There was also the anguish felt by those who had lost friends and comrades. Lieutenant Henry Slingsby was one of the survivors from the KOYLI: 'After the battle was over we assembled together some miles away, and to see the few that remained – My God, it was awful. Shall I ever forget it? I was very heartbroken after it, to think of our dear Regiment cut up like that. Words cannot simply express my grief.'[11]

On the 27th, Captain Arthur Osburn, the 2nd Cavalry Brigade MO, encountered individuals and small groups cut off from their units, some of whom were officers lacking maps or other directions. Among the stragglers were 'five privates blackberrying, without caps, packs or rifles, declaring they were all that was left of the 2nd Whiteshires and had nothing to eat for forty-eight hours.' Osburn also noted that 'some of these unarmed stragglers were evidently not unwilling to be "found" by the Germans', which he put down to their 'extreme fatigue'. [12]

The exhaustion of the troops seemed total. 'We walked along as if in a dream,' wrote Lieutenant Tower of the 4th Royal Fusiliers, 'seeing only the backs of the men in front and longing for the end of it all.'[13] In the 2nd Royal Irish Rifles, Corporal Lucy revealed how the strain was pushing some individuals to breaking point, among them Captain J. C. Colthurst: 'One captain turns his whole company about and marches back towards the Germans. The commanding officer gallops after him, and the captain tells him he is tired of retreating. It is bad for the morale of the troops, so he prefers to fight and perish if necessary. The unnerved captain is relieved of his command [sic], and his gallantly docile company comes back to us under a junior, and joins the tail of the column.'[14]

But within the confused mass surging south, staff officers worked hard to impose order, directing lost soldiers to their regiments and holding open separate routes for the three divisions and the 19th Brigade. Attempts were made to provide the men with food, whether through hot meals from the battalion 'cookers' or simple food dumps placed alongside the road. Captain James Jack of the Cameronians commented on how, 'in the twinkling of an eye organisation and food produced a happier air'.[15] Maurice Baring, private secretary to RFC commander Brigadier-General Henderson, also observed the restorative powers of a hot meal:

> The remains of a broken division was said to be arriving. It did arrive and was supplied with food by our transport officer, St John. How he did this was a miracle. These men arrived in a state of the greatest exhaustion, but it was curious how quickly they recovered. One man, who seemed to be a state of utter collapse, as soon as he had been given some food, produced a small hand looking-glass, which he put up on a lorry and began to shave. As soon as he had shaved he said he felt quite restored.[16]

For the pilots of the RFC the retreat developed into a series of last-minute hops from airfield to airfield to stay ahead of the German advance. Lieutenant Louis Strange had become separated from his squadron, and during the evening of the 27th he helped a hard-pressed staff officer direct stragglers:

> We stood at the junction of four cross-roads, sending the men of various divisions to their proper rallying points. We heard many stories that night – grim tales of whole regiments wiped out, while it was a terrible sight

to watch the return of those splendid troops who had marched up to Mons so recently. Some were minus weapons, tunics, and boots, with their puttees wrapped around their feet. All were utterly worn out with ceaseless marching and fighting.[17]

Brigadier-General Aylmer Haldane, leading the remnants of his 10th Brigade on the night march to Voyennes on the 27th/28th, was certainly grateful for this staff guidance: 'The arrangements made for this march by the divisional staff officer were admirable. Every side road had been blocked by sending men in advance, so as to preclude the possibility of our losing the proper direction in the dark, and in addition a staff officer handed over to me a fresh guide at each village to which we came.'[18]

Haldane was fortunate that he and his men were marching along the recognized route for the 4th Division's retreat. Much of the rest of the 10th Brigade was scattered across a wide area, soldiers forced to make their escape as best they could. The group under the command of Major A. J. Poole – originally over 600 strong – were among the last to leave the Le Cateau battlefield, and spent much of their time hiding by day and marching by night. Among the party was Lieutenant Montgomery, who described the retreat in a letter to his parents:

> I shall never forget that march: we call it the 'Retreat from Moscow'. We were behind our own army and in front of the Germans; we had several narrow escapes from being cut up and at times had to hide in woods to escape being seen by Uhlan patrols. We had no food & no sleep, and it rained most of the time. We were dead tired when we started so you can imagine what we were like when we finished it. Our men fell out by the dozens & we had to leave them; lots were probably captured by the Germans.[19]

On the morning of the 28th they caught up with the BEF, and like many other stragglers were sent via Le Mans to rejoin their regiments. This first taste of action left a deep impression on the future field marshal: the incompetence of some of his superior officers and the fortitude of others (not least Major Poole), and the poor communications that existed at all levels within the army.

The 'Retreat from Moscow' was a first-class adventure for a young officer, but of more significance was the experience of the remainder of the lost troops of the 10th Brigade. The 5th Division and 19th Brigade had been instructed to pass through St Quentin on 27 August, but such was the confusion of the retreat that soldiers from all formations ended up in the town. Among them were substantial elements of the 1st Royal Warwickshires (Lieutenant-Colonel John Elkington) and 2nd Royal Dublin Fusiliers (Lieutenant-Colonel Arthur Mainwaring). Both of these battalions from the 10th Brigade were led by their colonels to St Quentin in the hope of being taken by train to the rear. But the exhausted and dispirited troops discovered that the last train had already left St Quentin; they also came across stragglers from other units in a decidedly mutinous mood. The Warwickshires and Dublin Fusiliers now refused to move.

In desperation, the two COs asked the town's mayor for assistance, but fearful of German retribution he demanded that they either leave immediately or sign a document of surrender. Elkington and Mainwaring erroneously believed the Germans to be on the outskirts of the town, and unbalanced by a lack of sleep and the drama of events they signed the document.

Fortunately for the British troops, Major Tom Bridges of the 4th Dragoon Guards was acting as the rearguard commander. On his arrival in St Quentin, during the hot afternoon of the 27th, he encountered hundreds of British troops milling around the town, many of them drunk. On hearing the news of the 'surrender' Bridges acted swiftly, tracking down the mayor and relieving him of the surrender document. His next step was to get the men away from eventual but certain capture in St Quentin.

Throughout the afternoon and into the evening Bridges and his rearguard collected all the horses and carts they could find to carry those men unable to walk. Of those gathered around the station, he encouraged, cajoled and threatened them to move, initially to no effect. Bridges also had to behave with considerable discretion; he knew both colonels and was, of course, junior to them in rank. After great effort, however, he managed to persuade the soldiers to form up and prepare to leave march away.

Over 400 troops from many regiments remained in the town square. Bridges described his novel method to get them to move:

> The men in the square were a different problem and so jaded it was pathetic to see them. If one only had a band, I thought! Why not? There was a toy-shop

handy which provided my trumpeter and myself with a tin whistle and a drum and we marched round and round the fountain, where the men were lying like the dead, playing the British Grenadiers and Tipperary and beating the drum like mad. They sat up and began to laugh and even cheer. I stopped playing and made them a short exhortation and told them I was going to take them back to their regiments. They began to stand up and fall in, and eventually we moved slowly off into the night to the music of our improvised band, now reinforced with a couple of mouth organs.[20]

Captain Arthur Osburn had helped round up the men, stop the drinking of alcohol and instead provide bread and tea or coffee. He recalled how Colonel Mainwaring had been persuaded to march at the head of the column:

My recollection is that he looked very pale, entirely dazed, had no Sam Browne belt, and leant heavily on his stick, apparently so exhausted with fatigue and heat that he could hardly have known what he was doing. Some of his men called to him encouraging words, affectionate and familiar, but not meant insolently – such as: 'Buck up, sir! Cheer up, Daddy! Now we shan't be long! We are all going back to "Hang-le-Tear"!' Actually I saw him saluting one of our own corporals who did not even look surprised. What with the fatigue, heat, drink and the demoralisation of defeat, many hardly knew what they were doing.[21]

Mainwaring and Elkington were court-martialled a few days later, found guilty and cashiered in disgrace. Mainwaring disappeared into obscurity, but Elkington enlisted in the French Foreign Legion (at the advanced age of 48) and served bravely as a private soldier in the bloody Champagne battle of September 1915, where he was badly wounded. When news of his exploits reached Britain, he was reinstated to his former rank by the King, his error of judgment on 27 August redeemed by personal bravery.

●

While II Corps was fighting at Le Cateau on 26 August, Haig's I Corps maintained steady progress, marred only by a rearguard encounter at Le Grand Fayt, which cost the 2nd Connaught Rangers 300 casualties.

Meanwhile, the remainder of I Corps continued to endure the painful discomforts of a day's march in sun and rain. Captain H. C. Rees, of the 2nd Welch Regiment, was angered at the order to dispense with their packs – 'neatly stored in a barn for the Germans to ransack at their leisure'[22] – but was reassured to discover the piles of rations dumped by the roadside: 'Every man took anything that struck his fancy. It was rather amusing to see what the men selected. One man near me had seven tins of bully beef and not a single biscuit. He threw one tin away per mile on the average as he grew tired.'[23]

On the 27th the rearguard of I Corps was assigned to the 1st (Guards) Brigade, with the 2nd Royal Munster Fusiliers, a two-gun section from the 118th Battery and a cavalry troop holding the most rearward position at Étreux. During the morning, units of General von Bülow's Second Army – pulled westward to close the gap with Kluck's First Army – collided with the British rearguard. The German attack began a little before 11 a.m. Under the resolute command of Major P.A. Charrier, the Munsters held their ground with relative ease, and with the main body of I Corps clear of Étreux by 1 p.m. orders were sent to the rearguard to retire. But as had occurred with the Cheshires at Élouges and the Gordon Highlanders at Le Cateau, the message failed to get through.

The Munsters were then surrounded. An attempt to break through the German ring failed; Charrier was killed and the remainder of his men overwhelmed by the Germans at around 9 p.m. There were so few survivors that the battalion was withdrawn from the line, replaced by the 1st Queen's Own Cameron Highlanders. Brigadier-General Ivor Maxse, the commander of the 1st (Guards) Brigade, earned Haig's displeasure: 'I consider that Brig-Gen Maxse committed an error in not withdrawing the Munsters before they were surrounded. The whole rearguard seems to have been placed in jeopardy owing to the large gap which existed between it and the main body before Brig-Gen Maxse commenced to withdraw from his first position.'[24]

Despite the setback at Étreux, I Corps kept to its timetable and by the 28th the main body was clear of the Germans. In fact, Bülow's Second Army, while trying to readjust to the westward movement of Kluck's First Army, had exposed its flank to I Corps. Aerial reports from the RFC had revealed this movement, and Haig saw the possibility for a counter-attack. He signalled to General Lanrezac that he would be prepared to use his troops to co-operate with any French assault on the German Second Army. Lanrezac – who was being firmly prodded by Joffre to attack – was gratified at this offer of support. Unfortunately for Anglo-French relations, Haig's offer was angrily rescinded by Sir John French, who would have nothing to do with Lanrezac. It was a missed opportunity, especially when the French Fifth Army counter-attacked on the 29th, and inflicted a sharp defeat on the Germans at Guise, bringing Bülow's Army to an abrupt if temporary halt.

For II Corps, 28 August was another gruelling day, but one which brought it behind the River Oise. French decided to spend the day visiting the troops. He had a great affection for his men, and he liked nothing better than to be in their company. He did his best to raise morale, addressing the retreating infantrymen at roadside halts, relaying Joffre's telegram of congratulation for their efforts. He wrote: 'The wonderful spirit and bearing they showed was beyond all praise – ½ a million of them would walk over Europe!'[25] French's own spirits were fortified by his day away from the cares of command, although he also saw that his soldiers were exhausted, and a rest day was ordered for the 29th.

If French was encouraged by the fortitude of his troops, he remained troubled by the overall military situation. He believed his losses to be greater than they actually were, and with his new and intense distrust of his French ally, he feared for the survival of the BEF. Aware of his responsibility to protect Britain's sole military force in being – as explained to him in Kitchener's Instructions of 6 August – he certainly did not want to be remembered in history as the man who lost his army. In his mind was a growing conviction that his forces must be allowed time to retire out of the line of battle to rest and refit.

This was a blow to General Joffre's new plan to contain and defeat the powerful German right wing. For the plan to work it was essential that the BEF hold its position between Lanrezac's Fifth Army (to the east of the BEF) and a new Sixth Army that was being assembled to the west and north. On 30 August French telegraphed Joffre with the news that the BEF's retreat would continue:

I feel it very necessary to impress upon you that the British Army cannot under any circumstances take up a position in the front line for at least ten days. I require men and guns to make good casualties which have not been properly estimated owing to continual retirement behind fighting rearguards. You will thus understand that I cannot meet your wishes to fill the gap between the Fifth and Sixth Armies.[26]

Not only did this undermine Joffre's strategy, but it also revealed a worrying despondency in French's hopes for the BEF. In an exchange of telegrams with Lord Kitchener, the Secretary of State for War, French outlined his fears, while Kitchener encouraged him to 'conform to the plans of General Joffre for the conduct of the campaign'.[27] Kitchener was sufficiently concerned at French's state of mind that on the evening of 31 August he obtained Cabinet authorization to travel to France to stiffen his resolve. At 2 a.m. Kitchener boarded the boat train from Charing Cross, a destroyer in readiness for a fast night sailing to Le Havre.

CHAPTER TEN

THE RETREAT CONTINUES

Lord Kitchener met Sir John French at the British embassy in Paris on the afternoon of 1 September. French bitterly resented Kitchener's presence – an unwarranted intrusion in his eyes. That Kitchener wore his Field Marshal's uniform, rather than civilian clothes, was seen by the touchy French as another attempt to undermine his authority. The meeting was an ill-tempered business, but Kitchener got his message across. He subsequently telegraphed the Cabinet in London: 'French's troops are now engaged in the fighting line, where he will remain conforming to the movements of the French army, though at the same time acting with caution to avoid being in any way unsupported on his flanks.'[1]

In his book *1914*, French suggested the meeting was an exchange of views among equals. He wrote: 'I would not tolerate any interference with my executive command and authority so long as His Majesty's Government chose to retain me in my present position. I think he began to realise my difficulties, and we finally came to an amicable understanding.'[2]

Kitchener left no account of the meeting but it was clear that he had ordered French to co-operate with Joffre. To underscore this point he sent a copy of the Cabinet telegram to French, with this addition: 'I feel sure that you will agree that the above represents the conclusions we came to; but in any case, until I can communicate with you further in answer to anything you may wish to tell me, please consider it an instruction.'[3] Reluctantly, French accepted Kitchener's order, replying on the 3rd: 'I fully understand your instructions ... I am in full accord with Joffre and the French.'[4] And yet the idea of getting away to preserve his army still remained in French's mind.

Even as Lord Kitchener was conducting his first exchange of telegrams with French, Kluck's First Army had made a further abrupt change of course. In the aftermath of Le Cateau, Kluck had ordered his troops to push forward in a broad south-westerly direction. Breaking through a French screening force, he encountered and drove back more French troops, which, unknown to him, were forming-up to become General Michel-Joseph Maunoury's Sixth Army. On 30 August, however, Kluck accepted a request from Bülow's Second Army to come to its assistance to outflank the French Fifth Army. Unable to 'find' the BEF, Kluck – the victim of poor intelligence and his own hubris – believed his success against Smith-Dorrien at Le Cateau had knocked out the entire BEF as a fighting force. As he saw it, the destruction of Lanrezac's Fifth Army would confirm his victory.

Kluck's troops – nearing exhaustion yet still battle-worthy – began marching towards the south-east, the long grey columns visible to the RFC as early as the 31st. Much has been made of First Army's change of direction, often described as a blunder that fatally undermined the 'Schlieffen plan' by not advancing to the west of Paris. But neither Kluck nor Moltke was following the plan as set down in Schlieffen's positional paper of 1905. Kluck was simply trying to outflank the Allied left, while Moltke was keeping his strategic options open, with an attempted breakthrough against the French centre a leading candidate. Moltke lacked sufficient troops for a wider enveloping manoeuvre around Paris; it would also have stretched Germany's already frayed lines of communication to breaking point.

Kluck's new line of advance was beneficial to the Allies in taking the pressure off Maunoury's still vulnerable forces, allowing what was a scratch army to be assembled in relative peace. More significantly, First Army failed in its mission to outflank Lanrezac's army, which found sufficient time to retire in good order. Kluck's manoeuvre also had the unforeseen consequence of bringing it back across the BEF's path to the south, with German advance guards clipping the heels of the retreating British on 1 September.

Field Marshal Sir John French, Commander-in-Chief of the BEF in 1914. His volatile temperament made him unsuited to the rigours of high command; Haig eventually replaced him in December 1915.

Lieutenant-General Sir Douglas Haig discusses matters with senior officers from I Corps in a French village during the 1914 campaign. They include, from left: Haig, Major-General Sir Charles Monro (GOC, 2nd Division), Brigadier-General Johnnie Gough (Haig's chief of staff) and Brigadier-General E. M. Perceval (CRA, 2nd Division).

A pre-war photograph of General Sir Horace Smith-Dorrien (centre), with Colonel G. T. Forestier-Walker (left), subsequently appointed as II Corps chief of staff, and Colonel Paul Kenna (right), the King's ADC.

Cavalrymen of the 18th Hussars – from 2nd Cavalry Brigade – question local civilians as the BEF marches northward towards the Belgian town of Mons; there it would encounter the German Army for the first time.

Clearly tired from a day's hard marching, soldiers of the 4th Battalion, Royal Fusiliers, rest in the town square of Mons on the eve of the battle. Along with the 4th Middlesex Regiment, they were assigned to hold the line around the village of Nimy, just to the north of Mons.

Private Carter of the 4th Middlesex stands on guard on the outskirts of Mons during the afternoon of 22 August 1914. The following day, the 4th Middlesex would be overrun by the Germans in defence of the Nimy salient.

Troops and horse-drawn wagons of the 1st Middlesex seek cover as they come under surprise shrapnel fire on the Signy-Signets road during the battle of the Marne, 8 September 1914.

A rare photograph from the battle of Le Cateau, 26 August 1914: Lieutenant-Colonel P. R. Robertson (standing, third from left) confers with his officers from the 1st Cameronians, part of the 19th Brigade that acted as Smith-Dorrien's general reserve.

Troops from the British 5th Cavalry Brigade help cover the retreat of the BEF from its position at Mons. The photograph was taken by Paul Maze, unofficial interpreter to the Scots Greys.

A pontoon bridge, assembled by Royal Engineers of I Corps, spans the River Aisne. The original bridge, destroyed by the retreating Germans, is visible to the rear.

Standing on the Menin Road, officers and men pose in front of one of
the improvised armoured cars that were a feature of British operations
in the early stages of the fighting in Flanders.

British wounded are loaded into ambulance wagons immediately behind
the front line at Gheluvelt, scene of the heaviest fighting during the BEF's
1914 campaign.

Top: Infantrymen from the Scots Guards escort a German prisoner to the rear near Gheluvelt, October 1914. Two battalions of the Scots Guards took part in the defence of Ypres.

Middle: Indian troops of the 129th Baluchis man a breastwork outside the town of Wytschaete, October 1914. The Baluchis, part of the Lahore Division, had been sent to restore the wavering line held by II Corps.

Bottom: A battery of 13-pounder guns of the Royal Horse Artillery in action during the defence of Wytschaete, 31 October 1914. The misty conditions seen in this photograph are typical of the period.

NCOs and officers of the 1st Cameronians scan German positions for the presence of snipers from the appropriately named 'cabbage patch trench' in the La Boutilleries sector of the front-line, 5 November 1914.

The crew of an 18-pounder field gun at their emplacement on the Armentières sector, 7 December 1914. Some of the men are wearing the goatskin jackets issued to front-line troops during the winter of 1914–15.

Wearing cap-comforters, soldiers of the 1st Cameronians pack a forward trench near Houplines, December 1914. A steel loophole plate is visible on the skyline.

Troops from the machine-gun section of the 11th Hussars overhaul their Vickers machine gun at Zillebeke, winter of 1914–15. By this stage of the war, the cavalry had become increasingly trench-bound.

The misery of trench warfare: soldiers from the 2nd Scots Guards shovel out mud from a water-logged trench near Rue Petillon, 19 November 1914.

The first of several encounters took place at Néry at dawn on the 1st, when the German 4th Cavalry Division attacked Brigadier-General C. J. Briggs' 1st Cavalry Brigade. Although a heavy fog hung over the British position, security was lax and the unprepared British were caught by surprise. The German commander swiftly deployed his machine guns and the 12 field guns of his divisional artillery.

The opening shots were fired at 5.40 a.m., the Germans concentrating on L Battery of the Royal Horse Artillery (RHA). After the battery commander was knocked unconscious, Captain Edward Bradbury took charge and returned fire. Only three of the battery's six 13-pounders could be brought into action, and two were swiftly disabled. Bradbury and a few other men continued to man the single gun in a very unequal contest with the German artillery. Bradbury was mortally wounded while bringing up ammunition, leaving just Sergeant Nelson and Sergeant-Major Dorrell to continue the fight until the arrival of reinforcements at around 8 a.m.

The 4th Cavalry Brigade, along with I Battery RHA and the machine guns of the 1st Middlesex Regiment, turned the tables against the Germans, who fled the battlefield in disorder, leaving eight guns behind (the remaining four guns were subsequently found abandoned). The German 4th Cavalry Division was temporarily removed from front-line service with II Cavalry Corps. On the British side, L Battery – having lost all its officers and a quarter of its men – was withdrawn to Britain to refit. Nelson and Dorrell – and Bradbury posthumously – were awarded the Victoria Cross for their exceptional courage.

Further to the east, German cavalry from IV Corps and a Jäger battalion clashed with troops from the 5th Division around the village of Crépy-en-Valois. The 1st Royal West Kents and 2nd Duke of Wellington's Regiment were ably supported by the three 18-pounder batteries of the 27th Brigade RFA, and after a short fire-fight the British troops continued their withdrawal. A more serious action took place in the forested region around Villers-Cottérêts, where the 4th (Guards) Brigade fought a confused but intense action amidst the wooded slopes of the forest.

The brigade was acting as the rearguard for the 2nd Division, with the Coldstream and Irish Guards heavily engaged from the outset. After an initial attack, the Germans launched a second, more intense assault against the Irish Guards at 10.30 a.m. Aubrey Herbert, a volunteer attached to the regiment, described the encounter: 'The German advance began very rapidly. The Coldstreamers must have begun falling back about this time. The Germans came up in front and on our left flank. There was a tremendous fire. The leaves, branches etc. rained upon one. One's face was constantly fanned by the wind from their bullets. This showed how bad their fire was. My regiment took cover very well, and after a first minute or two fired pretty carefully.'[5]

The close terrain made an organized withdrawal a difficult business; units were mixed up and some were left behind. The Irish Guards had been instructed to retire, but this was countermanded by a new order to return to their original position:

> The Germans were by this time about 250 yards away, firing on us with machine guns and rifles. The noise was perfectly awful. In a lull the CO [Lieutenant-Colonel George Morris] said to the men: 'Do you hear that? Do you know what they are doing that for? They are doing that to frighten you.'
>
> I said to him: 'If that's all, they might as well stop. As far as I am concerned, they have succeeded, two hours ago.'
>
> The men were ordered to charge, but the order was not heard in the noise, and after we had held the position for some minutes a command was given to retreat.[6]

As the Guards withdrew they began to take casualties, losing over 300 officers and men in the brigade. Among them was Colonel Morris, who was shot and killed, while the 4th Brigade commander, Brigadier-General Robert Scott-Kerr, was badly wounded. Herbert was also wounded, and left behind to be captured by the Germans – although he was liberated from his prison hospital when Allied forces re-took the hospital in September.

Despite the 'rediscovery' of the BEF, Kluck did not deviate from his advance on what he hoped would be the flank of the French Fifth Army. The British, meanwhile, continued to retreat south, thus ending this phase of hostilities, although GHQ ordered a punishing night march on the 1st/2nd to maintain a safe distance between the Germans and the BEF.

The small-scale cavalry actions continued, with the British generally holding their own against superior German numbers. The fear of being caught on the end of a German lance remained, and Captain Arthur Osburn experienced several close scrapes with German horsemen, on one occasion seeing, 'the black and white pennons of German Uhlans fluttering over the top of the hedges'.[7]

In the febrile atmosphere that seemed to envelop GHQ, the hovering anxiety that they might be overrun by German cavalry continued after the engagements of 1 September, all of which failed to encourage the sense of calm necessary in such an organization. On the evening of the 2nd, GHQ was billeted in a chateau at Dammartin, well away from the German line of march. According to volunteer driver C. D. Baker-Carr, GHQ's stay did not end well:

> The departure from Dammartin was a panic-stricken flight. Rumours of thousands of Uhlans in the woods near by arrived every moment. Typewriters and office equipment were flung into waiting lorries, which were drawn up in serried ranks in front of the *château*. It was a pitch-black night, lit by a hundred dazzling head-lights. With much difficulty I collected my quota of passengers and got clear of the seething mass of vehicles.[8]

The rumours were ill-founded, as Baker-Carr discovered on returning to Dammartin: 'Everything in the little town seemed quiet and peaceful, so seeking out my previous billet, I went to bed and enjoyed a good night's sleep.'[9]

●

On 30 August, Snow's 4th Division and the orphan 19th Infantry Brigade had been combined into a new III Corps under Lieutenant-General Sir William Pulteney. And yet, as August gave way to September, there was no let up in the rigours of the BEF's withdrawal. Major G. J. P. Geiger of the 2nd Royal Welch Fusiliers – one of the four battalions of the 19th Brigade – described a punishing night march:

> The hours that followed were, I think, the most exhausting I have ever experienced. We had already had a fairly tiring day, and marching by night is always the more tiring, there is no change in the landscape to keep one interested. All I can remember of this night is a seemingly endless ribbon of

straight white road with an occasional village, and passing the usual crowd of fleeing villagers who were to be met at any hour of the day or night. When the whistle blew for each halt officers and men fell down in the road like logs until it sounded again. Whoever was keeping the time must have had an iron will to keep himself awake.[10]

Cyril Helm, MO with what remained of the 2nd KOYLI, recalled an incident where the 'iron will' of his time-keeper failed during one of the short, hourly halts. The KOYLI were acting as the brigade rearguard during a night march on 3/4 September:

At one of these halts we all lay down and it appears we went fast asleep; at the end of about half-an-hour someone woke up and discovered that, with the exception of the last company, all the remainder had gone on about 20 minutes before. As at this time there was little distance between us and the enemy, it was deemed advisable to go 'hell for leather'. However, all's well that ends well, and we had had a half-an-hour's sleep into the bargain.[11]

The near-continuous marching strained traditional military discipline in a variety of ways. Clothing was torn (sometimes replaced by civilian items) and equipment lost. The troops' ragged appearance was complemented by the growing of beards. According to Sergeant John McIlwain of the Connaught Rangers, British soldiers had a tendency to throw 'away equipment and clothing. Men lost their caps, and girls' sun hats became quite a fashionable article of wear. These were looted from houses and shops.'[12] Captain Jack noticed that the troops had 'adopted the comfortable but unsoldierly straw hats as worn by the peasantry',[13] while Captain Brownlow commented on the 'outrageous spectacle [of] both men and officers wearing cloth caps, homburgs and panamas'.[14] Frank Richards of the Welch Fusiliers, having lost his cap and unable to find a replacement, improvised with a knotted handkerchief.[15]

For senior officers and those with strict views on all aspects of the soldiers' appearance, these sartorial excesses were indicative of a more widespread decline in military discipline. Brigadier-General Forestier-Walker, II Corps' chief of staff, reminded officers that 'No unauthorized articles of dress should be allowed. Articles of civilian pattern are absolutely prohibited. The French and Belgian national colours may be worn in the cap, but no trinkets. The crime of throwing away clothing must be severely dealt with.'[16] Brigadier-General Haldane of the 10th Brigade criticized his battalions' march discipline as being 'far from satisfactory' and was concerned that 'many young officers and even some older ones seem to forget that the more trying the conditions are, the stronger is the necessity for tightening the bonds of discipline'.[17]

A more fundamantal concern for military authority was the problem of stragglers. Even if a battalion looked like an armed mob, it remained a force capable of action if called upon. Stragglers were individuals lost to the BEF as a fighting force. While some men were physically incapable of maintaining the high pace of the retreat, others were, in McIlwain's words, 'observed falling out apparently as they wished, and often rejoining with units not their own'.[18]

Forestier-Walker and other senior officers in the 5th Division were much exercised in trying to distinguish between 'excusable', 'semi-excusable' and 'inexcusable' straggling, with a demand that regimental officers oversee medical inspections of the feet of men who were not with their units at the end of the day's march. If these officers failed in this duty, they were to be replaced by 'more junior officers in their battalion, who should be given a greater capacity for command than their seniors'. As for those found guilty, they were to suffer 'severe punishment'.[19]

Among those punished, though not severely, was Royal Welch Fusilier Frank Richards, who with 60 other fusiliers had become separated from their battalion during the retreat. When back with their unit they were paraded in front of the CO, Lieutenant-Colonel Delmé-Radcliffe, who refused to listen to any explanations for the cause of their straggling. 'He said that no man should have left the battalion, and punished us by giving us extra route marching in the afternoon to improve our marching.' Richards thought this 'very unfair' but as an old regular philosophically accepted it as part of the arbitrary nature of the soldier's lot.[20]

Despite the fears and misgivings of those on the staff, the officers marching with their battalions began to notice improvements in both the troops' physical condition and their morale. In a diary entry for 3 September, Lieutenant J. G. W. Hyndson of the 1st Loyal North Lancashire Regiment wrote that 'the men have quite recovered from the awful first days of the campaign, and are in splendid fighting trim. The combination of sun, rain and wind has given them a bronzed appearance, and they are extraordinarily cheerful.'[21] Captain Jack agreed, noting how the men were 'recovering their "spring" after the intense strain of August'.[22]

Lieutenant Alan Hanbury-Sparrow of the 1st Royal Berkshire Regiment believed the march had 'sweated the softness out of us' so that the 'reservists suddenly began to find the mile a less terrible distance'.[23] He also detected a sense of fatalism: 'The daily marching southwards has become our normal outlook. The mocking cry of "Back to the Pyrenees" no longer seems a taunt, but rather assumes the shadowy shape of destiny.'[24] But within a few days the retreat would be over.

•

As the German First Army advanced further south, so its right flank became increasingly exposed to a potential counter-attack from the west. Joffre had now got the measure of the German offensive, transferring troops from his right wing to create Sixth Army under General Maunoury, now in position just to the north of Paris. The French capital was the responsibility of the newly appointed and energetic military governor, General Joseph Gallieni, who like Joffre saw the weakness of the German right wing and advocated an immediate offensive.

Demonstrating remarkable calm in his recovery from the initial French disasters in the Battle of the Frontiers, Joffre also displayed remarkable energy in developing his new plan of attack. Lanrezac was replaced by the more dynamic and optimistic General Louis Franchet d'Esperey, while a new force – to become Ninth Army under the aggressive General Ferdinand Foch – moved to support Fifth Army on its right. On 5 September Joffre was ready to go over to the offensive, with his Sixth Army attacking the German IV Reserve Corps, acting as Kluck's flank guard. The only piece missing was the BEF.

Although Field Marshal French had been ordered by Kitchener to conform to Joffre's wishes, doubts remained as to how he would co-operate with his ally. An all-out offensive was planned for 6 September, embodied in the *Instruction Générale No. 6*. It had been sent to GHQ at 3 a.m. on the 5th, and after an agonizing delay GHQ signaled its acceptance of the plan. Joffre telephoned his thanks to GHQ and said that he would visit Sir John, ostensibly to thank him for his co-operation but actually to ensure that the BEF would conform to his plan.

Joffre arrived at GHQ in Melun at 2 p.m. and was ushered into a small room where he was met by French, with Murray and Wilson, with a few other staff officers in attendance. Among them was Lieutenant Edward Spears, who provided a dramatic record of the momentous meeting.

Joffre placed his cap on the table and addressed the British Commander-in-Chief: 'At once he began to speak in that low, toneless, albino voice of his, saying he had felt it his duty to come to thank Sir John personally for having taken a decision on which the fate of Europe might depend.'[25] Joffre then explained his plan in detail, that the Germans had marched into a trap that he was now about to spring:

> The atmosphere in the room grew tenser and tenser. General Joffre was talking now of the vital necessity of acting rapidly; the next twenty-four hours would be decisive. If not taken full advantage of at once, this great opportunity would never occur again.
>
> He spoke of the order he was issuing to his troops. The time for retreating was over. Those who could not advance were to die where they stood. No man was to give way even a foot.
>
> The still, even voice was eloquent now, with an intensity of feeling that drew our very souls out. British co-operation was demanded in words of exalted eloquence inspired by the feeling and the truth within the man. Everything the British could give, all they had, was asked for.
>
> Then, turning full on Sir John, with an appeal so intense as to be irresistible, clasping both his hands so as to hurt them, General Joffre said: '*Monsieur le Maréchal, c'est la France qui vous supplie [it is France that begs you]*.' His hands fell to his sides wearily. The effort he had made exhausted him.
>
> We all looked at Sir John. He had understood and was under the stress of strong emotions. Tears stood in his eyes, welled over and rolled down his cheeks. He tried to say something in French. For a moment he struggled with his feelings and with the language, then turning to an English officer, who stood beside him, he exclaimed: 'Damn it, I can't explain. Tell him that all men can do our fellows will do.'[26]

Staff officers immediately set to work on planning the coming offensive, with the British informing Joffre that the BEF would be late in turning to attack the Germans. Joffre shrugged his shoulders: 'Let them start as soon as they can. I have the Marshal's word, that is enough for me.'[27]

PART THREE

FROM THE MARNE TO THE AISNE

CHAPTER ELEVEN

TURN OF THE TIDE

Major Tom Bridges had participated in many key moments of the war so far, but on 6 September he was to be just a witness, although it was to a literal turning point in the 1914 campaign. Leading his squadron of the 4th Dragoon Guards to high ground by the village of Pecy, he was able to see German infantry standing by the roadside: 'An Uhlan patrol which reconnoitred us was hotly dealt with. I sent back a frantic appeal for guns. A German battery barked at us and set fire to a house. Then the phenomenon occurred. Under our eyes the enemy column began to wheel round in the road and retire to the north. It was the peak of Kluck's advance.'[1]

The offensive on 5 September by the recently formed French Sixth Army against the German First Army, produced a rapid and aggressive response from Kluck. His II Corps – closest to the BEF – immediately turned around to support IV Reserve Corps, now closely engaged by the French. Other formations were to follow, removing any remaining pressure on the British.

For the soldiers of the BEF it was a chance to take stock. Since they had moved out of the concentration zone around Maubeuge on 21 August, I and II Corps had marched and fought for 16 days, the infantry battalions covering anything between 216 and 244 miles in the process.[2] Although Kluck's infantry had marched further, it still remained an impressive feat of endurance, aptly summed up in this heartfelt comment from an anonymous officer: 'I would never have believed that men could be so tired and so hungry and yet live.'[3] Total losses – killed, wounded and missing – by 5 September stood at a little over 15,000 men.

The relentless trudging along the hard pavé roads of northern France had seared its way into the infantry's consciousness. For the cavalry, however, the variety of experiences they encountered helped compensate for their physical exertions. Colonel George Barrow, who had replaced Colonel Vaughan as the Cavalry Division's principal staff officer, described something of the exhilaration of campaigning on horseback:

> It may sound strange but I enjoyed nearly every minute of the retreat – the excitement, the movement, the villages and fine churches, the sight of the French cavalry, the absorbing interest of one's work, the novelty of fighting alongside French troops, the feeling of relief and satisfaction that the clash with Germany had come. And there was the realisation that I was present to take part in it. There were the breakfasts at any hour of the day or night, off an army ration biscuit and a glass of white wine, the omelettes and home-made cheese in a farmhouse or wayside estaminet, and the varied billets. I enjoyed the best of health. It was a grand life.[4]

As the retreat drew to a close, the BEF received its first reinforcements and resupply through the new lines of communication running from St Nazaire. That this had happened at all was a tribute to the soundness of the British logistical system. Reinforcements would typically arrive in batches 100-men strong, and by 5 September the 'first hundreds' had arrived for most battalions. This did, however, produce the anomaly that those battalions who had not been in contact with the enemy were now over-strength, but those that had suffered heavily still had great difficulty in making up their numbers; in II Corps some units and formations remained at half-strength even after the arrival of further reinforcements. Having lost 42 artillery pieces on the battlefield – as well as numerous machine guns and military vehicles – II Corps' operational capability would remain diminished for some weeks to come. And the psychological wounds of having lost a battle would take longer still to heal.

The Cavalry Division had proved unwieldy on campaign. During the retreat, Brigadier-General Hubert Gough had removed his 3rd

Cavalry Brigade from the division to operate with the 5th Cavalry Brigade protecting I Corps. This separation would be formalized during the advance to the Aisne. The 3rd and 5th Brigades would become, progressively, 'Gough's Command' and then the 2nd Cavalry Division on 16 September, with the newly promoted Major-General Gough its chief. The 1st, 2nd and 4th Brigades would form the 1st Cavalry Division under Major-General de Lisle, with Allenby, promoted to lieutenant-general, exercising overall command in what would subsequently become the Cavalry Corps.

●

From a German perspective, the first month of fighting appeared to offer hope of victory. The initial French attacks of the 'Battle of the Frontiers' had been repulsed with heavy losses, and the First, Second and Third Armies were now deep in France; for the furthest advanced troops, Paris was less than 20 miles away. Kluck and the other army commanders were loud in trumpeting their successes to Moltke. And yet, by 4 September Moltke was beginning to have doubts, as he explained to a visitor at his headquarters: 'We must not deceive ourselves. We have had successes, but we have not yet had victory. Victory means the annihilation of the enemy's power of resistance. When armies of millions of men are opposed, the victor has prisoners. Where are ours?'[5]

On the evening of the 4th, Moltke issued a general order changing the strategic emphasis of his offensive, with the First and Second Armies instructed not to continue their enveloping movement but instead turn westwards to face Paris, while the other armies concentrated on breaking through the French defences on either side of Verdun. The order arrived too late at First Army headquarters for Kluck to change the march orders for the 5th, but the French attack on his right flank called a halt to the German advance south.

Kluck counter-attacked Maunoury's Sixth Army with the greatest determination, and as the French fell back the still confident Kluck saw the encounter as an opportunity to complete a wider envelopment. But the inability of the Germans to break through at Verdun, and Moltke's awareness that the French were attacking along the entire front, became a cause of concern. Bülow's Second Army was held fast by the French

Fifth Army, and a gap was developing between the German First and Second Armies as Kluck's forces were dragged westward. Moltke, meanwhile, had problems communicating directly with his right-flank armies, but his roving emissary, Colonel Richard Hentsch, considered the situation sufficiently serious to order both the First and Second Armies to withdraw to less exposed positions further north. Thus began the battle of the Marne, which ended German hopes of a swift and decisive victory in the West.

Directly facing the gap between the two German armies was part of the French Fifth Army and the BEF. If the British advanced swiftly and purposefully into the gap, great damage would be done to the Germans who were now in some disorder. But as the Allied offensive got underway on the 6th the BEF was still turning around, before tamely marching back to what should have been its start position. On 7 September the British marched towards the Germans, III Corps on the left, II Corps in the centre and I Corps on the right.

While the British soldiers had largely recovered from the ordeals of the great retreat, Sir John French remained suspicious of the French armies on his flanks and was cautious of the outcome of Joffre's offensive. GHQ's operational orders issued for the 6th guardedly spoke of an advance with merely 'a view to attacking'. No decisive intervention would be forthcoming from the BEF.

For the troops, however, the realization that they were no longer retreating but advancing was an enormous boost to morale. Captain Jack summed up the general mood when he wrote on the 7th: 'This totally unexpected news almost passed belief after the long depressing retreat; all faces are bright as we march 16 miles north-east.'[6] The change of direction to the north-east would bring the BEF to a new operational area comprising a limestone plateau stretching westward from Reims, cut by a number of steep river valleys. During the coming week, the BEF would successively cross the Grand Morin, Petit Morin, Marne, Ourcq and Vesle, before reaching the Aisne on 13 September.

General von Kluck continued to believe the BEF to be a spent force, and had been content to leave Marwitz's Cavalry Corps along with several powerful Jäger battalions to cover the gap left by the transfer of his infantry divisions to attack the French Sixth Army. As the British cavalry led the BEF's advance, so the opening encounters became a series of mounted skirmishes. Among the first was the 2nd Cavalry Brigade's encounter at Moncel on the 7th, an action made notable as the last charge of lance-armed British cavalry against similarly armed opponents. Two troops of the 9th Lancers were attacked by a larger German force in a confused melee that saw Lieutenant-Colonel David Campbell, the Lancers' CO, thrown from his horse. Captain Osburn attended the wounded and found Campbell, who had led the ill-fated charge at Élouges, sprawled out amidst a field of clover:

> He had, if I remember rightly, a revolver wound in the leg, a lance wound in his shoulder, and a sword wound in his arm.
>
> 'I am sorry to find you like this, sir,' I said, kneeling down to dress his wounds.
>
> 'Not at all, my boy! Not at all! I've just had the best quarter of an hour I've ever had in my life!'[7]

Osburn bandaged Campbell's wounds, and within a few weeks he was back at the head of his regiment. Not all injuries were dealt with so easily. Osburn discovered a mortally wounded lancer whose stomach 'had been almost completely blown away'. Osburn considered himself a typical tough-minded medical officer, well-inured to suffering, but the wounded man's fate had a profound effect:

> I gave him big doses of morphia, but I began to think the drug had lost its power. Poor chap – for hours he refused to die! I had much to do, but went back to him several times; he was so completely helpless, and I had seen two large rough-looking dogs roaming about in the woods. As last I had to leave him, tying a piece of white bandage to a tree so that some advancing ambulance might find him.
>
> I picked up what was left of the bandages and gauze and stuffed them in my pockets. He had not long to live, so I covered his face with some gauze to keep the wood-flies from worrying and folded his hands over what was left of his blood-stained tunic. Out of pain now and scarcely conscious – he saw I was going. 'Goodbye B,' I said, 'you will soon be asleep. You will never have to do another charge!'
>
> It was beginning to grow dark as I got up to go, and then I hardly could. I had had to move him a great deal in trying to dress the huge, gaping

wound, and though I must have caused him the most intense pain he had been so patient, scarcely uttering a sound. There was something about that still form, and the white mask of gauze over its head, lying there so helpless alone in the darkening woodland that seemed to call me back. I did not know what made me do it – I had never done such a thing before – but I went back and kneeling down beside him, unable to say anything, I pressed his hand. I think he understood.[8]

•

If Field Marshal French was cautious in pushing the BEF north, then so too were his corps and divisional commanders. Senior officers were right to treat the Germans with respect, but failings in staff work, lack of co-ordination between the three corps and between artillery and infantry, and an unfortunate hesitancy in pushing units forward in case their flanks become exposed, all discouraged decisive action. In the light of his experiences with General Lanrezac, French remained fearful of being outflanked, but the operational situation in the first days of the advance was very different than that experienced by the BEF after Mons. The French Sixth and Fifth Armies were engaged in titanic clashes with, respectively, the German First and Second Armies. The BEF, advancing against a cavalry screen, albeit strong, had no real need to worry about its flanks, and could have been the Allied spearhead rupturing the German line.

In contrast to the attitudes of their superiors, the soldiers of the BEF were disconcerted at the seeming lack of urgency as they moved north. Memoirs of the period repeatedly displayed irritation and anxiety at what was considered a missed opportunity. On 8 September, Brigadier-General Aylmer Haldane chafed at the delays to the advance of his 10th Brigade (4th Division): 'My anxiety to get on the move in order to molest the retreating enemy was great, but for a long time I got no orders to move, though I went personally to solicit them.'[9]

Lieutenant Alexander Johnston, an acting staff officer in the 7th Brigade (3rd Division), noted in his diary that his brigade waited until 5 p.m. before making a move: 'I cannot understand this… Surely our duty is according to Field Service Regulations "not to spare man or horse or gun in pursuing the enemy etc".'[10] A few days later on the 11th,

Johnston was to write: 'No sign of the enemy the whole way: as I feared we have let the Germans get clean away with very little loss. Even though we may have got ahead of the other divisions on our right and left, and might even have risked getting an advanced guard knocked about, surely we should have harried the enemy as much as possible.'[11]

Johnston continued his diary entry with the prophetic words: 'I expect that we shall find that the enemy will have been able to retire more or less unmolested on to a strong fortified position further north which will give us a great deal of trouble.'[12]

The Germans deployed their rearguards in the classic manner, using mobile units to delay the enemy and so protect the withdrawal of the slower-moving infantry formations. They made intelligent use of artillery and machine guns to force the marching British columns to deploy into skirmish order. Once a fire-fight developed, the rearguard maintained a stiff resistance until, with the threat of being overwhelmed imminent, it withdrew to continue the fight at the next good defensive position.

The German tactics compared favourably with the emphasis on merely 'getting away' that had characterized the British retreat, with rearguard actions coming about through accidental collisions rather than deliberate policy. The point was made by Major-General Snow of the 4th Division: 'I have always blamed the authorities [GHQ] for the bolt we made of it. Had we retired more slowly, fighting rearguard actions, we should have taken immense toll out of the enemy and kept our men in better hand.'[13] On 9 September, Snow was badly injured, falling from his horse, and replaced by the lacklustre but well connected Brigadier-General H. F. M. Wilson.

During the crossing of the Marne on 9 September, Lieutenant C. L. Brereton of the 68th Battery found the infantry of Brigadier-General A. G. Hunter-Weston's 11th Brigade (4th Division) pinned down by a powerful rearguard on the opposite bank of the river at La Ferté-sous-Jouarre: 'All the houses on the north bank were loop-holed, and the place on the hill opposite bristling with machine guns which were most skillfully concealed. Was stopped the whole way by infantry officers trying to point out machine guns that they had discovered, and wanted me to turn my guns onto.'[14] Later in the day, Hunter-Weston ordered Brereton to support the infantry with his 18-pounders:

About 6.30 p.m. an East Lancs officer pointed out to me what looked like a section of guns on the north side of the river at about 1,800 yards range. It was getting dark and I could not see very well, but did what looked like very good shooting. There were some infantry just to the right of these retiring up the hill. Was much applauded by the East Lancs for my shooting. Discovered next day that these 'guns' must have been two bushes and the infantry were our own. I wounded two of [our] men and killed a German prisoner.[15]

This instance of 'friendly fire' typified the lack of good co-operation between infantry and artillery. Brereton understandably had a poor opinion of Hunter-Weston's knowledge of artillery matters: 'Struck me he hardly knew what he was talking about.'

More serious incidents took place on the right of the BEF's advance with I Corps. On 9 September, the artillery of the 1st Division fired on British cavalry on the far side on the Marne, an episode observed by Captain Jim Patterson of the 1st South Wales Borderers: 'Our cavalry, which has already crossed is fired on by R.A. – silly asses. It is quite obvious that they are not the enemy. We find 18 wounded cavalry by our guns. The officer of the R.A. responsible ought to be shot in my opinion.'[16] The following day two battalions from the 1st Division were hit by British artillery fire, causing several casualties that included the 1st Loyal North Lancashires' CO, Lieutenant-Colonel G. C. Knight. Also on the 10th, a similar 'friendly fire' incident occurred to troops of the 2nd Division, when fired upon by guns of the neighbouring 3rd Division. Such was the angst and confusion caused by these incidents that Haig ordered a temporary halt to the advance for the remainder of the day.

The Germans did not have everything their own way. On 10 September, having crossed the Marne, II Corps and the cavalry of Gough's Command managed to overrun German rearguards and capture well over 1,000 prisoners. Smith-Dorrien was understandably delighted with the day's action: 'there is real evidence of our enemy being shaken, for the roads are littered and the retreat is hurried'.[17]

Unfortunately for Smith-Dorrien, the day's promising haul of prisoners proved to be something of a one-off, and the littered roads were less a consequence of a shaken army and more a symptom of the sullen rage of the German soldiers, who, having been mercilessly driven forward by the prospect of victory, now found themselves tramping back in the wrong direction.

The heavy drinking of the German troops had become clearly evident to their pursuers. According to Captain Cyril Helm of the KOYLI: 'One could not lose one's way as there were thousands of broken bottles spread across the sides of the roads.'[18] There was also the inevitable looting from French civilians: Brigadier-General Gleichen came across German wagons abandoned on 10 September crammed with 'cases of liqueur and wine, musical instruments, household goods, clothing, bedding, trinkets, clocks ribbons, and an infinite variety of knick-knacks, many of which one would not have thought worth taking'.[19] But what surprised the advancing British was the scale and venom of personal destruction; household goods of no value were smashed to pieces, children's toys broken, and beds and female underclothes torn and defecated upon, the latter coming under the heading of 'filthy deeds too abominable to mention'.[20] Yet amidst this wanton destruction were occasional humorous notes chalked on walls and doors; Lieutenant A.V. Spencer came across 'an invitation for a Tango Tea in Paris on September 13th'.[21]

•

On 10 September the first signs of a break in weather were observed, confirmed on the 11th as the hot, humid, thundery days of the previous weeks gave way to the early onset of autumnal gales, driving rain and a sharp drop in temperature. This meteorological change meant the arrival of mud and reduced mobility, further reducing hopes of catching the Germans as they began to withdraw behind the ridge of hills to the north of the River Aisne known as the Chemin des Dames.

That the Germans had decided to make a stand on the Aisne was unknown to the Allies. The bad weather made aerial reconnaissance all but impossible, providing a cloak for the Germans not only to dig in along the Chemin des Dames but also to bring up reinforcements unobserved. A gale on the night of the 12th/13th had also wrecked many of the RFC's aircraft at their new headquarters at Fère-en-Tardenois. Louis Strange found 'the aerodrome strewn with smashed machines that had been wrecked by the storm that night, and I believe that barely ten were fit to fly the following morning.'[22]

Crucial to the German defensive plan – to help plug the gap between First and Second Armies – was the arrival of General Zwehl's VII Reserve Corps on the morning of 13 September, after a truly epic march from the fortress of Maubeuge that began on 10 September. Zwehl described how his reservists – 'unused to such great efforts' – covered between 20 to 25 miles on the first two days, and then 'close on 40 miles between dawn on the 12th and dawn on 13th'.[23] A quarter of his infantry fell out by the roadside during the march, but subsequently limped in to join their comrades now facing the British I Corps.

On 12 September the BEF moved forward towards the Aisne, a river sufficiently wide and deep to create a difficult natural obstacle. French's operational order for the day stated that the 'crossings over the Aisne will be seized, and the columns will reach the high ground overlooking the river'.[24] Unfortunately for the British, the Germans had already begun to blow the bridges and another day's atrocious weather made progress slow. Unaware that one last, desperate push might have secured the tactically vital high ground on the north bank, the BEF remained on the southern side of the river as darkness fell.

The only progress made by the BEF came from III Corps, on the far left of the line. Brigadier-General Hunter-Weston, leading his 11th Brigade as the advance guard of the 4th Division, was informed that the bridge at Venizel had only been partially blown and was capable of holding light loads. Hunter-Weston was to have something of a chequered career later in the war, but on this occasion, at least, he was highly enterprising.

At 11 p.m. he led his infantry to the bridge, where the men crossed over the river in single file, with ammunition unloaded from the wagons and passed over by hand. By 3 a.m. on the 13th, the entire brigade was on the north bank, and with bayonets fixed they advanced up the ridge. The Official History described the ensuing attack: 'The German outposts on the crest, completely surprised by the sudden appearance of the British, incontinently abandoned their trenches and fell back on their main line some hundreds of yards away.'[25] As dawn broke, the 11th Brigade was in a good position to develop the assault, but the remainder of the BEF was still on the south bank of the Aisne and would have to cross the river in full daylight against well-prepared German positions.

CHAPTER TWELVE

BATTLE ON THE AISNE: ASSAULT

On the morning of 13 September the BEF prepared to cross the River Aisne. The British force was sandwiched between the French Sixth and Fifth Armies, and Field Marshal French was in full accord with General Joffre's instruction for a determined advance to capture the high ground to the north of the Aisne valley. British cavalry patrols had confirmed the destruction of all but one of the seven main bridges in the section of the line allotted to the BEF, but closer inspection revealed that the damage was only partial and that soldiers could get across the river, even if only travelling in single file. Meanwhile, the Royal Engineers worked feverishly to repair the crossings, as well as laying their own pontoon bridges to allow free passage for cavalry, guns and wagons.

The ground held by the Germans comprised a long west-to-east limestone ridge – the Chemin des Dames (the 'ladies' road', built for the daughters of Louis XV) – running parallel with the river some 2 to 3 miles to the north. From the ridge projected a series of steep-sided but flat-topped spurs, which acted as forward strongpoints for the German defenders. Thick woodland covered the upper slopes, while the whole area was honeycombed with caves and quarries. The German positions were between 300 and 400 feet above the river valley, and in most instances had good fields of fire on the British below. By hugging the ground at the foot of the spurs, however, the British could find some degree of concealment, as a result of the convex nature of the slopes and the belts of trees ringing the spurs.

But there was no cover to escape the plunging fire from German heavy howitzer batteries on the Chemin des Dames that searched these hidden positions. The Germans deployed large numbers of 15cm (5.9in.) heavy howitzers just behind the Chemin des Dames, to be joined by even more powerful 21cm (8in.) howitzers. These guns were well hidden and beyond the range of British field artillery south of the river, with the exception of the few 60-pounder heavy guns available at divisional level (although their flat trajectory made it difficult to hit targets behind hills). British batteries deployed in the Aisne valley, especially north of the river, were vulnerable to the heavy guns on the ridge and to cross-fire from field artillery on the spurs. Some protection was found by pushing the guns close to the spurs but such positions were only suitable for howitzers, with their high angle of fire, and not the more numerous field guns.

The British artillery contribution was further hampered by the absence of a fire-plan for 13 and 14 October. GHQ's orders for both days were for 'pursuit' rather than 'attack', and as a consequence little attention had been paid to how the gunners should support the infantry beyond engaging targets of opportunity. Overall, the British artillery commanders had little idea of German dispositions; consequently, their batteries would be forced to advance under heavy fire, adopting whatever fire positions they could find before trying to locate concealed enemy targets.

On the British right, Haig's I Corps made relatively good progress in crossing the Aisne. During the day, the 1st Cavalry Division, 1st Division and 5th Brigade of the 2nd Division moved over to the north bank, with the remaining two brigades of the 2nd Division ready to cross at dawn on the following day. Advance units fought their way northwards a couple of miles towards the Chemin des Dames. After encountering increasing resistance from German infantry, they halted along a line from Paissy (on the extreme right of the British line) to Verneuil, in readiness for a major push on the 14th.

The crossings of the other two corps proved more difficult. In the centre, II Corps advanced with the 3rd Division on the right and the 5th

Division on the left, the two divisions divided by the Chivres spur that ran down to the river bank. Major-General Hamilton's 3rd Division began to cross the river at Vailly, but progress over the damaged bridges was slow. By the end of the day only the 8th Brigade was on the north bank, with the 9th Brigade forced to cross during the night (the 7th Brigade was left on the south bank in reserve). The bridgehead established by the 3rd Division was dangerously shallow, as well as being isolated from I Corps to its right and from the 5th Division on the left.

The 13th Brigade of Major-General Fergusson's 5th Division crossed the Aisne using the available damaged bridges, while a 60-man-capacity raft was constructed to transport the 14th Infantry Brigade to the far side, with the 15th Brigade following after dark. Above them was the Chivres spur that dominated the river valley to both west and east, as well as directly to the south. Its defensive potential had been realized by the French in the immediate aftermath of the Franco-Prussian War (1870–71) with the construction of the Fort de Condé. Proof against anything the BEF's gunners could throw at it, the fort gave the Germans a secure base that also had a potent offensive capability provided by three batteries of field artillery. For II Corps to make any headway, the Chivres spur would have to be captured.

Further to the left, III Corps – comprising just the 4th Division as the 19th Infantry Brigade was kept in reserve – made modest progress: the 11th Brigade had already established itself on the north bank and was later joined by the 12th Brigade; in the face of heavy fire they sheltered in the lee of the high ground rising from the Aisne flood plain. But they were, at least, in direct contact with the 5th Division on their right.

Captain Walther Bloem of the German 12th Infantry Regiment – which had suffered heavy casualties at Mons – had followed the British during the great retreat and then fallen back to the Aisne with the rest of his 5th Division. On 13 September his company had been ordered to join the defences along the Chivres spur. Using his field glasses he looked to the west to see a line of extended dots: British infantry from the 12th Brigade marching across the water meadows from their crossing at Venizel towards the spur. He was impressed by the tactical finesse of the attacking British troops, advancing in several well-dispersed lines that minimized casualties from German artillery fire: 'More of our batteries came into action; but it was noticed that a shell, however well aimed, seldom killed more than one man, the lines being so well and widely extended. Our guns now fired like mad, but it did not stop the movement: a fifth and sixth line came on, all with the wide intervals between men and the same distance apart. It was magnificently done.'[1]

Lieutenant George Roupell of the 1st East Surreys crossed over the river on the Royal Engineer's raft later in the afternoon:

> We carried out the finest advance in open order I have ever seen. Each platoon formed a line with an interval of five or six yards between each man and 50 yards distance between lines. We were one of the last platoons to leave the cover of the trees along the river and saw all the plain in front; it was a wonderful sight and the occasional shrapnel which burst over the plain at intervals added a finishing touch for a war picture.[2]

Bloem's narrative was avidly seized upon by the British Official History, with an extended account translated and included in the first volume. But advancing across the flat meadows of the flood plain was the easy part, especially when, as Roupell noted, German artillery fire was not heavy. The real fighting began when the troops began to clamber up the hills towards the German positions, the orderly lines disrupted by the rough terrain and an ever-increasing volume of enemy fire of all types.

•

The weather had improved during the afternoon of the 13th, but as the BEF prepared for the major assault on the following day the rain returned, along with a thick, clinging fog. This had the advantage of concealment but also the potential for confusion as the troops advanced over unknown terrain. In Haig's Corps, the 1st Division was ordered to spearhead the assault, supported by the 2nd Division, which would bring the remainder of its units over to the north bank during the morning.

The 1st (Guards) Brigade and 2nd Brigade led the 1st Division's attack and by 9 a.m. had forced the Germans back up to the Chemin des Dames road. The 1st Coldstream Guards crossed over the road to fight their way into Cerny, and such was the confusion of fog and battle that soldiers on both sides mistook each other for friendly troops. On the right, the 1st Queens advanced even further north to La Bovelle farm.

The Battle of the Aisne, 15 September 1914

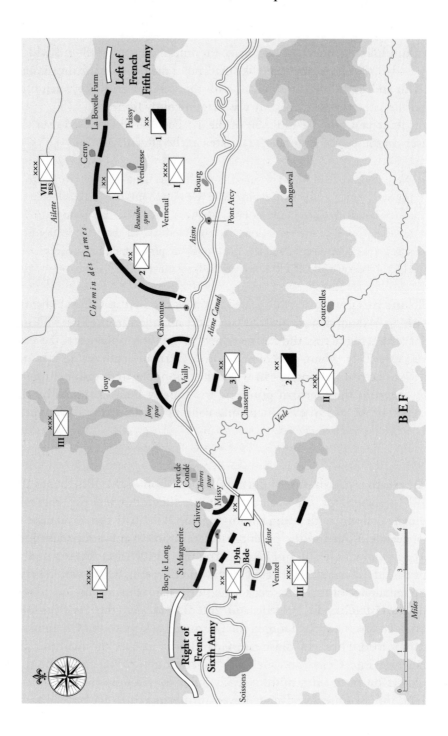

Both battalions had broken through the German line, and had the visibility been better they would have seen the Ailette valley stretching out below them.

For the Germans this was the critical moment of the battle. Their intention had been not merely to defend the line but throw the British back over the Aisne, and so attack was met with counter-attack. German reserves were immediately despatched to repulse the British advance and, despite the fog, artillery concentrated on where the British were likely to be, even if it meant hitting friend and foe. The British infantry were also fired upon by their own artillery. The gunners were semi-blinded by the rain and fog, and confused by the rain capes worn by the attacking troops that apparently gave them the appearance of German soldiers.

The 1st Loyal North Lancs (2nd Brigade) had been held in reserve during the initial attack but was rushed forward to help hold the line. A platoon commander in C Company, Lieutenant J. G. W. Hyndson described the heavy German artillery and machine-gun fire as he and his men came up to the crest of the ridge:

> We continue to double forward, although as yet I can see nothing of the enemy. We pass scores of our dead and wounded, and many of the latter are calling out for water, but it is impossible for us to help them and we have to go on. Suffering severe losses, we at last reach the firing line and mix up with the regiments from the Guards and our own brigade. Here the casualties are appalling, and our men are literally lying on the ground in heaps. We lie down in the open, as there is not a vestige of cover of any kind. I order the men to use their hand shovels to dig themselves into the ground. The noise of battle is, however, so great that only the men nearest me can hear me, and I therefore have to crawl round to give them my instructions.[3]

From their shallow trenches, the North Lancs and the remainder of the 1st Division endured determined counter-attacks, supported by machine guns and artillery. Hyndson's platoon was steadily reduced from 56 to 20 unwounded men:

> Once more the Germans pour a terrific fire of all arms into us. Our numbers diminish but we hang on grimly, digging ourselves farther and farther into the ground, until the whole of our bodies are under cover of mother earth.

In anticipation of being attacked again, I order the men to get all the ammunition they can from the dead and wounded, as there is no other method of getting a fresh supply. At the same time, I myself acquire a rifle in exchange for my sword, which I discard in order to camouflage myself as much as possible. We have learnt by now how adept the Germans are at picking out the officers.

The duel continues until about three o'clock, when a fresh attack is launched by the Germans. It meets with the same fate as the last one on our particular section of the battlefield, but succeeds in forcing back the troops on our right, thus enabling the Germans to break through, and we can see them advancing on in dense masses, far to the rear. It is an awful moment, and I picture life as a prisoner of war, that is, if I am fortunate enough not to be killed before I am taken prisoner. However, fresh troops from our reserves counter-attack and bring the Germans to a standstill.[4]

Overall, the North Lancs suffered the loss of 14 officers – including their new CO, Lieutenant-Colonel Walter Lloyd – and 500 other ranks on the 14th – half the number that entered the battle in the morning; Hyndson's platoon was reduced to just three unwounded men. Although the 1st and 2nd Brigades had managed to hold their positions during the day, their heavy losses forced them to retire to more defensible positions when dusk fell.

The 3rd Brigade – initially in reserve – was flung into battle on the left during the late morning, just as the fog was beginning to disperse. But even as they marched up to the start line they came under German artillery fire, as recalled by Private Samuel Knight of the 2nd Welch Regiment: 'Shrapnel shells burst over our heads. Roofs of neighbouring barns rattle like kettledrums. I hear a peal of laughter from my comrades near me for, as a result of an unconscious action, I had raised the collar of my coat. I laugh myself. We are now in the thick of it.'[5]

The Welch Regiment and the 1st South Wales Borderers were at the forefront of the 3rd Brigade's attack, and while the Borderers were delayed by thick woodland, the Welch managed to gain a good foothold on the Beaulne spur. Captain H. C. Rees, after rallying some soldiers of the Highland Light Infantry, took part in the attack: 'I found a very hot action in progress. We were holding a steep bank on the near crest of the ridge, with the Germans among some corn stooks, only about 150 yards away. Incautiously putting my head above the bank, I drew the immediate attention of a machine gun at point-blank range. Eventually we rushed the Huns and the remnants of them fled.'[6]

The battle on 14 September was the first offensive action undertaken by the BEF. As a consequence, the advancing British troops began to take prisoners, and through the determination of their attack they did so in large numbers. But in the confused nature of the fighting on the spurs and valleys leading up to the Chemin des Dames, the act of surrender became fraught with danger – to both sides. During the initial advance by Brigadier-General Bulfin's 2nd Brigade, the 2nd Sussex Regiment outflanked a German defensive line; after a short fire-fight, 'large numbers of Germans threw up their hands in the token of surrender'.[7] As the Sussex infantry advanced from cover to secure their prisoners they were fired on from positions higher up on the ridge. Troops from both sides were hit by this fire, although some 300 prisoners were successfully bundled away to the rear.

Similar incidents occurred along the British line over the next few days. To the left of the 1st Division's attack, the 2nd Division had been making slower progress but it too captured large numbers of Germans. An account by Major G. D. 'Ma' Jeffreys of the 1st Grenadier Guards provided a guardsman's view of the 'partial surrender' phenomenon:

At 12 o'clock the order was given to advance, but as our men got up to go forward a large number of Germans (at least 200), who had been lying flat in the root field, suddenly rose to their feet and ran forward with their hands up. It was said further away to the left a white flag was raised, but I did not see this. Unfortunately men of all units – Grenadiers, Coldstream, Connaught Rangers and Irish Guards – rushed forward to seize the prisoners, and though both [Major] Matheson and I shouted to them to stand fast, we could not stop them and a confused mass of British and Germans soldiers was the result. On this mass the Germans in rear at once opened fire, causing a number of casualties. I don't believe there was any intentional treachery on the part of the Germans. Their leading line had had enough and meant to surrender. Incidentally they had hardly any ammunition left. Their supports in the rear, however, had no intention of surrendering and opened fire when they got a good target. I had no idea what good cover a root field could give to men lying down: they were as invisible in it as partridges.[8]

Jeffreys was correct in ascribing an innocent cause for such incidents, which happened on both sides of the line. German infantry advancing on the British at Le Cateau repeatedly protested that fire continued after troops had waved white flags or put up their hands in surrender. This was confirmed by Lieutenant G. C. Wynne of the KOYLI, who carried on firing when he saw white handkerchiefs being raised by the Suffolks: 'My platoon continued firing at the Germans near them and it never occurred to me that I might be breaking some international law by so doing, nor do I understand how a few white flags mean the surrender of a whole line.'[9]

Wynne was right to continue fighting until he received orders to the contrary, but the Germans would not necessarily distinguish between two units. Indeed, the troops being fired on understandably felt highly aggrieved and often ascribed sinister motives to the enemy's action.[10] Lieutenant Osborne-Smith of the 1st Northhamptonshires wrote to the 2nd Brigade headquarters to describe two 'partial surrenders'. In the latter, 'a party of the enemy put up the white flag. Captain Savage went out to parley with them and was shot by them.' In all likelihood, the officer was shot by other, nearby German troops.[11]

In the heightened tension of the battlefield, swift retribution might easily follow. At Le Cateau, Terence Zuber described an instance of the German 26th Regiment's 8th Company, not only being shelled by their own artillery but apparently being fired on by British troops who had asked to surrender: 'The Germans once again complained that the British feigned surrender: the commander of 8/26 was allegedly killed by this trick, and in consequence 8/26 stopped taking prisoners.'[12]

The Germans were not the only ones to take summary action. At dawn on 15 September, the South Wales Borderers were improving their defences when a large body of armed Germans moved towards them. Such was the mistrust engendered by recent events, and by the previous engagement at Landrecies when the Germans had apparently approached the British under pretence of being French, that the British were extremely suspicious of the advancing soldiers. Captain Jim Patterson described the ruthless British reaction:

One of the [German] officers called out to us that he wished to speak to an officer, but after the episode at Landrecies with the Guards, we weren't having any of that. I have no doubt that they really did wish to surrender but they must do it properly, as one man did this morning and march up with his hands above his head and no arms upon him. So we opened fire, and although we lost some men we wiped them out at 200 yards, and there they lie in front of us. Poor devils.[13]

•

While I Corps had made an impressive advance on the right of the BEF's line, progress was halted by a succession of German counter-attacks. Haig had hoped to push on again in the late afternoon, but lack of fresh troops and the fading light brought the hope of a decisive advance to an end. Losses were also substantial; according to the Official History, I Corps had suffered 3,500 casualties in the day's fighting.[14] Also of concern had been the inability of the left of I Corps to link up with the 3rd Division, isolated in the centre of the British line around the town of Vailly.

Understrength and still battered by its experiences at Mons and Le Cateau, too much was expected of the 3rd Division as it took part in the general pursuit on the morning of the 14th. The 8th Brigade (on the left) was ordered to advance to the north-west of Vailly and take up position on the Jouy spur, while the 9th Brigade (on the right) was to push forward in a north-easterly direction and link up with I Corps. Artillery support was inadequate for the task: the guns on the south bank had great difficulty in finding suitable targets in the morning fog, and the three 18-pounder batteries of the 40th Brigade RFA, which had crossed over the Aisne at Vailly, were too close to the spurs pushing down from the Chemin des Dames to locate the German positions above them.

Emerging through the dripping wet woods on the flank of the Jouy spur, the 8th Brigade suddenly encountered well-manned German trenches on the spur's plateau. They were halted in their tracks by vicious fire, made worse when the Germans on the extended Chivry spur located their presence in the mist and poured machine-gun fire into their left flank. A German counter-attack forced the 8th Brigade off the spur and back towards Vailly. On the right, things were little better as the 9th Brigade was counter-attacked just as it began its advance. The 1st

Lincolnshires gave way first, followed by the other two forward battalions and then the reserve battalion.

Desperate messages were sent to the 7th Brigade on the south bank to reinforce the position. On reaching the damaged railway bridge, the leading troops of the 7th Brigade found the single-file crossing blocked by fleeing individuals from the Lincolns. Fortunately for the British, the Germans did not press their advantage, providing time for the 1st Wiltshires and 2nd Royal Irish Rifles to arrive on the northern side and buttress the British line, reduced to holding a tight perimeter around Vailly.

While they crossed the Aisne, the troops of the 7th Brigade had come under fairly heavy shrapnel fire, and Corporal John Lucy of the Irish Rifles observed how Lieutenant-Colonel Bird, the battalion CO, had 'with his usual bravery, stood upon a height on the south bank during the whole time taken by his battalion to cross over.'[15] Lucy was intrigued by the behaviour of his officers under fire, but with an ambivalent attitude to their very public displays of courage:

> The acme of officer leadership seemed to be to expose oneself in the most dangerous positions as an example to the men. All very gallant, but not very practical, and useless to us. We did not require any good example to fight in those days. Some of us resented the implication in such an attitude. Their presence certainly did inspire us, but a little more directing, and less examples of studied bravery, would have suited us better.[16]

To be a successful leader, an officer had to be courageous in front of his men. Private Frank Richards of the 2nd Royal Welch Fusiliers wrote: 'We always judged a new officer by the way he conducted himself in a trench, and if he had guts we always respected him.'[17] But the question remained: how was an officer to show his men that he had the necessary guts?

The martial expression 'to stand and fight' gained its resonance because that was how soldiers had fought over the centuries. At Waterloo, when the British Army last waged war in western Europe, soldiers were required to stand to load and fire their muskets, and alongside their officers they stood and fought together, whether facing the onslaught of French cuirassiers or the cannonballs of Napoleon's massed artillery.

The revolution in firepower during the late 19th century, which included the introduction of the breech-loading rifle, made it unnecessary for the soldier to stand to load and fire his weapon, and, more to the point, the greatly increased lethality of weapons compelled him to lie down and take cover if he was to survive. The officer, however, ideally needed to be upright to carry out his two key functions: to direct his men by voice and gesture and to inspire them in the face of the enemy. But in so doing he was liable to bring about his own demise.

The officers who fought at Mons, Le Cateau and on the Aisne tended to adopt the heroic model of Waterloo, whatever their personal reservations. When under heavy fire in the Nimy salient at Mons, Captain Wollocombe of the 4th Middlesex regarded it essential that he and his fellow officers not duck down, believing it would undermine the resolve of their soldiers (see page 67). During the advance to the Aisne, Captain James Jack had been shelled by German artillery while standing alongside his new brigade commander, Brigadier-General F. Gordon: 'The shelling is most disagreeable but relatively harmless; it lasts for perhaps half and hour. Although there is not the least sign of unsteadiness in the ranks, General Gordon and [Captain] Heywood persist in standing about (I cannot well do otherwise) with the salvoes constantly bursting almost in our faces.'[18]

Calmly standing in the face of enemy fire – especially when ranges were close – led to rising casualties. This was recognized by Field Marshal French, who, while not wishing to dampen the martial spirit of his officers, was concerned by the high rate of their losses, especially relative to other ranks. Although replacement officers were sent out to the front from Britain, their numbers were insufficient and they lacked vital battlefield experience. The shortage of proficient officers would become increasingly problematic towards the end of 1914. Writing to his corps commanders, French accepted that in 'the kind of warfare in which we are engaged, such losses may be, and probably are, inevitable', but he asked them 'to impress upon all ranks of leaders under their command the vital necessity of avoiding undue exposure themselves and of taking cover whenever possible'.[19]

French was well aware that this was an extremely delicate matter, especially in the way it might be communicated to the regimental officers in question. It was consequently no surprise that the dismissive handwritten comment on the note sent to Haig was simply: 'Seen by GOC. No action to be taken.'[20] But in the light of the growing toll of officer casualties, a more prudent, managerial style of leadership – as suggested by John Lucy – would be forced on front-line officers.

●

On the left of the British line, the 4th and 5th Divisions had also been ordered to continue the pursuit, their main focus being the capture of the Chivres spur by Fergusson's 5th Division. The division's three brigades were all across the Aisne by the morning of the 14th, but the cumbersome plan of attack involved readjustment of formations and units that took up most of the day, much of it clearly visible to the Germans and all the time under artillery fire. A mixed force from the 13th and 14th Brigades was instructed to attack the spur from the west, from St Marguerite, while the 15th Brigade, which had marched from St Marguerite and past Missy, would attack from the south-east. It was only at 4.30 p.m. that the 15th Brigade was in position for the assault to begin in earnest, approximately 12 hours too late.

The attack from the west side had begun earlier, but the advance from St Marguerite to Missy had been stalled by fire from the Chivres spur and by enfilade fire from German artillery and machine guns in the village of Chivres and further up the valley. From Missy, companies of the East Surreys and Bedfordshires had begun to advance up the southern tip of the spur. When the main attack was launched in the late afternoon – with the 15th Brigade – the British struggled up the steep wooded slopes, made more troublesome by the presence of fences and wire nets.

The British infantry were spread out in a rough half-circle, advancing inwards to a central point. In such a situation, control of the troops was virtually impossible: as they clambered up the spur, units were forced inwards on each other and the inevitable confusion was made worse by repeated friendly fire incidents. Brigadier-General Gleichen, of the 15th Brigade, described the difficulties faced by his soldiers:

> They surged on to a horse-shoe shaped road further on in the wood, and some men lost their direction and began firing in front of them at what they thought were Germans. But they were others of our own, and these began firing back, also without knowing that they were their friends. Consequently, although casualties were few, an unpleasant situation arose, and numbers of

men turned about and retired down the hill into Missy, saying that our artillery was firing into them.[21]

The British infantry had had enough, and while a few groups continued with the attack increasing numbers of soldiers turned back down the hill. The Official History correctly described how the 'confused advance gave way to a confused retirement',[22] and with failing light, Gleichen accepted the inevitable and ordered the rest of his men back to the foot of the spur. Many of them retired to the village of Missy, which had now become a magnet for German artillery fire, although not particularly effective. The three brigades of the 5th Division began to dig-in at the foot of the spur, intending to resume the action on the following morning.

If the attack of the 5th Division could be criticised for poor planning and bungled execution, it was still an attack. The 4th Division – under the command of Brigadier-General (later Major-General) H. F. M. Wilson – on the far left of the line, did virtually nothing, despite being the best-placed BEF formation. During 13 September, the 4th Division had consolidated its position on the high ground above the spring-line villages of Bucy le Long and St Marguerite, with the 11th Brigade on the left and the 12th on the right, the latter being in a good position to lend support to the 5th Division's attack on the Chivres spur. During the night of the 13th/14th the 10th Infantry Brigade had crossed over the Aisne and moved up to support the 11th Brigade, otherwise somewhat thinly spread.

While the 5th Division was throwing itself against the jutting prow of the Chivres spur, the 4th Division calmly stood its ground. The provision of good artillery support was a problem along the entire British line; the 4th Division's direct allotment was modest on the 14th – two howitzer batteries and two gun batteries, plus one two-gun detachment – but was similar to the three gun and one heavy battery deployed by the 5th Division.[23] It would appear that Wilson used the shortage of guns as an excuse for inaction, as implied in the guarded words of the Official History: 'The difficulty of giving artillery support to a direct attack by the 4th Division was so great that the divisional commander hesitated to commit himself to such an operation unless the 5th Division on his right or the French on his left should make a decided forward movement.'[24]

The division was subject to intermittent artillery fire throughout the day, causing light casualties to the 10th Brigade, among them Lieutenant-Colonel Sir Evelyn Bradford, the CO of the 2nd Seaforth Highlanders. Bradford's commanding officer, Brigadier-General Haldane, wrote: 'His death was a great loss to the brigade and to myself personally, making the fourth and last of my battalion commanders who was to become non-effective since it landed in France, though he alone fell in action.'[25]

The Official History also recorded (its criticism now barely coded) the way in which the 4th Division fought off a German attack at midday. It required just a single company of the Royal Dublin Fusiliers: 'This company advanced for half a mile, engaged hostile infantry in a beetroot field at four hundred yards' range, and by sheer marksmanship silenced its fire. This practically ended the active work of the 4th Division for the day.'[26]

On 15 September the British offensive stuttered to a close, although the 5th Division was to make a last attempt to gain the Chivres spur. The 3rd Division also saw limited action, as the 7th Brigade reinforced the front line. Due to a mix-up in communications A and D Companies of the Royal Irish Rifles launched an unsupported attack against the German line. John Lucy, in A Company, took part and described the devastating impact of fire – especially from machine guns – against men advancing in the open without fire support. Lucy's platoon officer waved his sword for the men to advance:

> With a sinking heart I realised that our extended line made an excellent target, as we topped a slight rise, and went on across flat country without the slightest cover. The Germans were waiting for us, holding fire. As we cleared the crest, a murderous hail of missiles raked us from an invisible enemy. The line staggered under this ferocious smash of machine-gun, rifle- and shell-fire, and I would say fully half our men fell over forward on to their faces, either killed or wounded. Some turned over on to their backs, and other churned about convulsively. With hot throats the remainder of us went on, as there is no halt in the attack without an order.[27]

As casualties mounted the advance began to waver and eventually the men threw themselves down on to the ground for protection:

> Hardly had we done so when a machine gun raked the whole line, a weak and feeble line now, and shot accurately home into it. Some of the men flapped about, others, shot through the head, jerked their faces forward and rapidly lay still. I trembled with fear and horror. This was a holocaust. The relentless spray of the deadly machine gun traversed back along the line from the left towards us. The Catholic soldiers blessed themselves in a final act of resignation.[28]

Fortunately for Lucy and his section the German machine gun's traverse stopped just short of their position. Lucy had sufficient presence of mind to locate the machine gun's position some 600 yards in front of them: 'With all my strength I shrieked the range, described the target, and ordered five rounds rapid fire.'[29] To his relief and delight, the enemy fire ceased, the machine gun either knocked-out or withdrawn. The survivors of the attack were then ordered to retire; the 'total casualties were not far short of 150, chiefly wounded'.[30]

Reinforcements had been ferried over the Aisne for the 5th Division's assault on the Chivres spur on the 15th, but as the British troops fought their way up the wooded hill for a second time, they found the Germans had improved the defences and the attack was repulsed. The increase in British numbers was causing problems in the confined space between the river and the German-held high ground. The village of Missy, at the foot of the spur, once again proved a bottleneck for troops moving either west or east; its crowded streets were pounded by German howitzers, causing confusion and a lengthening casualty list. Continuation of the assault was called off, with troops withdrawn to the south bank to ease the congestion in Missy. Any further plans to take the Chivres spur were abandoned, confirming the BEF's transition from attack to defence.

CHAPTER THIRTEEN

BATTLE ON THE AISNE: ENTRENCHMENT

Field Marshal Sir John French's order for 16 September accepted the reality of the end of mobile operations on the Aisne by stating that he wished 'the line held by the Army to be strongly entrenched'.[1] This marked the first stage in the development of trench warfare, which by the end of the year would dominate military operations and provide a new name borrowed from the Germans for the static battlefield: the Western Front.

As the intensity of the first phase of fighting on the Aisne died down, Major-General Henry Wilson asked each corps to provide GHQ with information analysing the conduct of the war so far and asking what lessons might be learned from it. The replies provided an insight into the way in which the British Army was attempting to come to terms with the demands of modern warfare.

Both I and II Corps stressed the accuracy and destructive power of German artillery. II Corps wrote: 'Perhaps the most unexpected feature of the present war has been the arresting power of modern artillery, and especially of howitzers and heavy artillery, both as regards their material and moral effect.'[2] I Corps agreed: 'It is the most formidable arm we have to encounter.'[3]

In the initial phase of the battle, the British gunners were at a marked disadvantage. The shortage of heavy, long-range pieces firing high explosive was an obvious problem, but this was compounded by an inability to locate the well-hidden German guns on the reverse slopes of the Chemin des Dames, while their own gun positions were too often visible to aircraft and the excellent German forward observers scanning the Aisne valley. And from 17 September onwards, the first concerns were raised over what would develop into a chronic and sometimes acute shortage of artillery ammunition (German gunners were also complaining of ammunition shortages, although this would have surprised the soldiers of the BEF).

German artillery domination was clear to all. Lieutenant Alexander Johnston of the 7th Brigade remarked: 'I cannot help feeling that we are being rather let down by our gunners: they do not seem to be as nearly as scientific as these Germans.'[4] Medical Officer Arthur Martin, an observer of the artillery battles around the Chivres spur, wrote: 'The Germans never refused an artillery duel, and when our batteries seemed to wake up the Germans did too, and hurled across their shot at a tremendous pace.'[5] General Haig was even more forthright: 'The enemy's big guns possess a real superiority for some of our gunners! In fact, our gunners cannot "take on" the enemy's heavy batteries.'[6]

The solution to the British artillery's predicament lay in concealment and indirect fire with either terrestrial or aerial forward observers. Battery commanders were firmly instructed to ensure their guns and attendant gun flashes were to be hidden from both ground and air. Each battery needed its own aircraft spotter and all firing was to cease when an enemy machine was located in the vicinity. Horses and limbers were to be removed from the battery area and all wheel tracks erased. Alternative emplacements were to be constructed, as were dummy batteries (with logs as gun barrels) to confuse German aerial observers. On a more homely note, the instructions concluded: 'Tins should not be left about near the guns, nor should washing be hung about in the vicinity.'[7]

Unable to see their targets, the battery commanders required a forward observation officer (FOO) who would direct and correct fire by telephone from a vantage point that overlooked the target. As cables were easily cut communications could be sporadic at the most critical moments, and signallers repairing the line became a regular feature of trench warfare. Despite this continuing weakness – only resolved through the introduction of effective wireless radio – there were few other alternatives.

Lieutenant Robert Money, the machine-gun officer of the 1st Cameronians, witnessed an instance of the effectiveness of indirect fire under the control of an FOO from a howitzer battery operating in front-line trenches held by the 4th Division: 'One day we spotted the flash of German guns. The young officer at the end of his telephone got his guns on to them straight away, knocked the Germans out. His guns were about 1,000 yards in the rear.'[8]

The use of the telephone extended beyond the artillery to the whole command structure, as senior officers tried to maintain direct contact with their forward troops. At this early stage of the war, the demand for telephones far outstripped supply. Artillery officers were reminded of the telephone receiver's vulnerability and rarity: 'The equipment should, therefore, be treated as if it were made of glass, and if it were as valuable as diamonds.'[9]

No matter how well placed the FOO might be, he lacked the panoramic overview provided by aircraft. The Germans had pioneered the use of aircraft for artillery co-operation, but on the Aisne the RFC and Royal Artillery began to catch up with their opponent. An RFC squadron each was assigned to I and II Corps, along with a few aircraft fitted with wireless transmitters. Techniques for aircraft to guide artillery to their targets had been developed pre-war, but they were used for the first time on the Aisne. In a somewhat complex process – demanding good visibility – an aircraft would fire a flare to alert the guns to the presence of its target, and when the battery began to bombard the enemy position further flares would be fired to indicate the fall of shot.

Rather more effective were the aircraft fitted with wireless, and which through morse-code allowed the pilot to transmit detailed instructions to a battery several miles distant. Commanders were appreciative; Haig noted that 'machines fitted with wireless have been particularly successful, and each day has shown improved results as experience has been gained. The good results are apparent.'[10]

Captain Louis Strange flew several flights a day, weather permitting, accompanied by his observer. Strange's log-book entry for 3 October read: 'Went up with Captain Furze at 12.15 p.m. to observe artillery fire, and made flight in one hour twenty minutes. Put the 36th Howitzer battery on to four targets; thirty-two rounds were fired, with four direct hits.'[11] Although Strange and other flyers preferred more direct action, dropping small hand-held bombs onto the Germans below or taking pot shots at enemy aircraft, their artillery co-operation duties took precedence. The following day, low cloud forced Strange down to 3,500 feet. He suddenly encountered a blizzard of ground fire, and was subsequently relieved to have returned safely to base: 'At one time the shells were simply all around us; in addition to the deafening roar of their bursts we could easily hear the whistle and shriek of bullets, which was all very awe-inspiring. I am getting used to being shelled now, almost indifferent to it, in fact; it is simply marvelous that we don't get hit more often.'[12]

German anti-aircraft fire – nicknamed 'Archie' by one of Strange's 5th Squardon pilots after a risqué line from a music-hall song, 'Archibald, certainly not!' – became an increasing nuisance to the British flyers, especially when the range of the Germans' guns extended from 4,000 to 10,000 feet. The BEF, by comparison, was equipped with 1-pounder pom-pom guns, universally judged to be useless in an anti-aircraft role. Archie was not the only problem faced by British flyers over the Aisne. Maurice Baring described a tragic incident:

One of the [RFC] pilots was practising and dropping lights. He was flying quite low over our trenches backwards and forwards. The machine, as so often occurred later during the war, was thought to be behaving in a 'suspicious manner' and was fired at by our troops, and before the men could be stopped firing it was brought down amid the cheers of the men. When the machine crashed they saw that the pilot was an Englishman and that he was dead.[13]

In addition to their work assisting the guns, the RFC maintained its vital reconnaissance role, informing GHQ of changes in German deployment, the construction of new trenches or the arrival of reserves. For the first time, on 14 September, during a gap in the bad weather of that day, a

British machine took photographs of previously hidden gun emplacements as it flew over the German lines. This was a private initiative, but, with assistance from the French aviation service, photographic reconnaissance became the best means of providing the commander with a view – literally in this case – of 'the other side of the hill'.

•

The advances made in artillery deployment and target acquisition were augmented by the introduction of a more flexible artillery command system, although shortages of telephones and cable prevented its full implementation. In I Corps, Haig and Brigadier-General H. S. Horne, his senior artillery adviser, pioneered the use of corps artillery 'groups' that took batteries from both the 1st and 2nd Divisions and concentrated their fire on specific points along the frontage of the corps. This system was used as early as 16 September, when I Corps massed 152 of its guns against the enemy. Haig wrote: 'The air reconnaissance had given us the dispositions behind the ridge. The firing was kept up for 20 minutes and seemed effective. The enemy did not reply very effectively so I hope we warmed him up.'[14]

These improvements could not, however, hide the fact that the BEF was severely deficient in heavy artillery firing high-explosive shells. This was partially remedied by the arrival of four four-gun batteries of 6in. (155mm) howitzers on 23 September (followed by two more batteries a week later). First introduced in 1896, the 6in. (30cwt) howitzer had seen service in the Boer War and by 1914 was nearing obsolescence. Captain John Mowbray, an artilleryman on the 2nd Division's staff, was concerned at the high number of 'prematures' from these guns, noting that the 'shells are too old and not really safe'.[15] But whatever its failings, the 6in. howitzer was the only such weapon then available to the BEF, capable of lobbing a 100lb high-explosive shell at German positions.

Given the dominant role of artillery in the 1914 campaign, it is perhaps surprising to discover numerous first-hand accounts from British soldiers downplaying the material effect of German shelling. That German shrapnel regularly burst too high was commonly acknowledged, but it seemed counter-intuitive to dismiss the destructive power of high-explosive shells.

At the battle of Le Cateau, Lieutenant G. C. Wynne had come under heavy German artillery fire – shrapnel and high explosive – while holding the forward line with the KOYLI, and yet he wrote: 'It seemed indeed that only a direct hit by a shell had mortal effect. Time after time shells burst on the road or in the turnips within ten or twenty yards of me, having no more effect than to cover one with clods of earth and turnip leaves.'[16] These observers commented on the localized nature of shell damage, as well as its potential to lower morale. Captain White of the 39th Brigade RFA ammunition column wrote on the 15th that 'the big siege gun has a demoralising effect but does little damage',[17] while Lieutenant Money described how 'the big shells are impressive – they whistle for ages before they arrive and then make an immense bang; however, it is very local. I have seen hundreds fall and do no damage to anyone.'[18]

This view was subsequently confirmed by Captain Patterson of the 1st South Wales Borderers at Ypres: 'We are shelled from every side and the big coal boxes are almost more than flesh and blood can bear, though the damage they do is next to nothing unless one lucky shot happens to get in the middle of a mass of men.'[19] But it took a brave and seasoned soldier to withstand an artillery bombardment with equanimity. Inexperienced soldiers, by contrast, were especially affected by shell fire. Infantry from the 7th Infantry Brigade had been unnerved when under heavy howitzer fire for the first time within the confines of the village of Caudry during the battle of Le Cateau. On the Aisne a panicked reaction was witnessed by MO Captain H. B. Owens, while supervising the withdrawal of horse-drawn ambulances over the river on 16 September:

Around the corner of a bend in the road came a most appalling sight – heavy wagons, water carts, cavalrymen, spare horses, riderless horses, cavalry limbers, all coming hell for leather [going] past like mad. Most extraordinary sight. They wouldn't stop for me. Thought the Germans must really have burst through and it was a case of 'sauve qui peut' ['every man for himself']. Went back to see what had happened and found they had shelled the tail lot of some cavalry. Dropped about five shells among them. Some of our men were hurt, but horses were scared and bolted.[20]

That the effect of shell fire as a whole was as much moral as physical should not disguise the devastating consequence of just a single shell if it exploded 'in the middle of a mass of men' – made worse if it happened in a confined space, where the blast was concentrated back onto the victims. Such incidents happened on a number of occasions on the Aisne. On the 16th, a howitzer shell landed in a quarry sheltering infantry from the 2nd Grenadier Guards and the 2nd Oxfordshire and Buckhamshire Light Infantry, killing and wounding at least 80 men. On 29 September a chance shell hit the 9th Lancers in their billets at Longueval, over 2 miles south of the River Aisne. It was an exceptionally fortunate shot from a German perspective, fired from a position at least 9,000 yards from the village. Captain Arthur Osburn, temporarily acting as the Lancers' MO, had just passed a detachment of new reinforcements in a parade yard when the shell exploded. His description reveals the visceral horror of such an event:

> Fragments of stone, manure, pieces of clothing and hair came falling about me as I ran through the archway into the yard and beheld one of the most heart-rending sights I have ever seen, even in war. The detachment of 9th Lancers had almost completely disappeared. In the centre of the yard where I had seen them but a moment before, there was now a mound four or five feet high of dead men and horses, yet still they were moving, men and horses twitching and sliding over one another with slow writhing movements, the men's faces purple, crimson or ash-grey. For a moment, rooted to the ground, I stared at this heap – a moving mound of death.
>
> Then, from all sides of the yard, a chorus of screams, shouts and groans. Around this central heap of dead men, the wounded lay on all sides. Some had been blown to the other end of the yard, their backs broken. One sat up dazed and whimpering, his back against the wall, holding part of his intestine in his hands. Those nearest to the heap, with terrible stomach wounds, or with legs and arms torn away, were only moaning and writhing; it was those further off, comparatively speaking the least damaged yet terribly injured, who shouted and screamed in agony. For a moment or two, alone in that desolate scene, I ran hither and thither, hardly knowing what to do or where to begin. I began to shout to my groom outside to go for assistance, to my corporal to fetch bags of dressings and chloroform.[21]

Officers and men from the Lancers and 4th Dragoon Guards then ran into the yard to help, as Osburn began tending to those strewn on the outer edges of the blast who might have a chance of survival. Osburn continued to work – 'oblivious to time' – until only the dead remained. All told, the 9th Lancers lost 40 officers and men.

•

As the BEF adopted a defensive position on the Aisne from 15 September onwards they were subjected to German assaults of varying intensity that lasted to almost the end of the month. These attacks were a result of a fundamental change in the strategic direction of the war by Germany and France. Even in open warfare, neither side had been able to achieve a breakthrough; with a line of entrenchments running from the Swiss border to just north of the Aisne, any such breakthrough was now all but impossible. Consequently, the Allied and German commanders looked to the open northern flank that stretched more than 100 miles to the English Channel. Apart from German cavalry and French Territorials the whole northern flank was virtually empty of troops.

Both sides desperately began to transfer forces in an attempt to outflank the other, but in a strange symmetry an advance by one side was almost immediately and proportionally countered by one from the other, again producing stalemate. During September and into the first half of October a defensive line advanced steadily northward – the 'Race to the Sea' – until reaching the Channel.

Both sides adopted a policy of making limited offensives against the existing trench system, to hold enemy troops in place and deter their redeployment to the vital northern sector. This reasoning lay behind the attacks against the BEF on the Aisne, although at the time the British reasonably believed them to be genuine attempts to break through their lines.

On 16 September, the 6th Division (Major-General J. L. Keir) had arrived at the front, its progress delayed by autumn storms during its sea voyage to St Nazaire. As a temporary measure the division was broken up to support the formations already in place on the Aisne: the 16th Brigade to the 3rd Division and the 17th and 18th Brigades to I Corps. On the 19th another batch of general reinforcements arrived, along with a first consignment of 18-pounders to replace those lost at Le Cateau.

The Germans instigated a fairly long constant bombardment as a prelude to the assault on 20 September against the 3rd Division and I

Corps. The gap that had formerly existed between these two formations had been virtually closed, so that the 4th (Guards) Brigade (on the left of I Corps) was able to provide fire support to the right of the 3rd Division. The German assault on the 3rd Division opened with a diversionary strike against the 9th Brigade followed by the main attack on the 7th Brigade. The two forward battalions – the 2nd Royal Irish Rifles and the 1st Wiltshires – held firm in their trenches but the Germans broke through on their right, pressing forward on brigade HQ, which deoloyed two weak companies of the 2nd South Lancashires in reserve. Captain Alexander Johnston was caught up in the action after he had rallied one of the South Lancs companies unsettled by shell fire:

> We called up the last company of the 2nd South Lancs, who were in the cutting below us, but had great difficulty in getting them to go forward. The situation now seemed serious, the Germans were right in our position now, the wood within 150 yards of brigade HQ was full of German snipers picking men off as they showed themselves. They had a Maxim there too which was doing a lot of damage, and one could hear the German officers collecting their men probably for a further advance. All this time heavy firing continued in the wood which told us that anyway someone was holding out in front all right.[22]

The Germans in the woods were then shelled by accurate fire from the guns of the 4th Brigade, forcing them to retire. But immediately, as the German infantry began to retreat, the British came under a fierce bombardment, another example, Johnston recalled, 'of the excellence of the German artillery'.

This brought the action against the 3rd Brigade to a close, although there was more serious fighting still going on along the line held by I Corps. An attack against the 2nd Division was repulsed after some hard fighting, but that made on the 1st Division seemed, for a time at least, to threaten a British collapse.

On 19 September the 1st and 2nd Brigades were withdrawn and replaced by the newly arrived 18th Brigade. For security reasons the change-over took place at night, with the new units having very little idea of the nature of their surroundings until daybreak. The most vulnerable position was taken by the 2nd West Yorkshire Regiment, holding a series of unconnected rifle pits on the far right of the British line just north of Paissy. To their right was a unit of French colonial troops with whom they had yet to make contact. It was the novice West Yorkshires' misfortune that the Germans made a determined assault against both British and French units at first light.

In accordance with French practice, the colonial troops fell back in the face of the German attack with the intention of regaining their trenches in a subsequent counter-attack – which duly took place. This behaviour perplexed the West Yorkshires – especially when they were briefly fired upon by the returning French – but they managed to fight off the initial German attack in the midst of heavy rain and hail. As the Germans pushed harder, however, the two forward companies gave way. The regimental history maintained that they had been 'first tricked and then shot down or taken prisoner' and that 'the whole affair was a mystery'.[23] But what was clear in the confusion of battle was a lack of determination among the troops of the battalion; the officers were unable to rally their men, many of whom were captured with comparative ease. As the Germans advanced into the British trenches they turned enfilade fire on the flank of the 2nd Durham Light Infantry and then on the 1st East Yorkshire Regiment, who, due to heavy artillery fire, were pinned down and unable to mount a counter-attack.

The BEF's cavalry was acting as a mobile reserve for the trench-bound infantry, and Major-General de Lisle was with the 2nd Cavalry Brigade when he heard the sound of battle. In his report on the action he wrote: 'I then saw part of the West Yorkshire Regiment retire from their trenches and expected them to halt on reaching the cover occupied by the ½ battalion in reserve. Instead of this I saw them running in disorder down the valley. I then hurried down to meet them and sent my ADC to turn out a squadron to bring them back to their position.'[24] He then encountered the West Yorkshires' dazed and wounded CO, Lieutenant-Colonel Towsey, and ordered him to turn his men around, promising to provide cavalry support, which was supplied by some troopers from the 18th Hussars and most of the 4th Dragoon Guards.

In the forefront of the cavalry counter-attack was, perhaps inevitably, Major Tom Bridges. His squadron galloped up to the scarp where the infantry were sheltering, dismounted and then advanced towards the Germans: 'I ran up to the crown of the hill which was bare stubble, and seemed quite deserted until I saw a German officer's head coming up the other side. I saw him wave to his men, and I did the same to mine, giving the signal to "double". We met the "pickelhaubers" almost face-to-face, and standing up poured rapid fire into them which put them to flight.'[25] The counter-attack gained momentum with the arrival of more cavalry and two infantry battalions, so that a new line was established in advance of that originally held by the West Yorkshires.

In the ensuing inquest, blame was laid at the door of the West Yorkshires, although Brigadier-General Congreve (18th Brigade) and Major-General Lomax (2nd Division) pleaded mitigating circumstances of general misfortune and inexperience. Haig was furious and his handwritten comment on Lomax's report fizzed with indignation: 'I find it difficult to write in temperate language regarding the very unsoldier like behaviour of the W. Yorks on the 20th inst: Apparently they fled from their trenches on the appearance of some 150 Germans. This is the worst incident of which I have heard during the campaign.' He was for sacking the unfortunate CO on the spot, only relenting in the light of his subordinates' entreaties, but he recommended that Colonel Towey's 'battalion be strongly rebuked and that they be told that it rests with them to regain the good name and reputation which our infantry holds'.[26]

●

Further German assaults were launched against I Corps positions between the 25th and the 27th. The British were well prepared and the Germans were beaten back, the fiercest fighting taking place on the 26th around the position held by the South Wales Borderers, their resolute defence earning praise from Haig. After 27 September, offensive actions ended, both sides improving the trench systems they had first begun in mid-September. Trench warfare developed on the Aisne with remarkable swiftness, many of the features that were to become standard in 'mature' trench warfare being evident in the first two or three weeks of combat.

That the Germans were well ahead in the materials and techniques for waging trench warfare came as little surprise. Apart from the German Army's greater awareness of the requirements of modern warfare, the German Supreme Command had devoted much time and energy to the problem of breaking through the formidable enemy defences stretching along the French and Belgian frontiers, and experience gained in the preparation for siege operations translated easily into trench warfare. The British soldier, looking up towards the ridge of the Chemin des Dames, faced an enemy not only well equipped with large-calibre howitzers, but also with trench mortars, grenades, rifle grenades, illuminating flares, searchlights and an array of entrenching tools and materials.

The British, by contrast, had to improvise; the only useful items arriving at the front were sandbags, some coils of barbed wire and new supplies of picks and spades to supplement the infantryman's 'grubber'. The cavalry – now acting as mounted infantry – had not been issued with entrenching tools, and particularly welcomed any digging implements. Arthur Osburn, with the 4th Dragoon Guards, recalled, 'passing along to the left a message that came to me from my right: "Will A Squadron lend C Squadron *the spade?*"'[27]

The first imperative for the men of the BEF was to dig themselves out of danger. Formerly, an acceptable trench was one excavated to a depth of 3 feet 6 inches with the spoil shovelled in front as a makeshift parapet 2 feet above ground level. This was clearly insufficient to protect men against artillery fire. In the light of the infantry's experiences at Le Cateau, an officer from the 5th Division wrote: 'A bad trench is worse than none at all. Trenches must be narrow and deep.'[28]

Instructions were also issued to construct trenches with traverses, especially as long sections of the British line were vulnerable to enfilade fire from German artillery and machine guns sited on the spurs projecting from the Chemin des Dames. More thought was given to the siting of trenches, with the emphasis placed on concealment. The firmly worded directives on this matter from the corps commands seemed to have filtered down the line. Ammunition supply officer Captain C. A. L. Brownlow encountered some recently dug reserve trenches: 'They were placed behind the crest, with a very restricted field of fire, of about a hundred yards, instead of being placed beyond the crest with a wide field, according to pre-war ideas. This was done in accordance with a new theory that at all costs our trenches must be concealed from enemy artillery.'[29]

Trenches were dug deeper and short sections joined up, although a continuous, unbroken trench line remained in the future. Second-line support trenches in vulnerable areas also began to be excavated, with plans for communications trenches to connect them. The trenches were also made more comfortable, as men installed rudimentary drainage systems and hollowed-out 'funk-holes' in the trench sides to rest and shelter. Captain Patterson and a fellow officer from the South Wales Borderers constructed their own 'dug-out' (the name being sufficiently new to require quotation marks): 'A good cave into the hill-side with three doors which the Germans pulled off their hinges in the village. These doors [placed] over the top and about a foot of earth on top, very cosy [in] this cold weather and proof against anything except a "coal-box" or percussion shell.'[30]

The quarried-out limestone caves, dotted along the slopes of the Chemin des Dames, were invaluable as shell-proof temporary hospitals for the treatment of the wounded. If sufficiently close to the front line they were also used to protect soldiers against the heaviest fire. 'Our procedure,' wrote Sergeant John McIlwain of the 2nd Connaught Rangers, 'was to occupy the caves when bombardments began; have a half-platoon or so on duty near the exit to rush out when the shelling ceased, occupy the entrenchments and stone breastworks and await an enemy attack.'[31]

The static nature of the fighting encouraged sniping, which in this early phase of trench warfare ranged from bored officers taking pot shots at enemy troops to more scientific methods using marksmen with a knowledge of fieldcraft, and armed with accurate rifles, some fitted with telescopic sights. The Germans were once again in the ascendency. The British sniper authority, Major H. Hesketh-Prichard wrote: 'These Germans, who were often Forest Guards, and sometimes Battle Police, did their business with a skill and a gallantry which must be very freely acknowledged.'[32] The British approach was exemplified by Lieutenant V. E. C. Dashwood of the 2nd Sussex, who noted in his diary for 30 September: 'Did some sniping and believed I bagged a couple.' But the following day he admitted the uncertainty of the amateur sniping process: 'Several of us claim bull-eyes as the result of sniping, but of course we don't know what we bagged.'[33]

The strip of ground between the British and German front-line trenches would soon take on that most resonant of names: No Man's Land. And it was here that another feature of trench warfare emerged, the patrol or, in its aggressive form, the trench raid – usually conducted at night. The width of No Man's Land during the war varied enormously

– in some places, less than a dozen yards, in others, several hundred yards. On the Aisne the distance between the two trench lines might typically range from 100 to 400 yards, within which was dead ground, woods, hay stacks and farmers' huts – features that provided concealment for those operating in No Man's Land.

Trench raids were partly intended to gain information about the enemy (especially from the capture of prisoners) but were also to overawe them and encourage an aggressive spirit among the troops making the raid. Senior officers in the BEF showed an ongoing concern for any signs of the weakening of the soldiers' resolve. Brigadier-General Forestier-Walker, II Corps' chief of staff, was a pessimist in this matter. He wrote: 'During the occupation of a defensive position, the morale of officers and men is apt to deteriorate to an alarming degree unless drastic steps are taken to counteract the tendency.' This decline in morale, he continued, 'leads rapidly to a loss of initiative, and the desire soon becomes apparent, not only to avoid attacking but even to do nothing which will tend to draw the enemy's fire.'[34]

The remedy, according to Forestier-Walker, was 'probably to insist on small local attacks and enterprises, even with the knowledge that they must entail loss of men on missions of minor importance'. It was this latter aspect that caused ongoing controversy. Critics rejected the whole notion that military effectiveness and sound morale were a direct product of an overtly aggressive attitude, and saw the casualties from trench raids as wasteful rather than reluctantly necessary. But it was the view propounded by Forestier-Walker that typically prevailed in the British command during the war.

On the Aisne, trench raids were certainly necessary to prevent the Germans dominating No Man's Land at the BEF's expense. German snipers needed to be dissuaded from adopting forward positions, as their accurate fire chipped away at a battalion's strength and its morale. More dangerous still were the intrepid German artillery observers, whose careful observation of the Aisne valley brought down a swift and accurate bombardment from the hills above whenever a British unit advanced from cover. It was this seemingly uncanny phenomenon that exacerbated the already strong spy mania of the period, a belief that undercover agents within or behind British lines must somehow be signalling detailed information of British movements to the Germans.

The better British battalions contested control of No Man's Land with the enemy. Lieutenant Rees of the 2nd Welch Regiment recalled how he and his men were plagued by a German battery deployed behind a ridge close to their part of the line:

> The German observer established himself on a haystack 300 yards away, and our guns with whom there was not telephone connection, failed to hit him. We tried to dislodge him with rifle fire, but as he usually gave us a dose of shrapnel in reply it was not very popular. The observer became such a public nuisance that a sergeant crawled out to the haystack at night, bayonetted the German on guard, put a match to it and made good his escape. A fine performance. The smoking heap next morning was a very gratifying sight.[35]

Rees briefly alluded to another aspect of trench warfare that so concerned Forestier-Walker, the tendency of troops not to initiate offensive operations to avoid enemy retaliation. This developed into the 'live and let live' system that became common in 'quiet' sectors of the Western Front. A fully formed example of this tendency, from early October, can be found in an account by Arthur Mills, who had just arrived as a reinforcement officer in an unnamed battalion on the 5th Division's front, where fighting was minimal:

> It did not take more than an hour or two to pick up the rudiments of trench life. We passed the morning sitting in the dug-out reading a few old papers and smoking and talking. By eleven the sun was high enough to peep over the parapet and warm us, and it all seemed to me a very pleasant, lazy sort of existence. There was no firing except for an occasional 'ping' from a sniper [Captain] Goyle kept posted at the corner of the trench, and an answering shot or two from the German side. Rifle fire seemed a matter of tacit arrangement. When our sniper was joined by a friend, or fired two or three times in a minute instead of once every three of four, the German fire grew brisker and life in the trench less tranquil. Our sniper was thereon reproved by Goyle and was silent, whereupon the German fire died down.[36]

The peaceful equilibrium of 'live and let live' was easily disturbed, however, whether through the actions of real snipers (rather than Sunday sharpshooters), the (subsequent) installation of trench mortars with plenty of ammunition or a bellicose attitude towards the enemy from the more aggressive company and battalion commanders.

•

Wars in the past had typically comprised long periods of manoeuvre culminating in the short, concentrated experience of battle and its immediate aftermath, to be followed by a period of respite. Trench warfare, by contrast, was continuous. The intensity of the fighting would vary over time and place, but the front-line soldier was always exposed to danger, whether through the sniper's bullet or a random shell blast. Combined with the often grim conditions of trench life, soldiers had to endure levels of physical and psychological pressure rarely encountered before.

Lieutenant George Roupell of the 1st East Surreys recorded how his troops were suffering 'from the continual strain of never being out of the reach of the enemy's guns. It is scarcely surprising that under these conditions traces of panic and loss of self-control occasionally appeared.'[37] Roupell also believed that the continual stress of trench warfare had eroded the initiative of his NCOs. In one rather irascible diary entry he wrote: 'The few remaining officers did *everything*. NCOs were there but could not be relied on to do anything but the most simple and unmistakable directions.'[38] This comment may well have been a result of Roupell's own feelings of strain, but it was also indicative of the pre-war army's failure to encourage NCOs to develop and use their initiative.

Roupell's concerns also extended to officers, in particular his company commander: 'Torren's nerves were really terribly bad at this time and I was practically assuming command of the company, but his presence made things difficult, and it was very bad for the men.'[39] Sergeant McIlwain of the Connaught Rangers was one of the other ranks who had to endure an officer close to breaking point. Lieutenant de Stacpoole, whose brother had recently been killed, was the sole officer in McIlwain's company: 'He was in a bad way indeed. He could not give an order without shouting at the men. This habit of uncontrolled yelling I soon found to be infectious at times of stress and alarm. It was bad for discipline and I succeeded in resisting it. De Stacpoole was almost beyond control, and was sent away just in time.'[40]

Officers overwhelmed by psychological stress – especially if the taint of cowardice hung in the air – were swiftly and discretely removed from the front line. Senior officers correctly reasoned that if field officers were seen to fail this ultimate test of leadership in battle, then the whole edifice of command was in danger of collapse. Accordingly, Roupell's company commander was removed and sent to brigade HQ. Arthur Osburn became aware of the 'growing effect of nerves' for the first time on the Aisne. Meeting one officer with this affliction his response was justifiably cynical: 'My companion had influence. Fear in high places usually meant a job at the Base and "happy ever afterwards".'[41]

The other ranks did not fare so well. Although personal honour was the prime motivational force binding both officers and other ranks, the latter were also subject to punitive disciplinary measures if their courage wavered. In McIlwain's company, a sergeant was repeatedly discovered to be skulking in the rear areas, and was finally court-martialled, reduced to the ranks and sentenced to two years' imprisonment. There were, of course, more serious punishments: for those convicted of 'desertion in the face of the enemy' the firing squad was a real possibility. A few days before the start of the Aisne battle, Smith-Dorrien recorded in his diary that one of his soldiers had been shot for desertion.[42]

A partial solution to the problem of battlefield exhaustion lay in the rotation of units from the front to the rear on a regular basis, providing an opportunity of recovery for both the individual and the unit. Haig was quick to realize the necessity of replacing exhausted front-line battalions with fresh troops. He had lobbied Field Marshal French for such a system, even before the arrival of the 6th Division provided the BEF with an opportunity to carry this out in a comprehensive manner. By the end of September unit rotation had become a standard practice. But at the start of October a more fundamental change of scene was being proposed, as plans were drawn up for the wholesale removal of the BEF from the Aisne to a new zone of operations in Flanders.

PART FOUR

DECISION AT YPRES

CHAPTER FOURTEEN

THE OPENING MOVES

The determination of the French and Germans to achieve a military decision in the north was mirrored by a British desire to redeploy the BEF in Flanders. To remain in position along the Aisne, in what was now a quiet sector, would condemn the BEF to a peripheral role subordinate to French strategic interests. Sir John French and GHQ chafed at such a restriction and saw the northern flank as an opportunity for the British Army to return to open warfare with a greater degree of national autonomy. The fighting on the Aisne had little to show for 13,500 British casualties.

In Britain, Lord Kitchener and Winston Churchill, First Lord of the Admiralty, saw a redeployment of the BEF as a means to secure Belgium's Channel ports and to support the Belgian Army and the fortress city of Antwerp. In addition, by moving north the extended lines of communication via St Nazaire would be shortened to a simple cross-Channel link, and the next wave of reinforcements – the 7th and 8th Divisions and the Indian Corps – would have sufficient space to fight alongside the BEF.

A formal application for an immediate transfer of the BEF was put to General Joffre on 27 September. Although he had misgivings about the timing of the move – interfering with the movement of his own forces – he acceded to the British request, his only stipulation being that the transfer be conducted covertly and in stages.

Britain's interest in Belgium predated the BEF's transfer from the Aisne. As early as 27 August, a small force led by three battalions of Royal Marines had landed in Ostend. The Marines marched along the front and then re-embarked for England four days later. A section of naval aviation and an improvised armoured-car detachment under Commander Charles Samson remained behind, however. Throughout September, Samson enjoyed the unusual experience of true independent command, flying reconnaissance missions and sending out motorized patrols in an attempt to deter German cavalry sweeps being made across northern France and Belgium.

A somewhat more serious British intervention came on the night of 19/20 September, when Brigadier-General George Aston landed at Dunkirk with a brigade of Royal Marine infantry, comprising a core of trained soldiers but with many overage reservists and inexperienced recruits. The Marines were joined by the Oxfordshire Hussars, a company of Royal Engineers and a consignment of motor cars and buses. Aston had a rather vague brief to act as a vanguard for a larger British force, but as he waited for reinforcement a Marine battalion marched to Lille to briefly fly the flag, while enterprising officers began to operate their own roving patrols. Major Norman Burge of the Marines' Portsmouth Battalion described in a letter how he led one such patrol, attended by the typical confusions of competing 'private armies':

> I would take about 20 of my men on bicycles, and also commandeer a French subaltern with 20 of his cyclists. Following in rear we'd have a big motor lorry with 20 Marines and 2 Maxim guns to support us. We'd hear of perhaps 50 uhlans who had been terrifying the country. We'd go and make careful plans for rounding them up and driving them back into the arms of our friends the French, when generally the infernal fellow Samson, the flying man, would dash up in armoured motor cars – chivvy off the uhlans and spoil the whole blessed show for us. However, one morning we bagged 8 or 10.[1]

This Boy's Own interlude came to an end with the German assault against Antwerp on 28 September. General Hans Hartwig von Beseler's III Reserve Corps had initially acted as a screening force to contain the Belgian Field Army within the Antwerp area. The change of strategic focus to the north and the freeing up of German heavy artillery after the fall of Maubeuge on 8 September sealed Antwerp's fate. The devastating 30cm and 42cm (Big Bertha) super-heavy howitzers were turned on the city's outer ring of forts, while the redeployment of the German besieging force threatened to encircle the city and trap the Belgian Army.

On 30 September the Belgian government informed the British and French that without reinforcements they would be forced to retire from Antwerp. General Joffre's preference was, in fact, for a withdrawal of the Belgian Army to take up position alongside his own troops, and his response for assistance was accordingly lukewarm. The British were ostensibly more positive. On 1 October, the government agreed to send the 7th Division to support the city's defence, although at the time the formation was not ready to cross the Channel.

Winston Churchill, eager to escape the tedium of desk-bound operations, travelled to Antwerp on 3 October to assess the situation personally and to encourage the Belgians to fight, in the widespread but erroneous British belief that Belgian morale was wavering. The Belgians, however, required immediate and substantial material reinforcement, and this the British were unable to supply.

A token effort was made instead. The Royal Marine Brigade already in Belgium arrived to man the city's defences on the 4th, although it was understrength with just 2,000 fighting men. Two poorly equipped brigades of naval infantry, raised from shore-based naval personnel and untrained volunteers, joined the Marines. Their unsuitability for land operations was evident to all who saw them. 'Both men and officers are splendid material', wrote Major Burge as kindly as possible, 'and very good and nice fellows but absolutely untrained and with no discipline. No trained officers or petty officers, 90 per cent of the men had never fired a rifle and they were very badly equipped.'[2]

The Belgian Field Army – its position increasingly vulnerable – began its retreat westwards from Antwerp on 6 October. Two days later, the Germans, having broken through the outer defences, were in a position to bombard Antwerp itself; they also threatened to cut through the western corridor and trap any forces remaining within and around the city. In scenes of the utmost confusion, the Royal Marines and naval brigades joined the masses of refugees fleeing the German guns. In the ensuing disorder, three battalions of the 1st Naval Brigade crossed the border into the Netherlands, where they were interned, while a Royal

Marine battalion became lost and was forced to surrender to the enemy. On 10 October, Beseler formally accepted the surrender of Antwerp. The British intervention had been a dismal diplomatic and military failure, displaying a manifest inability to match intentions with resources.

•

The British 7th Infantry Division disembarked at Zeebrugge on 7 October, too late for any hope of saving Antwerp. The following day it was joined by the 3rd Cavalry Division, and under Lieutenant-General Sir Henry Rawlinson the two formations were somewhat grandly designated as IV Corps. The 7th Division (Major-General Thompson Capper) had been hastily assembled in Britain from troops withdrawn from overseas garrisons, and while it contained few reservists the infantry were not march-hardened and the constituent units had not been given a chance to bed down. The division was also short of artillery. Instead of the normal complement of 72 field guns and howitzers and four 60-pounders, it was supplied with just 48 field guns (36 18-pounders, 12 13-pounders) and eight 4.7in. guns of Boer-War vintage. The 3rd Cavalry Division (Major-General Julian Byng) was understrength and short of supporting arms, fielding two small brigades and a single battery of horse artillery.

Once assembled on Belgian soil, IV Corps marched forward to Ghent to support the right of the line established by the Belgian Army along the Schelde canal. But in the face of growing German pressure, the Belgian position became too exposed for serious defence, and on the 11th and 12th the Belgians retreated to a new line on the Yser River. Rawlinson's Corps then retired in stages towards Ypres, where it would join the main body of the BEF, now in the process of moving north from the Aisne. The hard pavé roads soon took their toll on the infantry of the 7th Divison, as they had on the men marching to Mons just a few weeks earlier. Patrick Butler, an ADC to Major-General Capper, described the departure from Ghent:

That night march was a most miserable affair, and what made it worse was that the men were tired out even before they started. When we had gone about eight miles the men started falling out in parties of threes and fours. I could see them just quietly leaving the ranks and sitting down on the side of a steep bank that ran down from the roadway; and no efforts of entreaty or upbraiding on the part of their officers could move them.[3]

On 14 October the soldiers of IV Corps arrived at Ypres, among them Robert Lloyd of the 1st Lifeguards:

> Ypres was carrying on with its normal peace-time activities. The town had the day before received a visit from a body of German cavalry, and a few shrapnel shells had been burst over the outskirts. The inhabitants received us with open arms and made a tremendous fuss of us. Not one of us who admired the ancient town then, with its imposing buildings, tree-bordered streets, rows of handsome shops, and spick-and-span townsfolk, could foresee the ghastly dust-heap to which it was doomed to be reduced in the next few months.[4]

As the British entered Ypres, a German Taube aircraft flew over the city on a reconnaissance mission. It was met by a mass fusillade of ground fire that damaged the craft and forced it to land, the pilot and observer unharmed and subsequently captured. Commander Sansom of the Naval Air Service was called to interrogate the German airmen: 'On arriving at headquarters I found that everybody had brought the Taube down, including Sir Henry Rawlinson who had seized a rifle and fired five shots at it with the cut-out closed. The total bag was counted up to be one Hun aeroplane, five sparrows, three windows and most of the telegraph wires in the main square.'[5]

The 7th Division took up a line a few miles to the east of Ypres, in preparation for a general push deep into Belgium. On its left, the 3rd Cavalry Division advanced past Passchendaele towards Roulers.

The other formations of the BEF were now completing their redeployment from the Aisne. The withdrawal was carried out in secrecy, the Germans apparently unaware of the move until the British divisions had been replaced by units from the French Army. Given the complicated nature of the transfer north – the BEF competing with the French Army for rail access – progress was relatively slow. II Corps was not in position until 11 October, followed a couple of days later by III Corps, while I Corps completed its detrainment at Hazebrouck on the 19th.

Field Marshal French and his staff at GHQ established themselves at St Omer on 13 October. The BEF now came under the auspices of the newly formed Northern Army Group, commanded by General Ferdinand Foch, who was given responsibility for the co-ordination of the French, Belgian and British armies in Flanders. Although Foch had no direct authority over the BEF, he was well known to senior British officers and had forged a good relationship with Sir John French. Foch was an unashamed exponent of the offensive and his enthusiasm was taken up by French, who now saw this new theatre of operations as an opportunity to return to open warfare.

●

One of the last casualties of the battle of the Marne had been the German chief of staff, General Helmut von Moltke. On 14 September he was ordered to report sick, soon to be replaced by the Minister of War, General Erich von Falkenhayn, a confidant of the Kaiser. Falkenhayn redeployed Crown-Prince Rupprecht's Sixth Army with orders to overwhelm the French in the Somme region. But the arrival of French forces directly opposite him in early October forced Rupprecht to look further north to envelop the enemy's line. And it was there, between La Bassée and Ypres, that Sixth Army would encounter the BEF.

The German Sixth Army could only be stretched so far, and a gap remained between it and the Channel coast. During September and into early October the space had been filled by German cavalry – eight divisions in total – but they lacked the power to take and permanently hold positions in the face of enemy infantry and artillery. The pre-war failure to increase the size of its army to meet its strategic demands had now come back to haunt Germany.

A solution of sorts lay in the large pool of serviceable manpower that had been left behind when the German Army first marched to war. Comprising reservists, volunteers and other non-front-line troops, six new reserve corps were hastily assembled during August, and four were ordered to Flanders to join Beseler's III Reserve Corps. They would form a newly constituted German Fourth Army commanded by Duke Albrecht of Württemberg. The four new reserve corps would be deployed between Sixth Army and Beseler's III Reserve Corps, now pressing the Belgians along the Yser.

Falkenhayn was taking a gamble in using troops poorly prepared and equipped for war. While trained reserve formations such as Beseler's corps lacked the combat edge of the regular divisions, they were still able to hold their own in the front line. By contrast, the four new reserve corps were third-grade formations, relying on enthusiasm and bravery to make up for their other very obvious deficiencies. Some infantry units marched to war in the old blue uniforms, only receiving rifles at the last minute, with training confined to simple parade-ground drill. Of the officers, many had little knowledge of the more recent tactical and technical advances, and some were clearly too old and unfit for the rigours of campaign.

Even at the time, Rupprecht considered their deployment en masse a mistake: 'It would have been better to have used the available manpower to reinforce existing corps, whose manpower has been subject to attrition. There, working with experienced soldiers, better performance could have been expected.'[6] But for Falkenhayn, lacking trained divisions to throw into the battle, it was a risk worth taking if a decisive result could be achieved.

*

On the Allied side, Sir John French – influenced by Foch and egged-on by Wilson – was once more in a dangerously buoyant mood. He believed the Germans to be a spent force, and would brook no contradiction. On 10 October he had agreed to join Foch in a combined Anglo-French offensive. His II and III Corps were now moving up to their start positions for an advance to a line stretching from La Bassée in the south to Armentières in the north, with the Cavalry Corps pushing into the gap between Armentières and Ypres.

The terrain over which II and III Corps were to advance was a mixture of industrial and agricultural. In the area around Béthune and La Bassée – the responsibility of II Corps – Brigadier-General Headlam, the CRA of the 5th Division, wrote: 'I very well remember as we topped the ridge on the march from St Pol to Béthune, and suddenly came in sight of the "Black Country" lying before us, how our hearts sank at the prospect of more fighting among the slag heaps as at Mons. It was a real damper to our spirits.'[7]

Moving north from La Bassée, the countryside became increasingly rural, a landscape of small fields cultivated with beetroot, hops, corn and tobacco, and bound by thick hedges and drainage channels, all of which favoured defensive operations. In the words of the Official History, 'The water-courses and wells were contaminated by manure heaps close by, the odour of which contended for the mastery with the sickly smell of refuse beetroot, preserved for winter cattle food; and in most villages there was endemic disease.'[8] During October the soft ground became progressively water-logged, confining artillery and other wheeled vehicles to the roads. And the high water table existing in the low-lying areas turned trenches into drainage ditches, a further misery for the hard-pressed infantryman.

The advance by II Corps began late on the afternoon of 11 October, with the 5th Division on the right and the 3rd Division to its left. The following day the corps encountered resistance from German cavalry units whose responsibility was to delay the British until the arrival of Rupprecht's Sixth Army. The Germans adroitly utilized the defensive advantages of the terrain, their machine guns slowing the British advance to a snail's pace. Lieutenant Alexander Johnston, the signals officer with the 7th Brigade, deployed in the centre of the 3rd Division, fumed at the lack of progress:

> I must say it has been a most disappointing day: here we are a whole division held up by a few Jaegers & horse artillery practically all day. We seem to have plenty of guns which apparently do not help us at all even though they outrange and are heavier than the few guns against them. As far as I can see, everyone is expecting the unit on their right or left to do the hard work: we have been doing practically nothing because we are waiting for the action of the 8th Brigade on our left to take effect, they probably think the same of us and so nobody gets on. Surely the best way of helping the 8th Inf Brigade on is to push ourselves, and if we make headway the people in front of them are bound to give way.[9]

Although Johnston was underrating the difficulties of troops advancing against a resourceful enemy, he correctly highlighted a lack of resolve now evident in II Corps, whose two divisions had seen the most fighting in the BEF's campaign so far. This wariness among officers and men was hardly surprising, but other factors – poor communication at all levels and continuing failures in infantry-artillery co-operation – also compromised II Corps' progress.

The slow linear advance revealed a tactical shortcoming common throughout the BEF. The British Army had traditionally made something of a fetish of fighting in line: the thin red lines that had defeated Napoleon's columns in the Peninsula or repulsed the Russian cavalry at Balaclava had entered British military DNA. Lieutenant George Roupell had admired the steady advance of his East Surreys in successive lines over the water meadows of the Aisne (see page 175), and, as his opponent Captain Walther Bloem readily acknowledged, if well spaced, they were a good defence against artillery fire. But maintaining a regular line could be a painfully slow business over anything but the most perfect terrain, and as the infantry line closed with the enemy, it became vulnerable to machine-gun fire, suicidally so if the attack was not covered by an accurate artillery barrage. As Corporal John Lucy had discovered on the Aisne, a well-hidden machine gunner had merely to traverse his weapon against oncoming enemy lines to bring an attack to a grinding, bloody halt.

An intriguing solution to the problem had already been suggested in mid-September by Brigadier-General J. E. Gough, I Corps' chief of staff. A thoughtful yet aggressive soldier (he had won a VC in Somaliland and was killed at the front in 1915), Gough had put forward this proposal for a change in tactics:

> Thick, regular rigid lines of infantry advancing to the attack merely afford targets which suffer severely the moment they come under fire. Loose and irregular formations with men at 8 or 10 paces interval disposed so as to adapt themselves to any irregularities of ground suffer comparatively little, and are quite as effective as the denser formations. In other words a number of 'clouds of skirmishers' as opposed to a rigid and straight firing line.[10]

In part, Gough was warning against the tendency of an infantry line to close-up in combat, but his argument for the deployment of small, irregularly deployed tactical groups looked back to some of the ideas posed by McMahon and the radicals of the School of Musketry and forward to German stormtroop tactics and the combined-arms sections developed by the British towards the end of the war. In the meantime, the British would persevere with simple linear tactics in offensive operations, with attendant high casualties – as the first day on the Somme would only too graphically illustrate.

•

On 13 October the Germans mounted a fierce counter-attack against Brigadier-General Gleichen's 15th Brigade (5th Division), which was then advancing just to the north of the canal running from Béthune to La Bassée (with the 13th Brigade on the canal's southern side).[11] The 1st Cheshires, on the left of the 15th Brigade, were the first to be attacked, with both the temporary battalion CO, Major Vandeleur, and his second-in-command unwisely taking part in a forward scouting operation. The Germans ambushed the scouting party and captured the survivors. Having lost its two senior officers, the Cheshires were without effective leadership and made little other contribution to the day's fighting. In the centre of the line, the 1st Bedfordshires holding Givenchy were subjected to a heavy bombardment that forced them out of the village. In a disorderly retreat, the Bedfords lost both their machine guns and failed to inform the 1st Dorsets on their right of their withdrawal.

The Germans, having captured Givenchy, now turned their fire on the left flank of the Dorsets who were also heavily engaged in repelling a frontal attack. To make matters worse, the Dorsets, believing their right flank to be protected by the 13th Brigade, suddenly came under fire from Germans on the south side of the canal. Unsurprisingly, the Dorsets broke, suffering as many as 500 casualties in the encounter, leaving just five officers with the battalion at the end of the encounter.

The battered 15th Brigade was reinforced by the 2nd Devonshires in what Gleichen called 'a damnable day', but fortunately for his brigade the Germans did not push further. If nothing else, the encounter was indicative of the problems facing II Corps, that the men were fundamentally tired and that there were not enough experienced officers to manage a crisis and provide inspirational leadership. The strain burdening regimental officers was described by the 5th Division despatch rider William Watson, in a rather despairing note made on 15 October: 'The infantry officer after two months of modern war is a curious phenomenon. He is probably one of three survivors of an original twenty-eight. He is not frightened of being killed; he has forgotten about it. But there is a sort of reflex fright. There are very few, indeed, who retain a nervous balance and a calm judgment.'[12]

On Gleichen's right, the original commander of the 13th Brigade, Brigadier-General G. J. Cuthbert, had recently been replaced by Brigadier-General W. B. Hickie, who, on the morning of the 13th, had declined to advance alongside the 15th Brigade. This hesitancy by Hickie led to his immediate removal in favour of one of his battalion commanders, Lieutenant-Colonel A. Martyn. A further brigade replacement had taken place in the 14th Brigade, with Brigadier-General S. P. Rolt giving way to Brigadier-General Stanley Maude. Such repeated turnovers of senior officers, albeit often necessary, did nothing to maintain continuity and stability of command, but there was to be another, more fundamental change in the 5th Division. Both French and Smith-Dorrien had lost faith in the division's commander, Major-General Sir Charles Fergusson, and following the setback on the 13th, a decision was made to replace him with Major-General T. L. N. Morland, who took over command on 18 October.

Lieutenant-Colonel Lord Loch, the liaison officer between GHQ and II Corps, considered Fergusson to have been made a scapegoat for more general failings within II Corps, a view subsequently supported by historians such as Nikolas Gardner and Ian Beckett. But it should not be forgotten that Fergusson had failed miserably at Le Cateau and been ineffectual on the Aisne. His departure (albeit temporary) was of little loss to the BEF.

The fighting on 13 October brought the 5th Division's advance to a halt. The 3rd Division, on the left of II Corps, had made slightly better progress, although on the 14th its commander, Major-General Hubert Hamilton, was killed by shrapnel while inspecting forward positions. Hamilton's death came as a professional and personal blow to Smith-Dorrien, who wrote to his wife: 'Hubert was a giant, believed in by all – I have lost my right arm.'[13] Hamilton's successor, Major-General C. J. Mackenzie, assumed command on the 15th but he proved inadequate to the task and was temporarily replaced at the end of the month by Major-General F. D. V. Wing. Finding senior officers capable of exercising effective command would remain an enduring problem.

On the night of the 15th/16th the Germans withdrew to better positions a few miles to the east. The troops of II Corps slowly pushed up to the Aubers ridge, but on the 18th the British advance began to falter, a consequence of the arrival of Rupprecht's Sixth Army.

While II Corps had struggled in its advance it, at least, benefitted from close co-operation with the French Army, with French infantry and artillery units 'loaned' to the British on numerous occasions. Previously, the two armies had fought apart, but during the Ypres battles the soldiers of the two armies would develop a new awareness of each other, a point made by Brigadier-General Headlam:

> During the Retreat, and on the Marne and the Aisne, there grew up a general feeling that we were being left to do all the fighting, and one often heard very bitter remarks about the French. The fighting in October knocked all that nonsense on the head. We were together in a very tight place, and we were helping each other every day. Our men saw with their own eyes the gallantry of the French infantry in attack, the French saw the tenacity of our defence. [14]

Further to the north, the 4th and 6th Divisions of III Corps encountered less strong opposition and made better progress against the German screening force. The initial encounter – the attack against Meteren on 13 October – did not go smoothly, however. Artillery support was conspicuously lacking – excused by the Official History as a result of 'wet and misty' weather and enclosed terrain [15] – and the assault by the infantry of the 10th Brigade was made against an entrenched enemy well equipped with machine guns. The British suffered over 700 casualties fighting for control of the village; the battle went on for much of the day until the Germans withdrew.

Among the attackers was Lieutenant Bernard Montgomery of the 1st Royal Warwickshires. As he closed on the enemy trenches, sword in hand, he recalled a large German soldier preparing to shoot him. 'An immediate decision was clearly vital,' he wrote, and throwing himself forward he kicked the German hard in the testicles: 'He fell to the ground in great pain and I took my first prisoner!' [16] His platoon then adopted a new line, but while checking his defences he recklessly walked forward out of cover, and turning around was shot in the back by a German sniper:

> I collapsed, bleeding profusely. A soldier from my platoon ran forward and plugged the wound with my field dressing; while doing so, the sniper shot him through the head and he collapsed on top of me. I managed to shout to my platoon that no more men were to come to me until it was dark. It was then 3 p.m. and raining. I lay there all afternoon; the sniper kept firing at me and I received one more bullet in the left knee. The man lying on me took all the [other] bullets and saved my life.[17]

When it was dark, Montgomery was rescued and taken to an advanced dressing station. At the time there seemed little hope for his survival – he later wrote that a 'grave was dug for me' – but he somehow survived, to be evacuated to England. Montgomery was promoted to captain and awarded a DSO for his courageous leadership, and on recovering from his wounds returned to Flanders as a staff officer.

After withdrawing from Meteren, German cavalry units continued their slow retreat to the Lys River, which they crossed on 15 October to take up positions on the higher ground to the east. III Corps followed, while to the north, Allenby's Cavalry Corps secured the ridge between Messines and Wytschaete. On 17 October III Corps occupied Armentières and then moved 2 miles beyond the town.

This progress greatly encouraged Field Marshal French. In his mind, even though II Corps had suffered setbacks, III Corps seemed in a good position to help the Cavalry Corps cross the Lys, while the 7th Division was due to march on Menin. He ordered an all-out push on the 18th, but contrary to his expectations the advance stalled. Germans captured by the British were no longer just those from cavalry units; increasingly they were regular infantrymen which suggested a change in German deployment. Dogged by a combination of morning fogs and low cloud, reconnaissance missions made by the RFC were unable to provide GHQ with any definitive answers regarding German movements, and both British and French high commands were unaware of the scale of the German forces about to enter the battle.

CHAPTER FIFTEEN

STORM OVER YPRES

Field Marshal French's operational orders for 18 October called on Major-General Thompson Capper's 7th Division to 'move on Menin'.[1] French intended this as a direct assault on the town (12 miles south-east of Ypres), but Capper and Lieutenant-General Sir Henry Rawlinson, IV Corps commander, interpreted this in a more circumspect manner and advanced less than 3 miles. French already had a poor opinion of Rawlinson, and this apparent failure to carry out his instructions only confirmed his misgivings.

The following day GHQ issued orders for an aggressive resumption of the advance, but as the 7th Division attempted to capture Menin, it encountered stiff German resistance. Major-General Julian Byng's 3rd Cavalry Division, guarding Capper's left flank, was pushed back to a line between Zonnebeke and Poelcappelle. This left the 7th Division dangerously exposed, forcing it to retire to a line guarding Ypres. Rawlinson's Corps had been attacked by the vanguard of the four reserve corps of the German Fourth Army. They were marching westwards to join forces with Beseler's III Reserve Corps, already engaged with the Belgians and French along the Yser River.

Colonel George Macdonogh, GHQ's senior intelligence officer, had warned French of the growing numbers of German troops advancing on Ypres, but his reports, and those from IV Corps, were dismissed by French and his operational staff at GHQ. Disappointed by IV Corps' performance, French pinned his hopes on Haig's I Corps, which was forming up to the east of Ypres and would soon lead the advance on the left of IV Corps.

The entire Allied line was about to bear the weight of Falkenhayn's offensive. The German Sixth Army was ordered to attack the Franco-British defences to the south of Ypres, while the German Fourth Army was to act as a battering ram to break through the Franco-Belgian-British line between Ypres and the Channel coast. In the coming weeks the British Army would undergo the most intense and sustained experience of combat so far in its history.

Ypres and the terrain running due north of the city was flat and low-lying. A few miles to the south of Ypres, a gently sloping ridge ran in a north-easterly direction from Wytschaete and Messines in the south to Passchendaele and beyond in the north. It was on this ridge – dotted with chateaux, woods and coverts – that the 7th Division would receive its baptism of fire.

During the morning of 20 October, the 7th Division went over to the defensive as it waited for the arrival of I Corps. The 22nd and 21st Brigades held a line from just north of Broodseinde that ran due south to the Menin road. The 20th Brigade continued the line south of the Menin road to Kruiseecke. There the line abruptly turned westward by 90 degrees to the far side of Zandevoorde where it met up with the Cavalry Corps.

The two Royal Engineer companies allotted to each division helped the infantry with the siting and construction of trenches, but the engineers were few in number and their resources limited. Lieutenant Kerrich RE assisted the 1st Grenadier Guards, holding the right-angled position around Kruiseecke. Barbed wire remained in desperately short supply: 'Not one coil of new wire was to be had,' wrote Kerrich. 'The whole lot had to be collected from neighbouring fences, and the amount of work done by one section in a day was heartbreakingly small.'[2] The infantry were often forced to dig with their entrenching tools, there being insufficient picks and shovels in the battalion and brigade reserves. As a consequence, the British defences consisted of short, isolated sections of entrenchment.

Kerrich had also attempted to clear the foreground immediately in front of the trenches to give the infantry an improved field of fire. There was very little time available, however, and during the morning of the

20th he was warned that the enemy was close at hand. 'Not so long afterwards,' he recalled, 'someone shouted, "Here they come", and the R.E., having orders not to fight, faded away to our farm.'[3]

The defensive line taken by the 7th Division was subsequently criticized because its trenches were dug on forward slopes visible to the German guns. This was taken as an example of the inexperience of the division in the latest tactics; these had been learned the hard way by the other infantry divisions at Le Cateau and on the Aisne. There was some truth in this, especially as regards the 22nd Brigade, but a withdrawal by the other two brigades to suitably concealed positions would have entailed a substantial withdrawal onto the main ridge, which, no doubt, would have brought down the wrath of the Commander-in-Chief.

The prime weakness of the 7th Division's position was not so much the siting of its trenches as the length of line it had been ordered to hold. On the 20th, the division's three brigades were spread across a distance of just over 8 miles, and while this would be progressively reduced over the coming days, the infantry were stretched dangerously thin. By way of comparison, the two powerful divisions of I Corps would take up a near identical length of the line on the 21st.[4]

The shortage of field artillery would also be keenly felt, especially as one of the 13-pounder RHA batteries had been reassigned to the 3rd Cavalry Division, leaving just F battery and six batteries of 18-pounders to be divided up among the three infantry brigades. The division's heavy artillery comprised two four-gun batteries of 4.7in. guns. The near-obsolete 4.7in. gun was of limited value, however, as the Official History confirmed with only slight exaggeration: 'Its shooting was irregular and its shells unreliable. These characteristics earned for it the name of "strict neutrality", for shells fell on friend and foe alike.'[5]

The German assault against IV Corps began in the afternoon of 20 October but was too late to cause much damage. Byng's 3rd Cavalry Division was forced to retreat but the 7th Division held its line without difficulty. The following day, the 3rd Cavalry Division began to move behind the 7th Division to take up a position alongside the Cavalry Corps, south of Ypres. This was also the day that the Germans attacked the 7th Division in force: two reserve divisions from the east, plus a cavalry division pushing south of Kruiseecke. The German infantry were well supported by artillery that included 15cm and 21cm heavy howitzers.

Brigadier-General S. T. B. Lawford's 22nd Brigade, on the left of the line, was particularly hard hit. Sir Richard Sutton, a junior officer in the 1st Lifeguards (3rd Cavalry Division), described how his regiment was despatched to support the brigade: 'When we got there some of the infantry were leaving their trenches in spite of their officers trying to prevent them. They lost rather heavily in this. We took up our position in the support trenches and prevented any further retirement.'[6]

Sutton had yet to face real combat and he was unaware of the ordeal that the 22nd Brigade had just undergone. Inexperienced troops were invariably unnerved by a heavy artillery bombardment, which in the case of the brigade had been followed up by a massed infantry attack. The 1st Royal Welch Fusiliers had been struck the hardest, reduced in three days of fighting to six officers and 206 other ranks. The brigade fell back in disorder but rallied in front of Zonnebeke, aided by the arrival of a battalion of Irish Guards from I Corps.

Further south, a section of the 21st Infantry Brigade position was overrun by German reserve infantry, but, possibly through their own inexperience, the Germans failed to exploit the advantage. A company of 2nd Royal Scots Fusiliers repulsed the Germans, the British line restored. The 20th Brigade, holding Kruiseecke, fought off attacks by the German 3rd Cavalry Division, although because of its right-angled position it remained subject to constant enfilade fire.

The 20th Brigade was supported by F Battery RHA. Major J. S. Olivant, the battery commander, recalled how the signals officer of the 1st Grenadier Guards at Kruiseecke requested assistance in knocking out a German machine-gun position hidden in a nearby house. Olivant described a good if basic example of infantry–artillery co-operation: 'Just before dawn one gun, drawn by drag ropes over several hundred yards by practically all the battery detachments, was got into position from which, at the first streak of light, the target was visible. As soon as it could be seen rapid fire was opened, the house breached and machine gun silenced. The gun was successfully run back before it could be located.'[7] The Grenadiers were grateful for the artillery presence; their CO, Colonel M. Earle, considered the lighter 13-pounders to be more useful for close-support work than the standard 18-pounder field gun.

On 20 October I Corps began to arrive on the battlefield, the 2nd Division taking up a line to the north of the 7th Division and providing welcome reinforcement to the beleaguered 22nd Brigade. Once in position, it waited for the arrival of the 1st Division on its left. Large numbers of refugees passed through the British lines, proof of the imminent arrival of the Germans. The troops of the 2nd Division also encountered farm animals roaming wild, for some a source of food but for others a distressing sight. Sergeant John McIlwain of the 2nd Connaught Rangers wrote: 'All about that part of Flanders, the terrified cattle go wild about the fields; roaring every night in their hunger, fright and desolation, waiting to be milked yet running stupidly from our men who attempt to relieve them.'[8]

Haig and his divisional commanders did not share Field Marshal French's belief that they faced only weak forces. Their suspicions were confirmed by the fierceness of the German response to their advance. Major-General C. C. Monro's 2nd Division pushed forward only a short distance beyond the Zonnebeke–Langemarck road before taking up a defensive position at around 2 p.m. Major-General S. H. Lomax's 1st Division was preparing to march due east, but with news that Germans were pushing through the Houthulst forest it swung round in a northerly direction to face this potential threat, anchoring its left flank to the French Territorial divisions around Bixschoote, while an advance guard pushed past Langemarck to join up with the 2nd Division.

On the 22nd the Germans attacked along the full length of the I Corps line. Captain H. C. Rees of the 2nd Welch, a short distance in front of Langemarck, described the initial bombardment:

The Germans opened fire with eight 8-inch [21cm] howitzers on Langemarck and in about four hours reduced the town to ashes. It was really a splendid spectacle. A number of field guns were also employed. I saw a field-gun shell strike the spire of the church just above the cross and send the cross some twenty feet in the air. The church shortly afterwards caught fire, and went up in a sheet of flames.[9]

Wisely, the bulk of the British troops were deployed well forward of the town and suffered few casualties, although the psychological strain on the waiting troops was severe, as Private Samuel Knight of the Welch revealed: 'My nerves are taut. I was waiting for death. It is not a hand-to-hand struggle, but man pitted against a huge death-dealing machine. I am unhurt. But I wonder how much longer I could have withstood the strain.'[10]

The following day, the German 51st Reserve Division launched a mass infantry assault to capture Langemarck, as described by Rees:

> At the corner of the hedge, we had a machine gun. Colonel Morland [battalion CO] and I stood by this gun for about an hour. We actually saw the Germans form up for attack and opened fire on their first line at 1,250 yards. From that time onwards, we had every form of target from a company in mass, who tried to put a large haystack between us and them, but who formed on the wrong side of it, to a battalion in fours near the edge of the Houthulst forest. Sgt Longden, who was firing the gun, told me that evening that he reckoned he'd killed a thousand Germans. I put it at about four or five hundred casualties. I never saw the Germans make a worse attack or suffer heavier losses.[11]

The 2nd Oxfordshire and Buckinghamshire Light Infantry – holding a line directly opposite Poelcappelle – also faced the attack by the 51st Reserve Division. The British battalion had suffered fairly heavy casualties in the advance on the 21st, and spent the next day digging trenches. Captain Henry Dillon was concerned that his stretch of the line was too thinly held: 'The night came on rather misty and dark, and I thought several times of asking for reinforcements, but I collected a lot of rifles off the dead, and loaded them and put them along the parapet instead.'[12] As the light began to fade, the British line was subjected to a sudden and violent German bombardment:

> Presently the guns stopped, and I knew then that we were in for it. I had to look over the top for about 10 minutes, however, under their infernal Maxims before I saw what I was looking for. It came with a suddenness that was the most startling thing I have ever known. A great grey mass of humanity was charging on to us not 50 yards off. Everybody's nerves were pretty well on edge as I had warned them what to expect, and as I fired my rifle the rest all went off almost simultaneously. One saw the great mass of Germans quiver. In reality some fell, some fell over them, and others came on. I have never shot so much in such a short time.

At the very last moment they did the most foolish thing they possibly could have done. Some of the leading people turned to the left for some reason, and they all followed like a flock of sheep. My right hand is one huge bruise from banging the bolt up and down. I don't think we could have missed at the distance and for one short minute or two we poured the ammunition into them in boxfulls. My rifles were red hot at the finish.

The firing died down and out of the darkness a great moan came. People trying to crawl away; others who could not move gasping out their last moments with the cold night wind biting into their broken bodies and the lurid glare of a farm house showing up clumps of grey devils killed on the left further down. A weird awful scene; some of them would raise themselves on one arm or a crawl a little distance, silhouetted as black as ink against the red glow of the fire.[13]

The accounts by Dillon and Rees revealed both the tactical ineptitude of the German reserve infantry and their great bravery. Haig's I Corps weathered repeated attacks over a period of two days, inflicting severe losses on their enemy. The heavy casualties suffered by the reserve formations were later cynically manipulated as the 'Kindermord' ('Death of the Innocents'), a German nationalist myth that envisioned idealistic students marching towards the Allied lines, singing martial songs with arms linked and flags unfurled. The Langemarck Myth was subsequently taken up by the Nazis but it could not conceal the shortcomings of the German Supreme Command in sending poorly trained men into battle.

The German 46th Reserve Division did have some success against the 1st (Guards) Brigade around the Inn at Kortekeer on the 22nd, pushing in a section of the British trenches that left part of the 1st Cameron Highlanders cut off from the rest of the brigade. Brigadier-General E. S. Bulfin of the 2nd Brigade was ordered to retake the position the following morning. Well supported by artillery, the 1st Loyal North Lancashires and 1st Queen's (loaned from the 3rd Brigade) spearheaded the attack. Second Lieutenant J. G. W. Hyndson of the North Lancs described his part in the final stages of the assault:

We are now close to the 'Bosche' trenches, and must pause to wear down his nerves until he dare not show a hair, before we can complete the attack. We commence to fire for all we are worth at selected portions of their position.

Little by little we get the upper hand, but the slightest attempt on our part to work forward is met by angry bursts of fire.

And so the fight goes on until about one o'clock, when the firing from the enemy trenches almost dies down. The time has now come to put the finishing touches to the battle, and we work forward in small groups until only two hundred yards separate us from the enemy. From this point of vantage the whole regiment rises up, and with rousing cheers, which must have put fear into the hearts of the Germans, we surge forward with fixed bayonets and charge.

On we dash, yelling with all our might, passing over the front German trench, we bayonet the surviving defenders, and pass on to the reserve trenches. Here we expect to meet with stout resistance, but the Germans have had enough, and suddenly the glorious sight of masses of great-coated men standing up to surrender meets out gaze. The fight is practically over, and we gather some four hundred unwounded prisoners and send them under escort to the rear.[14]

The British attack could have come directly from Field Service Regulations, and underlined the disparity in the quality of the forces involved. According to Brigadier-General Bulfin, 'over 600 prisoners captured and one machine gun. 1,200 dead Germans left out in front, many of the German prisoners mere boys.'[15]

To the south of I Corps, the over-extended 7th Division desperately needed swift and comprehensive reinforcement if its line was to hold. The Franco-British allies agreed that I Corps' position would be taken over by the French, allowing it to move directly to support the 7th Division and to prepare for a continuation of the offensive. On 23 and 24 October, the 2nd Division moved out of the line, to be replaced by General Dubois's IX Corps. On the 25th, the 1st Division relinquished its trenches on the northern section of the salient, and briefly acted as an Allied reserve. The redeployment of the 2nd Division saved the 7th Division from almost certain collapse.

On 24 October the two divisions of the German XXVII Reserve Corps threw themselves against the 7th Division. The German 244th and 246th Reserve Regiments smashed into the 21st Brigade. Gaps

The Battle of Ypres, 25 October 1914

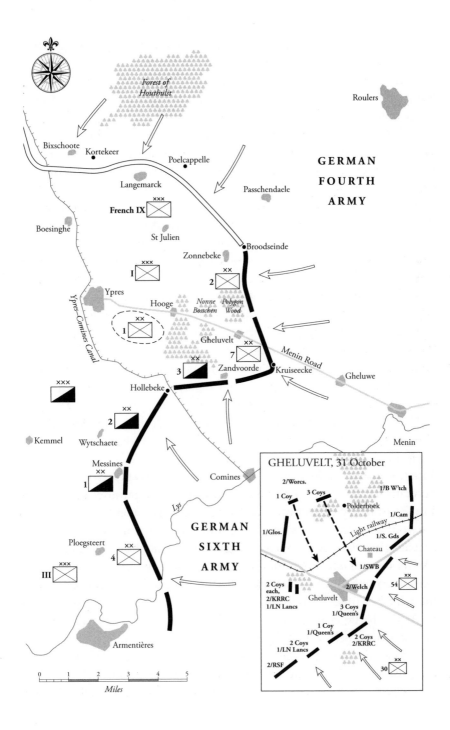

Forest of Houthulst

Roulers

GERMAN

FOURTH

ARMY

Bixschoote
Kortekeer
Poelcappelle
Langemarck
Passchendaele
Boesinghe
St Julien
French IX XXX
Zonnebeke
Broodseinde
I XXX
2 XX
Ypres
Hooge
Nonne Bosschen
Polygon Wood
1 XX
Gheluvelt
7 XX
Menin Road
3 XX
Zandvoorde
Kruiseecke
Gheluwe
Hollebeke
XXX
2 XX
Kemmel
Wytschaete
Menin
Messines
Comines
1 XX
Lys
Ploegsteert
4 XX
III XXX
GERMAN
SIXTH
ARMY
Armentières
Ypres–Comines Canal

GHELUVELT, 31 October

2/Worcs.
1/B W'tch
1 Coy
3 Coys
Polderhoek
1/Cam
1/Glos.
1/S. Gds
Light railway
Chateau
1/SWB
2 Coys each,
2/KRRC
1/LN Lancs
2/Welch
54 XX
Gheluvelt
3 Coys
1/Queen's
1 Coy
1/Queen's
2 Coys
2/KRRC
2 Coys
1/LN Lancs
2/RSF
30 XX

0   1   2   3   4   5
Miles

appeared on both flanks of the 2nd Wiltshire Regiment, through which the Germans advanced. Unaware that this had happened, the Wiltshires carried on firing to their front and were consequently attacked from both flanks and rear; the majority of the battalion was captured, with fewer than 90 soldiers reaching British lines.

German infantry now poured through the breach and into Polygon Wood. Once in the wood, however, the Germans became confused, unable to exploit their advantage. A series of vigorous British counter-attacks – firstly from the meager 7th Division reserves and then from the 2nd Division – repulsed the Germans and, at the point of the bayonet, threw them back to their own lines. The 2nd Worcestershires lost up to 200 men in the counter-attack through Polygon Wood, while the casualties suffered by the two German regiments provided further evidence of the ferocity of the combat. Jack Sheldon relates that on the morning of the 24th, 'the fighting strength of Reserve Infantry Regiment 244 had been 57 officers and 2,629 other ranks. By that evening they were reduced to six officers, 77 NCOs and 671 other ranks.'[16] The 246th Regiment suffered similar losses.

Major-General Capper was much praised for his bravery during the battle, encouraging his troops to fight wherever the danger was greatest. 'Capper himself seemed to bear a charmed life', wrote auxiliary driver C. D. Baker-Carr. 'Day after day he exposed himself in the most reckless fashion. He wasn't brave; he simply did not know what fear meant. His steely blue eyes, beneath a thick crop of dark, wiry hair, stared at one with the look of a religious fanatic.'[17] This style of leadership was certainly inspirational but could only directly affect a small number of troops. It also led to heavy casualties among senior officers – Capper was killed at the front in 1915 – and it took the commander away from his prime role of managing *all* his forces. Capper's ADC described how he raged against 'the modern practice of tying the general to the end of a telephone wire, but the complaint of his staff was that he was far too little at the end of the wire, but miles away in front'.[18]

As the battle continued so the RFC did its best to provide support for the troops below. The deteriorating weather, complete with regular low cloud, hampered aerial reconnaissance, and the initial developments in photography from the air made on the Aisne do not seem to have progressed much at Ypres. On the positive side, the RAF's Official

History explained how, 'good work was done in directing the fire of the artillery, and the few wireless machines were much in demand'.[19] Unfortunately, there were too few wireless-radio equipped aircraft, and artillery-spotting usually relied on more conventional methods that involved flying close to British artillery batteries. This, in turn, brought aircraft alongside the trigger-happy infantry. Major 'Ma' Jeffreys witnessed a tragic incident on the 26th, almost identical to that observed by Maurice Baring on the Aisne (see page 183). 'During the day,' Jeffreys wrote, 'a British aeroplane flying low over the lines and dropping lights was mistaken for a German and heavily fired upon by the Black Watch, who brought it down in flames, all the men cheering as it came down. A dreadful sight, as we were watching and realised it was British.'[20]

The aircraft had a large Union Jack painted on its underside, but as a French officer pointed out to the RFC, at height only the red cross was visible and was easily confused with the German Maltese Cross. It was suggested that the British should adopt the French circular markings. An RFC report on the battle for Ypres noted: 'The mishap of the 26th hasted the adoption of this suggestion and thereafter the French target was painted on British aeroplanes, with the alteration of the blue for red and red for blue, to preserve national distinctions.'[21]

•

The battle on the 24th had been a close run thing for the 7th Division, but the restoration of its line and the arrival of the 2nd Division encouraged Field Marshal French to continue offensive operations alongside General Dubois's IX Corps. The Anglo-French assault was slow in getting underway on the 25th and gains were limited. The advance of the 2nd Division between Zonnebeke and Polygon Wood had the unfortunate consequence of drawing away attention from the vulnerable 'right-angled' position of the 20th Brigade around Kruiseecke. Although the Germans had spent most of the 25th reorganizing after their setbacks on the previous day, the British command seemed unaware of a build up of German forces on both sides of Kruiseecke, which had included an exploratory night attack (repulsed) on the hamlet itself.

As the 2nd Division continued it slow advance on the 26th, the Germans opened a fearsome bombardment against the 20th Brigade.

Understrength and exhausted by several days' fighting, the defenders were overwhelmed in the subsequent German infantry attack. By midday the Germans had broken through on the southern side of the line, before taking Kruiseecke.

The capture of Kruiseecke had, in fact, removed a dangerous anomaly in the British line, but once the position had been lost, the 20th Brigade fell apart. In the space of a few hours the Germans had battered down the southern part of the British defences, so that the ridge position of Gheluvelt was now exposed. Haig, who had the 1st Division in reserve, rode out from his headquarters in the afternoon and was 'astounded at the terror stricken men coming back'[22] before sending up reinforcements that temporarily replaced the 20th Brigade and re-established a more effective line. The 7th Division had taken a battering. From just its three infantry brigades, up to 26 October, the division had lost 162 officers and 4,320 other ranks, which amounted to an unsustainable casualty rate of 44 per cent of officers and 37 per cent of other ranks.[23]

Haig had now taken over the direction if not the actual command of the 7th Division. Rawlinson had already lost control of the 3rd Cavalry Division (formally assigned to the Cavalry Corps on the 25th), and his increasingly anomalous position was neatly if sharply resolved by the disbandment of IV Corps on 27 October. Capper's 7th Division was absorbed into I Corps and Rawlinson sent back to Britain to prepare the 8th Division (now forming up) for trench warfare. French had been disappointed with Rawlinson, although a new IV Corps (7th and 8th Divisions) was reconstituted at the end of the battle for Ypres with Rawlinson again at its head.

Douglas Haig had been alone among senior British officers to enjoy the full confidence of his Commander-in-Chief, and over the course of the 1914 campaign his star would steadily rise. French had also given Haig more leeway in command decisions, so much so that Haig increasingly took control of operational matters. Haig's overweening certainty in his own abilities, his jealousy of potential rivals and sharp, sometimes unjust, criticism of colleagues and subordinates made him a less than attractive character, but his overall competence in military matters, his energy and, above all, his obdurate will made him the ideal commander for a defensive battle, when at times all seemed lost.

•

To the south of Ypres, the advance of Allenby's Cavalry Corps had been halted by the German offensive of 20 October. The British cavalry were opposed by elements of the German I, IV and V Cavalry Corps (plus four Jäger battalions), and in the face of superior numbers the British fell back to a defensive line stretching from Messines in the south to the right flank of the 7th Division around Zandvoorde. The Official History made much of the apparent German numerical superiority, but in terms of the cavalry-versus-cavalry combat, the greater German numbers were countered by the British advantage of holding a generally sound defensive position.

For the first two days of the offensive Allenby's cavalry was forced to weather the German storm, but with support from the 11th Infantry Brigade and the arrival of the 3rd Cavalry Division from the 22nd onwards, the British line was secured against a German breakthrough.

Where possible, each of the three cavalry divisions would hold back a brigade as a mobile reserve. Bob Lloyd of the 1st Life Guards – part of Brigadier-General Kavanagh's 7th Cavalry Brigade – described his brigade's role in glowing terms when called upon for help: 'It straight away galloped to the danger point, dismounted, and going in with the bayonet, put things again in order. It then held the line until relieved, after which it got back to its position in reserve. Our brigade seemed to get a call almost every time we were put, so we became known to the troops in the salient as "Kavanagh's Fire Brigade".'[24]

It was ironic that the cavalry had been so swiftly and efficiently transformed into mounted infantry, a role bitterly opposed by Sir John French and the cavalry school in the years before the war. This process had begun on the Aisne, when the infantry was desperately short of reserves and the cavalry found itself without any traditional cavalry functions to perform. But as the battle of Ypres continued the cavalry would be relegated to the position of 'dismounted' infantry, occupying the trenches rather than their saddles for increasingly long periods. When the 1st Connaught Rangers (from the Indian Lahore Division) arrived as reinforcement to the 2nd Cavalry Division on the 22nd, a staff officer observed how Major-General de Lisle 'ordered them to dig a trench to show them how it ought to be done properly'.[25] It was a portent of things to come, but it was much to the cavalrymen's credit that they so readily took up this new and unwanted responsibility.

While the Germans maintained a degree of pressure on Allenby's corps, a stalemate of sorts existed between the opposing cavalry formations. But on the 29th the situation would be transformed by an all-out assault on Messines and the Ypres salient by new German divisions. To the south, the soldiers of II and III Corps had already endured an offensive that had pushed them to the limit.

CHAPTER SIXTEEN

BATTLE IN THE SOUTH

Crown Prince Rupprecht's Sixth Army – operating in conjunction with the German Fourth Army's advance on Ypres – had been ordered to break through the British defences on the La Bassée–Armentières front. In this sector of the line, south of Ypres, the Germans fielded battle-hardened regular formations that were well equipped with heavy artillery. Although the British were aware of an increase in German strength, they were unprepared for the vigour of the assault on the morning of 20 October.

When the British II and III Corps had fought their way up to the Aubers ridge, a gap between the two formations was filled by French cavalry units. Although Anglo-French co-operation was generally good, there were inevitable exceptions. The 8th Infantry Brigade – on the far left of II Corps and adjacent to the French – had made a determined push on 19 October, with the 2nd Royal Irish Regiment capturing the village of Le Pilly. The British believed the French to have advanced on their left, but this was not the case, leaving the Royal Irish isolated in the village. Although the danger of the position was known to Major-General C. J. Mackenzie, the new commander of the 3rd Division, he was slower to react than his German opponents, who surrounded and then attacked Le Pilly on the morning of the 20th. British attempts to relieve the Royal Irish failed, and at 3 p.m., with the commanding officer dead, the survivors of the battalion surrendered; only 30 other ranks managed to get back to British lines.[1]

A similar disaster overcame the 2nd Sherwood Foresters, from III Corps' 6th Division. Like the Royal Irish, the Sherwood Foresters were holding an exposed forward position on the 20th, and were virtually destroyed in the German attack against Ennetières. Over the next two days, the 6th Division fell back to a new defensive line, which they were able to hold, albeit with some difficulty. On the 21st, the peripatetic 19th Infantry Brigade rejoined the division, taking up a linking position between II and III Corps. The 4th Division was briefly in trouble when its line was broken at Le Gheer on the night of the 20th/21st, but a robust counter-attack restored the position, and from then on the division was not especially hard-pressed by the Germans.

Meanwhile, the battered British II Corps, on the right of the British line, was to suffer heavily as the 13th and 14th Divisions of the German VII Corps continued their assault on 21 October. Covered by early morning mist, the Germans surprised the 2nd South Lancashires (from the 3rd Division's 7th Brigade). Lieutenant Alexander Johnston, the brigade's signals officer, heard a sudden outbreak of rifle fire: 'I rushed forward to see what was happening and was met by streams of the 2nd South Lancs coming to the rear, saying that the line had been broken and everyone was retiring.'[2] Johnston attempted to rally the South Lancs while leading his signals section and any other troops he could find to plug the gap, being awarded the MC for his prompt action.

Over the previous months, Johnston had gained a poor opinion of the South Lancs: 'They really are an awful lot and are a positive danger to the Brigade: one cannot rely on them for anything, and today is the fourth time during the war that they have bolted.'[3] He had a correspondingly high regard for the other battalions in his brigade, and on the 21st he was also full of praise for the support provided by the field artillery:

The gunners did splendidly all day and one incident impressed me immensely: when the line was broken I saw Major Bruce staying on at his O.P. in a haystack although the Germans were almost up to him, shouting

The Battle of Armentières–La Bassée, 19–27 October 1914

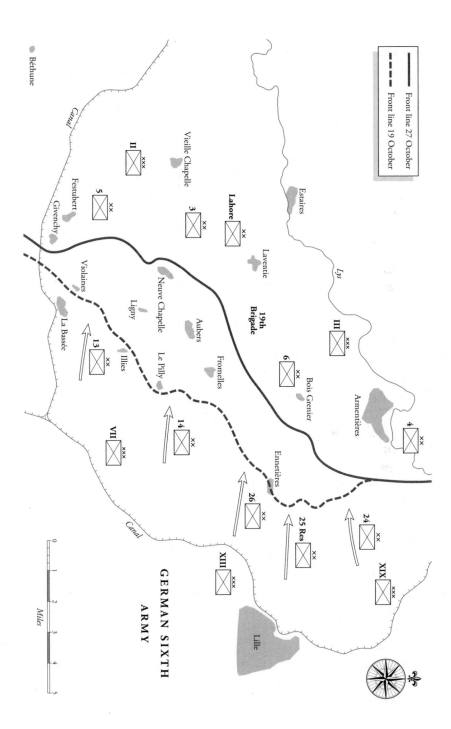

229

directions to his telephonist in an orchard just behind and calmly shooting his guns in great style if he was in no danger. Later in the day when the Regiment [3rd Worcestershires] was advancing, the gunners again did great work and simply mowed the Germans down and when they retired followed them up excellently.[4]

On the next day it was the turn of the 5th Division to buckle under the German offensive. A German attack on the understrength 1st Cheshires holding the line at Violaines caught the British battalion unawares; as it fell back it took part of the 1st Dorsets with it, and while the German advance was eventually stemmed, a British counter-attack failed to regain the original trenches. Both battalions had, of course, suffered heavy losses on 13 October, but the ease with which they were ejected from their trenches caused Smith-Dorrien concern. In a report sent to GHQ that evening (22nd) he wrote: 'There is no doubt in my mind that the regiments concerned in that fight did not put up a resolute resistance, and it was apparent to me that the spirit of other battalions of the Fifth Division, who were not closely engaged today, is by no means what it should be.'[5]

In this painfully frank submission, Smith-Dorrien continued with his wider concerns for II Corps, with special reference to the 5th Division. He described the physical tiredness of the troops: 'battalion commanders state that, in the event of a night attack, they fear it would be impossible to awaken their men to receive the attack, and that the men are really now too exhausted, even if awake, to put up a proper fight'.[6] He concluded: 'I have no confidence in being able to maintain the line … if the enemy presses his attacks with the same vigour as today and yesterday.'[7]

Smith-Dorrien had already ordered new defences to be established in front of Neuve Chapelle, a couple of miles to the rear of his present position; on the night of the 22nd/23rd, II Corps successfully withdrew to this line. Although overlooked by the Germans on the Aubers ridge, the trenches were systematically laid out by the Royal Engineers, and digging had begun using local civilian labour. But the line was unfinished. Communication trenches were merely marked out on the ground, thereby preventing movement to and from the front line during daylight. There were too few sandbags to revet the trench sides, so that enemy shelling and wet weather soon turned them into mud-filled ditches, and, according to a humourist in the 2nd Royal Welch Fusiliers, the few available strands of barbed wire were there 'to keep the cows from coming into the trench'.[8]

On 23 October the British gained some respite from the battle as the Germans moved forward to face the new British line and re-sited their artillery for a continuation of the offensive. Also on the 23rd, II Corps received limited reinforcement with the arrival of the Indian Jullundur Brigade and some divisional troops from the Lahore Division (Lieutenant-General H. B. B. Watkis). Indian formations, however, were not directly comparable with their regular British counterparts, being smaller in size and less well equipped. The infantry of the Jullunder Brigade – comprising one British and three Indian battalions – were sent into the line between the 8th and 19th Brigades, having had very little time to acclimatize to their new situation.

By the morning of the 24th the German guns were ranged-in and commenced an exceptionally heavy bombardment along II Corps' line. As well as the high volume of fire, the British defenders were disconcerted to find themselves targets for large-calibre shells that included those from the super-heavy 30.5cm (12in.) Skoda howitzers recently used in the sieges of Namur and Antwerp. Corporal John Lucy of the 2nd Royal Irish Rifles in the 7th Brigade trenches in front of Neuve Chapelle described the terrible noise made by the 630lb high-explosive shell as it began its descent:

> Every man in the front line ducked as the thing shrieked raspingly louder and louder down on us. There was a terrific thump which shook the ground, and quite a pause, then a rending crash, so shatteringly loud that each of us believed it to be in his own section of trench. A perceptible wall of air set up by a giant explosion struck our faces. The monster shell had burst well behind us in amongst the houses of the village. A huge black cloud rose slowly up and bits of brick and hot metal kept clattering to the earth, even as far as the trenches, for about half a minute.[9]

The infantry of II Corps had to endure the bombardment through much of the day, as Lucy and his men 'crouched wretchedly, shaken by the blastings, under a lasting hail of metal and displaced earth and sods, half-blinded and half-choked by poisonous vapours, waiting for the enemy infantry'.[10]

A number of exploratory German infantry attacks were made later in the day but made little impression on the British defenders. More serious were those made at dusk and during the night of the 24th/25th against both the 7th and 8th Brigades. While the troops of the 7th Brigade held firm, the 1st Gordon Highlanders of the 8th Brigade collapsed. The Germans took over their section of the trenches and were only forced out by a counter-attack from the 4th Middlesex. Smith-Dorrien was once again critical of his troops, claiming that the Gordons had failed to 'put up even the semblance of a fight', although he accepted that the battalion, which had suffered so disastrously at Le Cateau, was now filled with drafts from the Special Reserve and inexperienced officers, 'making it difficult to blame the battalion too much'.[11]

Such was the shortage of officers – at all levels of experience – that they were encouraged to disguise their appearance for their own protection. Most officers had already dispensed with their swords, which served no practical purpose except to draw enemy sharp-shooter fire, and preferred to pick up a rifle with a fixed bayonet. According to Lieutenant Arthur Mills, if an officer 'is holding his rifle, as the men always do, at the trail in an advance, he is indistinguishable to the enemy. Nowadays the wise officer keeps well in line with his men, and gives as few indications by hand signals to halt or advance etc. as possible.'[12] German officers were similarly ordered to make themselves look less conspicuous.

The German bombardment continued with even greater ferocity on the 25th, placing enormous mental strain on all those directly involved. Cyril Helm, the MO of the 2nd King's Own Yorkshire Light Infantry (KOYLI), had been tending the wounded in an increasingly packed cellar just behind the 5th Division's front line:

> The ground all round was by this time a mass of shell holes and both the fire and support trenches were mostly obliterated, the men occupying the shell holes instead. That day I had several who had gone stark raving mad and it was awful to have these poor fellows among the wounded as they were screaming the whole time and crying out that there was no hope for us, that we should all be killed. I think we all agreed with them but we did not want reminding of this fact.[13]

The British infantry, sheltering in their smashed-up trenches, believed the artillery battle had gone in favour of the Germans. The German infantry, for their part, held British artillery in high regard. The British gunners could not, however, match the Germans in terms of the heavy high-explosive shells that were achieving a new importance in trench warfare.

The 13-pounder and 18-pounder field guns had proved their worth in open warfare, but for most of the Ypres battle they were solely reliant on firing shrapnel shells that were largely ineffective against buildings and men in trenches. Several weeks of hard campaigning had also revealed a fundamental weakness in their recoil systems, and while this would be subsequently remedied, a small yet significant number of guns were rendered unserviceable during the final phase of the 1914 campaign. Added to this was a general shortage of artillery ammunition that had first become apparent during the fighting on the Aisne.

Pre-war assumptions on artillery expenditure had not taken into account the idea of a war being a continuous, or semi-continuous, battle. Field Marshal French had forcefully lobbied Kitchener and the War Office for a massive increase in the supply of all munitions, but this would take time to put into effect. Meanwhile, the gunners were given daily rates of permissible artillery expenditure.

These rates varied greatly and were sometimes used to paint the overall situation in a particularly bleak light. In his memoirs, General Robertson wrote: 'I had, with the Commander-in-Chief's approval, to issue orders restricting the expenditure to two rounds per gun a day.'[14] This figure seems not to have been adopted by the field commanders. On 25 October, the chief of staff of II Corps, Brigadier-General Forestier-Walker, allowed the 5th Division a daily expenditure per gun to rise to a maximum of 30 rounds for 18-pounders, 15 rounds for 4.5in. howitzers and 20 rounds for heavy artillery (60-pounders, 4.7in. guns, 6in. howitzers).[15] These figures still obscured the fact that in moments of extreme danger, a battery commander would fire all the shells he had in his limbers to protect the infantry to his front. Thus, when the Germans opened their offensive on 20 October, Lieutenant George Devenish of the 6th Battery (3rd Division) recalled that his battery of six 18-pounders had fired 1,500 rounds during the day.[16]

While the infantry seldom experienced a shortage of small-arms ammunition, the sand and clay encountered in the trenches got into rifle mechanisms. This problem was normally dealt with by thorough cleaning, but in the trenches, 4x2 cleaning rags and pull-throughs were in short supply. Worse still was a shortage of lubricating oil. This, and a very high expenditure of ammunition, had the unfortunate effect of 'baking' the dirt onto both bolt and breech, greatly slowing the rifleman's rate of fire.

This problem, widespread throughout the BEF, understandably caused the infantry great anxiety when facing an enemy attack. Private Edward Roe of the 1st East Lancashires (6th Division), holding the line in III Corps trenches at Le Gheer, had been ordered to fire on attacking German troops at 500 yards' range: 'We are reloading and firing like mad; still the advance continues. Our rifles get jammed with clay. With the utmost persuasion and much swearing we can only average about eight rounds per rifle per minute. We take our bolts out of our rifles and urinate on them, as we have no rifle oil.'[17] While fighting off a subsequent attack, conditions became even worse: 'One had to use brute force to load. When you fired you could not extract the empty case, you had to lift the bolt lever then hammer it back with your fist or your entrenching tool handle, to get the bolt back and empty case ejected.'[18] The best temporary solution was to grease the rifle bolts with vaseline or pork fat, a common by-product from the pigs caught behind the lines and on the battlefield.

•

The seeming ease with which German attacks caught British units by surprise was an on-going concern for Smith-Dorrien and his senior officers. The failure of the Gordon Highlanders to repel the Germans on the evening of the 24th prompted Forestier-Walker to remind battalion commanders to increase their vigilance in the hours of darkness.[19] That such an obvious directive needed to be sent at all was indicative of the problems facing II Corps.

The continuation of German attacks on the 25th – causing the 7th Brigade's position in front of Neuve Chapelle to wobble dangerously – led Smith-Dorrien to drive to GHQ in the evening to explain II Corps' position. According to Major-General Wilson, Smith-Dorrien warned French 'that he was afraid his corps might go in the night'.[20] This alarming news did little to improve French's opinion of Smith-Dorrien, but reinforcements – a cavalry brigade, artillery and a substantial French contribution of all arms – were redeployed to bolster II Corps' position, and to allow units to be taken out of the trenches and rested. French also confirmed that the Indian Corps would begin the process of taking over the stretch of line held by Smith-Dorrien's troops.

These reinforcements would not arrive in time to help the unfortunate defenders of Neuve Chapelle, who were subjected to the full force of a renewed German assault on 26 October. On the previous day, enemy troops had broken into a section of the trenches held by the Royal Irish Rifles but had been chased out after a short fight. On the 26th the brunt of the attack would again be faced by the Irish Rifles (half a battalion), plus the 1st Wiltshires and the 1st Royal West Kents, (temporarily part of the 7th Brigade; by this time the battalions of II Corps were increasingly mixed up). The bulk of the German 14th Division was directed at capturing the village, and during the afternoon their infantry fought their way into the British trenches, forcing the defenders back through Neuve Chapelle itself. During the evening, however, a British counter-attack regained most of the village.

Corporal John Lucy had been part of the counter-attack and he and his fellow riflemen had managed to retake the forward trenches they had formerly occupied, but their position was vulnerable, with German infantry close by. After a preliminary bombardment on the morning of the 27th, the German attack resumed:

> Once more, lines of German infantry, apparently inexhaustible, came over the field of dead, and again those of us still sound stood up to stave them off, but our strong ranks of riflemen were gone, and our weak fire caused alarmingly few casualties. We shot and shot, and we stopped them once more on our company front, but they got in again on the left, and to some purpose. Fugitives from the left company joined us, saying that the Germans had overrun them and were now in their trench, and presently we were horrified to see large numbers of field-grey soldiers moving steadily forward over the ground behind us, and then we found ourselves once again surrounded, and under German fire from front and rear.[21]

Now that the Germans had overrun their position, Lucy and his comrades found themselves victims of their own artillery, their position repeatedly hit by Lyddite high-explosive shells from British 4.5in. howitzers: 'Several British shells scored direct hits on our trench, and the poisonous heavy vapour hung about us. I moved left from a coming shell, and found Corporal Biganne dead in the next bay, his face up with open eyes staring skywards, and all his skin and clothes painted a ghastly yellow by the Lyddite shell that killed him.'[22]

The remnants of the Irish Rifles began to retreat, and although under enemy machine-gun fire, Lucy successfully scrambled back to British lines. The battalion had begun its defence of Neuve Chapelle with a strength of around 700 all ranks; on the evening of the 27th the battalion War Diary concluded that, including 60 new reinforcements, the 'fighting strength of the battalion was now under 200'.[23]

The Germans attempted to push on through the gap, but the West Kents held firm and a determined counter-attack by the 9th Bhopal Infantry (with support from field engineer companies of the Lahore Division) established a new line immediately to the west of Neuve Chapelle. The Germans were discovering one of the uncompromising truths of the offensive in trench warfare: while breaking into an enemy line took enormous effort and courage, the exploitation of that breakthrough was even more difficult, the pendulum of initiative swinging back in favour of the defenders.

Smith-Dorrien was determined to recapture Neuve Chapelle, and ordered the 14th Brigade under its new commander, Brigadier-General Stanley Maude, to spearhead a night attack. Maude, who was well aware of the exhaustion of his men, considered the terrain over which he was to attack and diplomatically declined: 'I thought it would be more prudent to delay action until daylight.'[24] The commanders of the 3rd and 5th Divisions also seemed less than enthusiastic but a scratch force was assembled for an attack on the following morning, comprising battalions from the two divisions, plus French infantry and troops from the 2nd Cavalry Brigade and the Indian Division. To have successfully co-ordinated such diverse forces at short notice would have taxed the most astute commander, and was certainly beyond the capabilities of Brigadier-General McCracken of the 7th Brigade, assigned to lead the attack.

According to the Official History, 'fog and mist prevented an early advance',[25] although, of course, it was usual for such weather conditions to be eagerly sought by an attacking force to disguise their initial movements from the enemy. A short but powerful artillery bombardment from four British and nine French batteries eventually opened the attack at 11 a.m., but when the Allied guns lengthened their range by 500 yards (an early form of barrage) the infantry failed to move, except for two companies of 47th Sikhs and two companies of Indian Sappers and Miners. In an exceptional display of courage and determination, the Indian troops charged across No Man's Land and broke through the German lines into the ruins of Neuve Chapelle. Through poor staff work and general tiredness, the remainder of the attacking force failed – in the measured words of the Official History – 'to render the support and assistance expected from them'.[26]

The Germans, estimated to be three battalions strong, were obviously surprised by the attack and fell back through the village. The Indians' situation became untenable, however, when the Germans mounted an organized counter-attack. The outnumbered Indian troops fell back across No Man's Land, suffering heavy casualties in the process: 68 men were rallied from the 289 Sikh infantry present at the start of the attack, while of the highly valuable Sappers and Miners – who should never have been included in the assault – all officers were either killed or wounded along with a third of the other ranks. The whole attack, which eventually cost the British over 1,500 casualties, had been a waste, especially as the Germans withdrew from Neuve Chapelle during the night of the 28th/29th, both sides considering the village too exposed to hold against enemy artillery fire.

While the struggle for Neuve Chapelle absorbed the energies of both sides, fighting carried on elsewhere along the line. The 2nd KOYLI, deployed immediately to the right of the Royal West Kents, continued to suffer from heavy German shelling and repeated infantry attacks, usually made at night. On the 26th/27th a large German force broke through a gap between the KOYLI and West Kents, and MO Cyril Helm had the unnerving experience of German troops running past his farmhouse-cellar dressing station, firing wildly in all directions in the darkness before being overwhelmed. Throughout the 27th, Helm tended both British and German wounded, the latter 'extremely grateful for any attention they got'.[27] Amidst Helm's constant, grinding round of work, one tragic occurrence stood out:

> A young gunner subaltern was on his way up to observe a machine-gun position. Just as he got outside my door a shrapnel shell burst full in front of him. The poor fellow was brought into me absolutely riddled. He lay in my arms until he died, shrieking in his agony and said he hoped I would excuse him for making such a noise as he really could not help it. Pitiful, as nothing could be done for him except an injection of morphia. I will always remember that incident, particularly as he was such a fine looking boy, certainly not more than nineteen.[28]

The following day a shell hit the farmhouse, burying Helm, his orderlies and the wounded in the cellar. 'There was a blinding flash and a roar,' Helm wrote. 'The next thing I knew was that I was leaning against a wall in pitch darkness with the air full of dust and acrid fumes. Shrieks and groans were coming from all around. It was a dreadful position to be in. We all thought it extremely unlikely whether any of us would get out alive.'[29] Despite the bombardment continuing above ground, rescuers dug down to the buried dressing station, pulling out Helm and the survivors.

The intensity of the German attacks began to lessen and during the evening of 29 October Helm and the KOYLI 'were relieved by the Garhwal Rifles, tiny little men like Gurkhas. They came up at the double, jumped into the trenches and started blazing away for all they were worth. They were so small that they had to get things to stand on before they could see over the top of the trench.'[30]

The arrival of the Garhwal Rifles marked the beginning of the replacement of II Corps by the Indian Corps under the command of Lieutenant-General Sir James Willcocks. The move was indicative of French's lack of confidence in Smith-Dorrien and his command. Over the next two days the units of the 3rd and 5th Divisions were withdrawn and informed that they would be given a period of rest. The artillery of II Corps remained on the battlefront to provide the under-gunned Indian troops with necessary additional firepower, while the 14th Infantry Brigade was swiftly returned to the front line when a shortage of Indian manpower to hold the extended line became apparent.

Smith-Dorrien's II Corps had received a severe mauling from the troops of the German Sixth Army, losing almost 14,000 men in the October fighting (III Corps' casualties were 5,750).[31] Few were sorry to go. Brigadier-General Gleichen of the 15th Brigade wrote: 'It was with a feeling of extreme thankfulness that we left the horrible mud-plain of Festubert and Givenchy, with its cold wet climate and its swampy surroundings and its dismal memories.'[32] William Watson, the motorcycle despatchrider with the 5th Division, was even more damning: 'We hated La Bassée, because against La Bassée the Division had been broken.'[33] The promised rest for the infantry of II Corps proved illusory, however; within days they were thrown into the front line to support their comrades around Ypres.

The anxiety experienced by British senior officers regarding the strength of their defences was countered by a rising sense of frustration among German commanders at their inability to penetrate the Allied line. As early as 23 October, Falkenhayn had criticized his two army commanders for their failure to make significant progress, and on the 27th he issued orders for the deployment of a newly organized force – Army Group Fabeck – to achieve victory by delivering a smashing blow to the BEF just south of Ypres. On this day, the heavy guns from Sixth Army were transferred north to support the new offensive. Fighting continued along the line held by the Indian Corps but the attacks made against them were subsidiary actions designed to prevent reinforcements being sent to Ypres, now the sole focus of German offensive plans.

CHAPTER SEVENTEEN

YPRES: THE TEST

The German failure to break the Allied line on the wide front that stretched from La Bassée to the Channel coast forced General Falkenhayn to revise his strategy, although brute force rather than tactical finesse once again lay behind German operational planning. The German Fourth and Sixth Armies would continue to apply pressure along the Allied line while Army Group Fabeck was to spearhead an attack between Zandvoorde and Messines, against Allenby's Cavalry Corps and Haig's I Corps. The German plan was to pierce the British line, gain the high ground around Kemmel and then drive northwards towards the Channel coast.[1] The seriousness of Falkenhayn's intent was made clear in the German Order of the Day for 29 October: 'The break-through will be of decisive importance. We must and will therefore conquer, settle for ever with the centuries-long struggle, end the war, and strike the decisive blow against our most detested enemy.'[2]

General Max von Fabeck had given his name to the force, comprising four new regular divisions, plus a division each from Fourth and Sixth Armies. They were joined by the 1st Cavalry Corps, 11th Landwehr Brigade, and six independent infantry battalions. This gave the Germans a numerical superiority of roughly two-to-one at the opening of the assault, but the trump card lay in the array of guns assembled by Army Group Fabeck: over 250 heavy howitzers (15cm and 21cm, plus a

30.5cm super-heavy howitzer) as well as nearly 500 field guns and howitzers.[3]

The BEF could do little to counter the German artillery threat with their own heavy guns, which at Ypres numbered just 54 pieces, the majority of them ageing 4.7in. guns and 6in. howitzers. Shortages of artillery ammunition also remained an underlying concern; battery commanders were instructed to use their daily allowances as circumspectly as possible and infantry officers were dissuaded from calling for help from the gunners unless essential.

The British did, however, enjoy the benefit of operating within an interior position inside the Ypres salient, which allowed their guns to be switched between targets with relative ease. This was made possible by improvements in control and communication between artillery and infantry commanders, so that, for example, on 24 October the entire artillery of the 2nd Division had been used to support the 7th Division, while, to the south, the guns of the 4th Division would fire into the flanks of the German infantry attacking the Cavalry Corps around Messines.[4]

Another positive sign was the arrival of high-explosive shells for the 18-pounders. First used by the BEF on 23 October, the supply of high-explosive shells was strictly limited but they made field guns far more effective as weapons for trench warfare. Although shrapnel remained the first choice for breaking up infantry attacks in the open it could do little against men under cover. Captain Alexander Johnston was told that German prisoners said, 'They prefer shrapnel while they are in the trench to rain, the latter makes them wet but the former merely makes a noise!'[5]

Army Group Fabeck's opening attack would be directed at the battered 21st Infantry Brigade (7th Division) and the three understrength divisions of the Cavalry Corps. The German offensive was planned for 30 October, but a preliminary assault by XXVII Reserve Corps was launched along the Menin road towards Gheluvelt on the 29th. Heavy morning fog provided good cover for the German advance, which caught the British by surprise. In a fierce day of fighting, early German gains were largely offset by British counter-attacks, although the Germans managed to take and hold the crossroads in front of Gheluvelt.

On the 30th, the guns of Army Group Fabeck concentrated their fire on the exposed trenches of the British line around the village of Zanvoorde, held by the 7th Cavalry Brigade and 21st Infantry Brigade. The trenches running around Zanvoorde were sited on a forward slope in clear view of the Germans, a 'death trap' according to one of the earliest historians of the battle, Ernest Hamilton.[6] Although not dug by troops from I Corps, these trenches came under Haig's command. Later historians highlighted Haig's failure to ensure they were sited to minimize the effect of German artillery fire, especially when he had been so critical of Rawlinson and Capper in the positioning of the 7th Division's trenches in the opening phase of the battle.[7] And yet, according to Brigadier-General S. R. Rice, I Corps CRE (Commander Royal Engineers), Haig had expressed his dissatisfaction with the trenches on the 28th, and after an inspection of the line, in conjunction with Major-General Capper, Rice recommended leaving them as dummy trenches to absorb enemy artillery fire, with a new line dug to the rear. But before Rice's proposal could be acted upon, the German offensive was underway.[8]

The German bombardment hit the 7th Cavalry Brigade especially hard, and from as early as 8.30 a.m. the cavalrymen were forced back from the front line. The advancing German infantry took over their smashed trenches, before attacking the 1st Royal Welch Fusiliers on the right flank of the 21st Infantry Brigade. The Fusiliers bravely held their position and were overrun; according to Hamilton, 'The exact number of survivors out of a battalion which a fortnight earlier had numbered 1,100 was 86, and these were shortly afterwards absorbed into the 2nd Queen's, their only remaining officer being the quartermaster.'[9]

British reserves were at hand to plug the gap. The 2nd Brigade, commanded by the newly promoted Major-General E. S. Bulfin, had been divided into two the previous day, with the 1st Loyal North Lancashires and 2nd King's Royal Rifle Corps (KRRC) despatched to help defend the Gheluvelt position. On the 30th, Bulfin was ordered to take the other half of his brigade – the 2nd Royal Sussex and 1st Northamptonshires – to shore up the line around Zandvoorde. Bulfin, not at all pleased on losing two good battalions, moved up to the front line: 'Found cavalry had retired early this morning leaving huge gap which the Germans could have marched through. My men working like bees went round first line with support trenches 400 yards behind. Heavy shelling all day, a few casualties. Made big dug-out for self and staff. Don't feel a bit happy, no sort of reserve.'[10]

Later in the day, Brigadier-General Lord Cavan's 4th (Guards) Brigade entered the line on Bulfin's right, and informally came under his command. The gap was now filled, with Bulfin's force extending to the Ypres–Comines canal, where it met Major-General Gough's 2nd Cavalry Division. Other infantry battalions from both the 1st and 7th Divisions were fed in to hold the defences just to the north of Zanvoorde. Haig had now deployed almost all of his reserves, but a request for assistance to General Dubois of the French Army brought an immediate response, with five infantry battalions, a cavalry brigade and an artillery group placed at the British commander's disposal.

Further south, the 2nd and 1st Cavalry Divisions were also attacked by troops from Army Group Fabeck, although in this part of the line the Germans did not press as hard as their comrades did against Zanvoorde. Gough withdrew his 2nd Cavalry Division, trading space for the maintenance of good order. The positions at Hollebeke and Oosttaverne were lost and a new line adopted that curved from the Ypres–Comines canal to Wytschaete. The assault on Major-General de Lisle's 1st Cavalry Division was concentrated around Messines, but was repulsed with little difficulty. Troops from the Indian Corps had helped bolster the Cavalry Corps' defences, while late on the 30th the first reinforcements from II and III Corps began to arrive on the battlefield.

*

German success on 29 and 30 October had been limited and some of the senior German commanders seem to have lost faith in the offensive, but Crown Prince Rupprecht – overall commander of Army Group Fabeck as well as his Sixth Army – was determined to break the Allied line. The Kaiser's arrival to visit German positions around Ypres on 31 October was taken as a further impetus for a final push that would see Ypres in German hands. The German plan of action comprised two simultaneous attacks: against Messines and along the Menin road towards Gheluvelt.

The German drive on Messines – held by Brigadier-General Briggs' 1st Cavalry Brigade – began with an attempt to seize the town by surprise while it was still dark. An attack south of Messines apparently involved Germans attempting to look like Indian troops – 'disguised by wearing turbans' – and while some Germans got into the British trenches they were either killed or forced out at bayonet point.[11] Other attacks against Messines and immediately to the north were similarly blocked.

Having failed to gain Messines by *coup de main*, the Germans subjected it to a heavy artillery bombardment, while maintaining rifle and machine-gun fire from nearby cover. Although the mixed holding force of British cavalry and Indian troops had been reinforced by the 2nd Inniskilling Fusiliers, they were hopelessly outnumbered by the German 26th Infantry Division. Shortly after 9 a.m. the Germans broke into the northern part of the town. Colonel Archibald Home, the senior staff officer in the 2nd Cavalry Division, was impressed by the determination of the men holding Messines: 'The 1st Brigade under Briggs held it against enormous odds. It was a wonderful defence by cavalry with the bayonet, fighting from house to house and street to street, defending a corner here and another there. All this time the place was being very heavily shelled, shells dropping about 50 a minute into the town.'[12]

The town of Messines and the ridge running due north to Wytschaete seemed about to fall to the Germans. But during the afternoon, reinforcements from II Corps were pushed forward, comprising the understrength battalions of KOYLI and KOSB. They were joined by a battalion of the London Scottish, which had been driven to Messines in a fleet of London omnibuses. The London Scottish were the first Territorial unit to see action in Flanders; over the coming weeks many more Territorial battalions would arrive to shore up the British line.

As they reached the crest of the ridge the London Scottish came under fierce artillery and machine-gun fire, but in a spirited debut they helped prevent an admittedly lacklustre German advance from closing on Wytschaete. In Messines itself, the British defenders managed to hold on throughout the day and into the night, despite the Germans bringing up artillery and combat engineers with demolition charges to blow apart the British defences. The weak British line had wavered but it had not broken.

The other main German thrust, to the north on both sides of the Menin road, would nearly bring Haig's I Corps to its knees. The village of Gheluvelt lay astride the Menin road on a distinct spur jutting out from the main ridge held by the British. It provided good observation of enemy positions to the east and south, but in its turn it was clearly visible to the Germans and the village became a magnet for their artillery.

The British defensive line was sited in front of the village – again on a forward slope that could be observed by the Germans and which left British troops leaving or entering the front-line trenches vulnerable to artillery and machine-gun fire. In this instance, Haig was arguably more at fault than he had been with the trenches in front of Zanvoorde. It would have been more prudent to have lost the vantage point provided by Gheluvelt and to have withdrawn the main defensive line onto flat ground behind the village, leaving the village as a lightly defended promontory to absorb German artillery fire and break up their infantry attacks.

Of the British infantry defending the Gheluvelt position, the 2nd Welch Regiment were deployed in front of the village, with the 1st South Wales Borderers and 1st Scots Guards to their left, defending Gheluvelt Chateau and its park. On the right of the Welch, to the south of the Menin road, were the 1st Queen's and part of the 2nd KRRC, along with two companies of the 1st Loyal North Lancashires and 120 men from the 2nd Royal Scots' Fusiliers. Two companies each of KRRC and North Lancs, plus 1st Gloucesters, provided the only reserve.

Throughout the 30th the British trenches had been heavily shelled, and during the night intermittent shelling and sniping continued with German infantry pushing up saps to act as jumping-off points for the coming attack. At first light, the German infantry advanced into forward positions, before an enormous artillery bombardment from guns of all calibres was made against the British line. Captain Marshall of B Company, 2nd Welch, recalled that at 'about 7.30 a.m. the German artillery started to bracket my trench. About 7.45 a.m. they got their range, and proceeded to blow the trenches to pieces.'[13] During the night, the Germans had established a machine-gun company in trenches directly opposite those of Marshall: 'Their fire was so accurate and heavy that we soon lost a lot of men, and found it impossible to fire on the parapet. We also found that there were only a dozen rifles that would fire, the remainder being either clogged with clay or damaged by shell fire.'[14]

The Welch fell back to a support line and then through the village, which received special attention from the German guns: the nearby windmill disintegrated, the church was reduced to ruins and the remains of the houses set on fire. The battalion's CO, Lieutenant-Colonel C. B. Morland, personally informed the South Wales Borderers, on his left flank, of his impending retreat, allowing them to withdraw to a reserve line. No message reached the 1st Queen's on the Welch right, however.

The Queen's (plus two companies of KRRC) also faced the devastating barrage of fire, and the withdrawal of the Welch left a gap, through which surged German infantry. While the remnants of KRRC withdrew from the front line (eventually to join the two companies in reserve) the men of the Queen's stood their ground. German troops attacked their left flank and then worked around to their rear, cutting them off from the rest of the British line; just two officers and 12 other ranks escaped the German net. Having fought so determinedly, the survivors of the Queen's suffered almost inevitable German retribution, some killed by their captors for having surrendered 'too late'.[15] The Germans then rolled up the line, taking the trenches held by the North Lancs and Royal Scots.

The withdrawal of the 2nd Welch from the front line and then through the burning Gheluvelt – still under heavy fire – caused enormous confusion, and units within the battalion became mixed up and lost. Captain H. C. Rees rounded up those soldiers he could find in the village and attempted to rejoin the main body under Colonel Morland. In the confusion, Rees became separated from the rest of his battalion, and retreating back along the Menin road with a small group of men he encountered the 54th Battery RFA under the command of Major Peel. Rees explained to Peel that only a hundred men of the 2nd Welch were left. 'He obviously disbelieved me,' wrote Rees, 'and I fancy seriously thought of putting me under arrest for spreading alarmist reports. I confess to being very badly shaken, the stock of my rifle had been shot through in two places and the strap of my water bottle cut.'[16]

Peel was understandably suspicious of Rees, as worryingly large numbers of soldiers were falling back from the front line. One of Peel's officers, Captain R. Blewitt, recognized Rees:

> The first group of men properly under control came back and I saw that it was Rees in the Welch Regt. He had, I suppose, about fifteen or twenty

men with him. The Major asked me who he was and whether I knew him
and whether he was the sort of man who would come back. As he had got
a DSO only a few days before I was able to convince the Major that he was
one of the best and there was no question of his coming back unnecessarily.
Rees then came over to the battery. I have rarely seen a man in a more
pitiable state, he was muddy and unshaven, of course, but barely able to walk
for sheer weariness, his equipment had for the most part been shot off him,
and he was absolutely stunned and almost speechless. By good luck we
happened to have some hot tea going in the battery and a cup and a slice of
bread and jam and a cigarette worked wonders.[17]

At Peel's suggestion, Rees and his men took up a position 200 yards in
front of the 54th Battery. Other stragglers falling back from the original
line were rounded up to form the beginning of a second defensive line.

With the loss of Gheluvelt at around 11 a.m., an order to retake the
village was issued to the nearest reserves: the two companies each of
North Lancs and KRRC. Lieutenant Hyndson of the North Lancs
described the counter-attack:

Leaving our trenches, we move forward to try to carry out our task. The ground
all around is literally alive with bursting shells, and about a score of our men are
struck down as they leave the trenches. However, on we go, in extended order,
and push into the village which is still burning, and German shells are bursting
against the houses, throwing bricks and dust in all directions. On reaching the
centre of the village, we are unable to make any further progress as the Huns
have firmly established themselves in the houses in front of us.[18]

As casualties mounted, the North Lancs and KRRC withdrew. The
British troops around Gheluvelt found themselves between a rock and a
hard place: the front-line trenches had been systematically pounded to
destruction with high-explosive shells, while the open ground behind
the trenches was raked with shrapnel and machine-gun fire. Such was
the ferocity of fire that, after some argument, the commanders of the
North Lancs and KRRC decided to temporarily fall back out of the
firing line towards the safety of Hooge, 2 miles to the rear.[19] The other
reserve unit, the 1st Gloucestershires, was unable to make any headway
against the German fire.

On the left of the British line around Gheluvelt, the South Wales Borderers fought on with stubborn determination. Once the German attacking force had established itself in the village, shortly before midday, it was able to pour devastating fire against C Company, holding the battalion's right-hand position. Lieutenant-Colonel Leach, the Borderers' CO, sent back messengers to ask for assistance, but it would seem most were killed or wounded by shrapnel. Brigadier-General Charles FitzClarence of the 1st (Guards) Brigade sent one of his staff officers, Captain A. F. Thorne, to assess the situation and report back to him. By 2 p.m. C Company had been virtually wiped out, and with relentless pressure to his front, Leach withdrew the battalion back to the relative shelter of a light railway line a couple of hundred yards north of the chateau park.

The Germans had suffered heavy casualties, but they taken almost 1,000 prisoners, three guns and a machine gun.[20] A wide gap had now opened up in the British line around Gheluvelt, and, for the time being at least, there were no reserves to fill the breach. On hearing reports of the situation, the 1st Division commander, Lomax, simply said to Monro of the 2nd Division, 'My line is broken.'[21] The two generals were conferring at their combined headquarters at Hooge Chateau, when at 1.15 p.m. the building was bracketed by fire from a howitzer battery. One of the shells hit the chateau: Lomax was mortally wounded and Monro badly shaken; many staff officers were killed or wounded. Such losses at this critical point represented a potentially disastrous blow to I Corps.

●

That part of the British line to the right of Gheluvelt – held by the remnants of Capper's 7th Division and the ad hoc collection of units that comprised Bulfin's Force – had similarly been pounded by the German guns. During the night of the 30th/31st the British had improved their defences. Lieutenant C. S. Baines, an officer in one of the two companies of the 2nd Oxford and Buckinghamshire Light Infantry in the front line, recalled how his men 'dug really quite good standing trenches' in contrast to the battalion on his left, where he saw 'only "lying" trenches, which provided their occupants with poor protection from the shrapnel to which they were to be subjected before very long'.[22]

The German assault opposite the 7th Division and Bulfin's force was relatively slow in getting underway, the first shrapnel shells bursting over the trenches at around 8.30 a.m. The bombardment went on for most of the day, with shrapnel giving way to high explosive. Baines considered this 'the worst shelling I had experienced, worse than the Aisne.'[23] It was not until after 3.30 p.m. that the German infantry made their attack against the position held by the Ox and Bucks, whose accurate rifle and machine-gun fire forced the attackers away to either flank. 'On the left there were swarms,' wrote Baines. 'Our men were shooting and shouting, "shoot them – shoot them!"'[24]

Although the battalions on both sides gave way, the Ox and Bucks held their ground, pushing out troops on either flank to minimize enfilade fire. But orders came for the light infantrymen to retire. The position held by Capper and Bulfin was under intense strain, and the collapse around Gheluvelt forced a re-adjustment of the line rearward. In his diary, Bulfin noted the sight of 'streams of Germans in unending numbers pouring over the ridge. As far as I could see to my north, there were endless glinting of spikes of German helmets. The roar of guns and rifles was incessant.'[25]

•

In the early afternoon, Sir John French visited Haig's I Corps headquarters at the White Chateau. Haig, although calm, was deeply apprehensive, explaining to French that the Germans 'have broken us right in ... and are pouring through the gap'.[26] In this instance Haig was being overly pessimistic; the Germans who had captured Gheluvelt were too exhausted to push on and there seemed to be no reserves to exploit this initial success. But the officers at I Corps headquarters were unaware of this, so that the arrival of news that a counter-attack by a battalion of the Worcestershires had retaken Gheluvelt and plugged the gap was greeted with almost rapturous enthusiasm. The only dissenter was Haig himself. According to his ADC John Charteris: 'DH pulled at his mustache and then said he "hoped it was not another false report".'[27]

Haig was also deeply frustrated at being unable to directly influence the conduct of operations. Shortly afterwards he called for his horse and rode up the shrapnel-swept Menin road in an attempt to personally assess the situation and to rally stragglers – hardly appropriate actions for a corps commander. Even though he could do little to directly influence the course of the battle, Haig enjoyed the great advantage of possessing able subordinates. The fighting on the 31st was a 'soldier's battle' – especially after the shelling of the divisional headquarters – with leadership devolved to the commanders of brigades and battalions, who, in turn, were able to rely on a solid core of field officers, NCOs and private ranks who simply refused to give way.

This attitude was evident in the actions of Colonel Leach and the South Wales Borderers, who in the early afternoon were still clinging to their position along the railway line just north of the Gheluvelt Chateau park. The retreat to the railway line had provided the Borderers (joined by some of the 1st Scots Guards) with a useful breathing space, but Leach realized that remaining in place would drain the resolve of the battalion (an officer had already been sent out to shepherd back those 'dribbling away'). With the only options being retreat or attack, Leach chose the latter. This choice was not as quixotic as it might have seemed, as the German troops who had captured the chateau had begun to relax in the belief that their job was done, and were now vulnerable to a counter-attack.

Leach's subsequent report described the ensuing action: 'There was no hesitation, no halting, only a dominating and fierce desire to take toll for the loss of so many gallant comrades and to restore the lost position.'[28] Caught by surprise, the Germans retreated across the park.

The earlier collapse of the British position on both sides of the Menin road had been observed by Brigadier-General FitzClarence of the 1st (Guards) Brigade, and at midday he instructed the 2nd Worcestershires to be ready to counter attack Gheluvelt. Despite the desperate situation, FitzClarence calmly made preparations for the Worcestershires' advance: A Company was sent on ahead to hold a blocking position along the light railway line, while scouts were instructed to clear the way for the main attack. The remaining three companies, under Major E. B. Hankey, discarded their packs, were issued with extra ammunition and fixed their bayonets.

At around 1 p.m. FitzClarence ordered the Worcestershires, stationed at the edge of Polygon wood, to attack Gheluvelt without delay. Guided by Captain Thorne, FitzClarence's staff officer, Hankey promptly led his three companies (just over 350 men) in column through a wood behind the Polderhoek ridge. As they emerged from the wood and deployed into line in readiness for the assault they encountered retreating soldiers, who unhelpfully warned them that 'it was impossible to go on, and that it was murder etc. to attempt it'.[29] But Hankey led his men over the crest of the ridge. Once exposed to view, they encountered a hurricane of shrapnel and high explosive; advancing at the double over a fire-swept 200 yards they swiftly sustained 100 casualties. The battalion adjutant, Captain B. C. Senhouse Clarke – who was alongside Hankey – wrote: 'The conduct and courage of the NCOs and men was magnificent, no leaders have ever been better supported.'[30]

Advancing into the grounds of the chateau a little after 2 p.m. Hankey and the Worcestershires were surprised to find the South Wales Borderers still carrying on the fight; between them the two units ejected the remaining Germans from the park and took possession of the sunken road. But this was a vulnerable position, with the Germans in the village of Gheluvelt able to pour fire on their right flank, as they had against the Borderers earlier in the day. Accordingly, an attempt was made to retake the village. Patrols entered the village and then at 3.45 p.m. a proper attack was launched by A Company from its reserve position.

Various Worcestershire narratives describe the Germans falling back under the attack,[31] although they make it clear that part of the village remained under German control, in contrast to the almost certainly erroneous assertion made in the Official History that 'Gheluvelt was definitely in British hands'.[32] By contrast, only one German account makes reference to a British attack of any kind.[33] The situation was certainly confused; Senhouse Clarke wrote: 'The village was burning merrily in several places, and both sides were shelling it – no health resort for either the Huns or ourselves.'[34]

Despite the absence of aggressive intent from the Germans holding Gheluvelt, the position held by the South Wales Borderers and the Worcestershires remained vulnerable. At around 5 p.m. I Corps ordered them to withdraw to the new, more secure line that had been established a few hundred yards to the west, now defended by survivors from the original Gheluvelt position, reinforced by reserves from the 2nd Division.

The British artillery presence remained strong throughout the day. Captain Blewitt of the 54th Battery successfully tried out the first of his newly issued 18-pounder high-explosive shells against a sniper's nest in a house at the edge of Gheluvelt: 'We were highly elated at the effect on the house which gave forth clouds of brickdust.' A short while later his 18-pounder knocked out a German howitzer hidden behind a barricade in the village; the British infantry were 'full of thanks and praise'.[35]

•

The position held by Capper and Bulfin had seemed on the verge of collapse, but by mid-afternoon the German advance began to lose momentum, partly because of the broken, wooded nature of the terrain and also through their debilitating losses, especially to the officers. Sensing this, Bulfin decided to launch his own counter-attack. He sent orders for the Gordon Highlanders, then in reserve, to move up with all the transport troops, orderlies and cooks that could be gathered together. Bulfin was somewhat disconcerted to find his reinforcements consisted of just 80 Gordon Highlanders, but as the woods largely hid the British positions from the Germans, he relied on subterfuge to conceal his weakness:

> I told the Gordons to form line and advance through the wood cheering like mad. I ordered the first line to open a one-minute rapid fire when they heard the cheering and told all first line to go for the Germans when the cheering proclaimed the arrival of reinforcements. The Gordons started cheering and the first lines opened fire. The Gordons, with fixed bayonets, came up to our first line and all cheered and went for the Germans, and rushed them back to our old line. No prisoners were taken but hundreds of Germans were lying bayoneted all through the wood, or shot by our own people.[36]

Bulfin had timed his attack with precision. The now demoralized German infantry fell back in the face of the British advance, showing little resistance. Lieutenant Baines of the Oxford and Bucks was part of the counter-attack, his men struggling through the thick undergrowth to get at the enemy: 'The Germans had collected in small parties, and as we advanced we found them quite ready to surrender, but they had a nasty habit of shooting at us from the undergrowth just before turning to run, or throwing down their arms and putting up their hands.'[37]

During a brief delay in the advance, Baines went over to the commander of the other company, Captain Henry Dillon: 'I found [him] at the top of his form, laughing and shouting and shooting, and very hot.'[38] Dillon described his part in the attack:

> Fixed bayonets and went straight in; we soon came across them and had the finest fight that ever was fought. I make no pretence at liking the ordinary battle, and anybody who says they do is a liar; but this was quite different. We first came on some fifty of the grey swine, and went straight in and annihilated them. We were very quickly into the next lot and in a few minutes we were shooting, bayoneting and annihilating everything we came across.[39]

Such was the enthusiasm of the British attackers that Bulfin was concerned they might overrun their original front line and be massacred by German reserves. But they halted near their old trenches and dug-in to improve the position. On Bulfin's left, the remnants of the 7th Division also pushed forward, while on his right, Brigadier-General Lord Cavan's 4th (Guards) Brigade regained lost ground by the end of the day.

*

Army Group Fabeck had managed to break into the British defensive line in places on the 31st but had failed to achieve the breakthrough required by the German Supreme Command. Both sides had demonstrated the highest military virtues, fighting each other to a standstill.

The charge by the 2nd Worcestershire Regiment soon passed into legend, the news of the attack arriving at the moment when the British command was at its most despondent. Sir John French was even reported to have said: 'The Worcesters saved the Empire.'[40]

The Worcestershires subsequently produced an exceptionally fine regimental history, and its indefatigable historian, Major H. FitzMaurice Stacke, elbowed his regiment's claim over others to the Historical Section, politely but firmly downgrading the importance the South Wales Borderers' counter-attack. In the same vein he graciously accepted that Major-General Bulfin's action was 'a most gallant feat of arms', but he considered it 'open to question' whether it was as 'remarkable' as the Worcestershires' counter-attack.[41]

Stacke concluded that 'in probability [the] counter-attack had saved Ypres from capture and the British Army from defeat'.[42] Stacke's claim made for a good story – hence its enduring popularity – but it was a ridiculous exaggeration. The 2nd Worcestershire Regiment's attack was just one of many fine actions carried out by front-line battalions: it was the sum of their contributions that saved the day. Major Hankey himself was a little bemused by the attention given to the counter-attack, believing the charge through Polygon wood on the 24th to be 'a finer show than Gheluvelt'.[43]

The price for this magnificent defence was high. After the battle, the 1st Queen's mustered about 50 soldiers; the 2nd Welch, 70; the 1st South Wales Borderers, 200; the 2nd Worcestershires, 260; the 2nd KRRC, 150; and the 1st Loyal North Lancashires, just 36.[44] These figures would improve with the return of stragglers and the lightly wounded, along with those men stationed in the transport lines, but they remained a grievous blow to the identity of the battalions concerned. Captain Rees could reasonably claim: 'On 31 October, the 2nd Battalion of the Welch Regiment was annihilated. No other term can describe the casualties.'[45] Higher ranks suffered too. The commanding officers of the Queen's and the Welch were both mortally wounded on the 31st, and the CO of the North Lancs was killed on 4 November.

•

Unable to penetrate I Corps' defences, Army Group Fabeck continued its assault against Allenby's Cavalry Corps. The Germans' lodgement in Messines on the 31st enabled them to exploit their superior numbers, and during the following day they ejected the British defenders. Having gained the village, the Germans then began to push northwards up the Messines ridge towards Wytschaete, as well as advancing due west beyond Messines.

The exhausted, understrength Cavalry Corps could no longer hold the line, and their position was progressively taken over by the French Army. The French 32nd Division replaced Gough's 2nd Cavalry Division on 1 November, although in the process Wytschaete was lost to the Germans. More French divisions came forward but the Germans pressed hard and over the following days created an alarming bulge in the Allied line. But by 8 November the French had stabilized the front and pushed the Germans back onto the Messines ridge. This allowed the Cavalry Corps an opportunity to rest and refit, although Byng's 3rd Cavalry Division remained in reserve at Ypres.

The British III Corps continued to hold its position around Armentières, the 4th Division receiving some reinforcements from the infantry battalions of the disbanded II Corps. The remaining II Corps infantry either remained with the Indian Corps or were sent north to Ypres to provide support to the Cavalry Corps or form an ad hoc formation called the 3rd Division that comprised three infantry groups (roughly 1,500 men each) commanded by Brigadier-Generals Shaw, McCracken and Gleichen. This formation, under Major-General Wing, replaced the 7th Division, whose normal infantry establishment of 12,552 had been reduced to 4,149 soldiers of all ranks. But the infantry units of the new 3rd Division, even though they had been out of the front line for a few days, were not in a much better state than those they replaced.

In retrospect, the battles of 31 October represented the high water mark of the German offensive against Ypres. At the time, however, this seemed far from clear. Having sensed the possibility of victory on the 31st, Falkenhayn and his commanders decided on a final push with fresh troops. More guns and extra ammunition were assembled, and while the German front-line units awaited the arrival of these new divisions they were instructed to maintain pressure on the Allies, to prevent them consolidating their defences.

These attacks were not pressed with their usual vigour, but the artillery bombardments continued with little respite. A German assault to the south of the Menin road against 3rd Division units on 7 November almost caused a British collapse. While under artillery fire, soldiers of Gleichen's and Shaw's groups simply left their trenches for safety in the rear. At this stage in the campaign, front-line infantry would sometimes temporarily vacate their trenches while the bombardment was at its heaviest, before returning to what remained of the trenches to repulse any enemy attack. This called for great self-discipline among the troops involved, which was now lacking in many of the 3rd Division units. The 1st Bedfordshires were the first to go, followed by men from the 1st Lincolnshires, 1st Northumberland Fusiliers and a few of the 1st Cheshires.

Captain Johnston, with McCracken's group, was outraged at seeing the men fall back without rifles or kit: 'Most of these men I believe were not out of the firing line at all but were in the support trenches and just bolted when they saw the firing line being attacked and a few men being hit, leaving their pluckier comrades (of whom there are still plenty thank goodness) in the lurch and thinking only of the safety of their own skins.'[46]

Johnston had considered the enemy fire to be relatively light, and he and fellow staff officers rushed out of their headquarters to round up the stragglers, who, on this occasion, seemed reluctant to return to their trenches. 'I had to threaten to shoot some of the men before I could get them to go on', Johnston concluded.[47] Although the Germans broke into the forward British trenches, they were unable to push on further.

Johnston's distinction between those soldiers being brave or cowardly obscured the complex reality of battlefield performance – where soldiers could rotate through both emotions in quick succession – but he was certainly correct in identifying a sufficiently large group of genuine warriors who would continue to fight. Some battalions were able to maintain an exceptional level of battlefield performance, despite repeatedly suffering terrible casualties.

Thus, on 8 November, a further German attack cleared what remained of the 1st Loyal North Lancashires (reinforced by some soldiers from the West Riding Regiment) from their trenches.[48] They immediately counter-attacked and regained the trenches, but were forced out and successfully counter-attacked again to finally hold their original line by the onset of darkness. Reduced to just two officers – Captain Prince and Lieutenant Hyndson – and about 100 men, the North Lancs then launched their own night attack and captured some nearby forward German trenches to establish an improved line for the following day. Prince was killed, leaving Hyndson to command the battalion. The survivors fought off German attacks during the night and the following day. The men of the North Lancs – a little-known regiment – did not carry out a specific action that brought them wider acclaim, but their thorough professionalism and bloody-minded determination never to be broken was representative of the best of the regular British Army.

•

The Allied defences would face one last great test on 11 November. This new German offensive was little more than a repeat of that made against Gheluvelt on 31 October. Once again, strong offensive action was to be conducted around the entire Ypres salient, with the battering ram provided by the two fresh divisions of General Karl von Plettenberg's Corps. The German 4th Division was to attack the British line to the south of the Menin road, while the German Guards Division, to its right, was to advance along the road and to its northern side. Both divisions were considered high-grade formations, although the Guards Division had suffered heavy casualties in the opening battles of the war and was filled with new recruits.[49]

The offensive had been planned for the 10th, but deteriorating weather had prevented Plettenberg's staff from making a proper tactical reconnaissance, and so it was postponed to the following day. The extra guns brought up by the Germans made this the heaviest artillery bombardment yet, beginning at 6.30 a.m and continuing to around 9 a.m. The German infantry then climbed out of their forward trenches and advanced across No Man's Land, partly hidden by the morning mist (to be followed later in the day by driving rain). The attack by the German 4th Division was an abject failure; despite their numerical superiority they proved unable to close with the understrength battalions of Shaw's and Gleichen's groups.

On the right of the German attack, the Guards Division did considerably better. According to Captain Thorne of the 1st Brigade, the German artillery fire was especially severe: 'Towards 9 o'clock it became so tremendous that even the observation men were forced to keep their heads down, with the result that the advance of the Guard to the attack was not noticed until in some cases they were right up to the wire entanglement.'[50] The Guards broke through the 1st Brigade's trenches, as they did against part of Shaw's group on the Menin road.

That the British front line had been so easily ruptured caused alarm at I Corps headquarters but the initial enemy success was deceptive. The failure of the German 4th Division left the Guards Division's advance isolated. The German Guards also seemed to have dispensed with contemporary tactical doctrine in favour of that practiced by Napoleon's Guard a century previously: their rigid close-bunched lines of advance appeared to the British as a vast massed column. Consequently, their casualties were fearful, and only their initial advantage of surprise, greatly superior numbers and raw courage enabled them to break into the British trenches.

The further the Guards advanced, the more disorganized they became. In part this was because of the broken terrain of woods, hedges and farms, but also through the siting of strongpoints by the Royal Engineers over the preceding days. Modest earthwork constructions, bounded by a few strands of barbed wire, they held 'garrisons' of up to 50 men; their presence was unknown to the Germans and so had escaped the preliminary bombardment. Colonel Hugh Jeudwine, the senior staff officer in the 1st Division, considered them, 'the saving of the day. The attackers blundered on them after they had broken through our line and were taken in enfilade and broken up and driven into woods and hollows for shelter.'[51]

The German advance divided into two, unsupported thrusts. The first, along the Menin road, was fairly easily contained, but the second, in a north-westerly direction, smashed into the three battalions of FitzClarence's 1st Brigade (totalling just 800 men). The six battalions of the German 1st and 3rd Guard Regiments penetrated the centre of FitzClarence's line but the British troops continued to fight on either flank. The German Guards advanced rapidly almost due north towards a small wood called Nonne Bosschen (Nun's Copse). They were now under intense British artillery fire and possibly sought shelter in the wood, but in so doing they had lurched into a cul-de-sac lined with hostile troops.

Major-Generals Landon of the 1st Division (Lomax's replacement) and Monro of the 2nd Division adroitly handled their reserves to deal with the German threat. The 2nd Connaught Rangers, from the the 5th Brigade of Monro's Division, moved to trenches in a blocking position close by Nonne Bosschen. Among them was Sergeant John McIlwain: 'Great bursts of fire and screams of delight brought us to the fire-step to a sight every infantry soldier dreams about. The Germans were lumbering over to us just 50 yards away, in any order, bunching together. We poured rapid fire into them. The dead piled up in heaps.'[52]

Despite their casualties, the Guards facing the Connaught Rangers returned fire while hastily scraping out kneeling trenches. The Germans within Nonne Bosschen were attacked by another battalion from the

5th Brigade, the 2nd Oxford and Bucks Light Infantry. Lieutenant Baines of B Company – considered a crack shot with a revolver – was surprised at the numbers of enemy soldiers within the wood:

> There seemed to be crowds of them, because they were in no sort of formation and were wandering about; and most of them put their hands up when they saw us. We moved slowly forward like a line of beaters and kept coming upon bunches of Germans. Some loosed off their rifles without bothering to take careful aim, thank goodness, then turned tail and ran. Others surrendered without much ado, I took pot shots with my revolver at those who ran. I fired 52 rounds through my revolver, and burnt my left hand in reloading. It is not difficult to understand when I say that the longest range at which I fired at a German was about 30 yards and that the huge bulk of the average Prussian guardsman made an easy target, even on the run.[53]

The Oxford and Bucks drove the guardsmen from the wood, suffering just five killed and 22 wounded. Continuing beyond Nonne Bosschen the light infantry came under French shell fire and were forced to end the pursuit at around 3 p.m. The counter-attack was a turning point in the fight, as, from then on, the Germans were in retreat, the onset of darkness bringing the British pursuit to a halt. The energetic FitzClarence wanted to resume the attack later in the night, but was killed while conducting a forward reconnaissance.

The Germans were able to hold some of their gains made during the day, but once more they had been unable to break the British line. Attacks continued over several days, but the idea of a decisive breakthrough was now abandoned. Added to the exhaustion of the German front-line troops was a growing sense of demoralization, confirmed by the large numbers of their men falling back from the front line as stragglers.

The increasingly severe winter weather also tempered thoughts of aggressive action. Several days of heavy, cold rain followed the 11 November battle; the first snow fell on the 15th, succeeded by heavy frosts before a snowstorm on the 19th left much of the battlefield covered in snow. The Official History described the soldiers' plight: 'Apart from the discomfort to the troops and the first appearance of frost-bite from their standing in trenches half full of water, the physical condition of the men was becoming desperate. Men were reported standing up in the trenches fast asleep under fire, although the opposing infantry was only a hundred or so yards away.'[54]

On 15 November the first stage of the much-needed relief of Haig's I Corps began, the French temporarily taking over the rest of the Ypres salient. The battle whimpered to an end, with desultory fighting continuing past the official British end date of 22 November, although it was on the 22nd that Captain Louis Strange at last achieved his first 'kill' – fire from his observer's Lewis machine gun bringing down a German Aviatik just behind British lines near Armentières.

For the remainder of 1914, the British Expeditionary Force held the line running south from Wytschaete to Givenchy, the old battle grounds of II and III Corps. Both sides settled down to endure the wretchedness of a winter in the trenches and, on the Allied side at least, make plans for a new offensive in the spring of the following year.

EPILOGUE

DEATH OF THE
OLD ARMY

The successful Allied defence of the Ypres sector – from Givenchy in the south, past the city of Ypres and along the River Yser to the Channel coast – represented the final act of the battle of the Marne. The German strategic plan to achieve a decisive military victory against the Allies in the West had failed. The Germans would now be forced to wage a war of attrition, where Allied advantages in the economic and diplomatic spheres would ultimately overcome German military strength. For their part, however, the French, British and Belgian armies of 1914 had been unable to defeat the German Army, thereby condemning both sides to years of trench warfare.

The overall performance of the BEF during the 1914 campaign was uneven. The peacetime failings in command and control had been ruthlessly exposed on many occasions, and the vital necessity for the separate arms to work closely together was a lesson that was painfully and sometimes inadequately learned. The morale of the other ranks had proved too dependent on the inspirational qualities of their officers; when officers became casualties, or otherwise failed as leaders, the men fell back from exposed front-line positions with alarming frequency. Good leadership at all levels was a precursor to battlefield success.

The accomplishments of I Corps compared favourably with those of other corps formations, most notably Smith-Dorrien's II Corps. Smith-Dorrien was popular among his troops and gained widespread public sympathy for his dignified response to the vindictive post-war campaign waged against him by Sir John French, but this should not obscure his flaws as a general. Whether at Le Cateau, the Aisne or in the battles fought to the south of Ypres he repeatedly failed to impose himself on the battlefield. The passive nature of his style of command seems to have passed down to his subordinates who so often made a virtue of inaction. At brigade level, for example, the sheer lack of grip found among II Corps brigadiers like Gleichen and McCracken, during both the Aisne and Ypres battles, made a poor contrast with the energy and decisiveness of Bulfin, Cavan, FitzClarence and others in I Corps.

But whatever the overall shortcomings of the BEF, during the fight against the German Sixth and Fourth Armies, the line held. And in the battle to defend the Ypres salient, the British Army made its first great contribution to the Allied cause, displaying a steely determination against great odds that won the respect of both Germans and French. But it had come at a price. BEF casualties at Ypres amounted to 58,155 soldiers killed, wounded and missing, a sizable proportion of the total casualty figure of 89,864 for the whole 1914 campaign.[1]

Casualties were not spread evenly, with some battalions losing more than their full peacetime strength in the battle. Of the long-suffering 1st Loyal North Lancashires, Lieutenant Hyndson wrote: 'During 23 days' continuous fighting we have lost 30 officers and 1,000 other ranks killed, wounded and missing – an appalling figure, including as it does all the trained officers and men in the regiment whom we shall never be able to replace.'[2] These losses of experienced officers and men would affect the BEF in the forthcoming year's fighting, but many of the wounded would return to their units, and the better battalions demonstrated the greatest combat resilience.

The survivors of the 1914 campaign who were still with their units at the end of the year certainly felt a profound sense of loss. The officers, NCOs and regular other ranks had developed a close *esprit de corps* in the years leading up to 1914, which in many units had been brutally and irrevocably destroyed.

At the end of November, Cyril Helm, the MO of the 2nd KOYLI, was shocked to find that, apart from the quartermaster, he was the only original officer remaining in the battalion: 'Many new officers had been sent up to replace casualties but had themselves been killed or wounded. It had been appalling seeing one's friends picked off one after the other, and I can only marvel now that I survived. At times, when I realised all my pals had gone, I nearly went off my head.'[3]

The remnants of the 2nd Royal Irish Rifles departed the front line at Ypres on 19 November. As he prepared to march out, Corporal John Lucy looked back at his old position:

My eyes weakened, wandered, and rested on the half-hidden corpses of men and youths. Near and far they looked calm, and even handsome, in death. Their strong young bodies thickly garlanded the edge of a wood in the rear, a wood called Sanctuary. A dead sentry at his post, leaned back in a standing position, against a blasted tree, keeping watch over them. Proudly and sorrowfully I looked at them, the Macs and the O's, and the hardy Ulster boys joined together in death on a foreign field. My dead chums.[4]

The British government recognized the contribution made by the soldiers of 1914, issuing a special medal for those officers and men who had served in France and Belgium between the declaration of war and midnight on 22/23 November. Some 365,622 individuals were eligible for this award – colloquially known as the Mons Star – an indication of the already substantial British involvement in the war to date.

The soldiers were proud to call themselves Old Contemptibles, after Kaiser Wilhelm's pronouncement of the BEF as a 'contemptibly small army'. Like many of his fellow veterans, John Lucy saw himself as a witness to the end of an era in the British Army's history. 'The old army was finished', he wrote at the close of 1914. 'We remnants stuck to each other in a necessary form of freemasonry. We drew nearer to each other than ever before in our lives, and we got to know and love each other as men never do in peace time.'[5]

APPENDIX A

BEF Order of Battle 1914
(Fighting Formations/Units)

Commander-in-Chief: Field Marshal Sir John French
Chief of Staff: Lieutenant-General Sir Archibald Murray
Sub-Chief of Staff: Major-General Henry Wilson
GSO 1 (Intelligence): Colonel G. M. W. Macdonogh

Cavalry Division (Allenby)

1st Cavalry Brigade (Briggs):
  2nd Dragoon Guards
  5th Dragoon Guards
  11th Hussars
2nd Cavalry Brigade (de Lisle):
  4th Dragoon Guards
  9th Lancers
  18th Lancers
3rd Cavalry Brigade (Gough):
  4th Hussars
  5th Lancers
  16th Lancers
4th Cavalry Brigade (Bingham):
  Household Cavalry (composite regiment)

6th Dragoon Guards
3rd Hussars
Artillery:
3rd Brigade (D, E Batteries) RHA
7th Brigade (I, L Batteries) RHA

5th Cavalry Brigade (Chetwode) – unattached:
  2nd Dragoons
  12th Lancers
  20th Hussars
  J Battery RHA

I Corps (Haig)
1st Division (Lomax)

1st (Guards) Brigade (Maxse):
  1st Coldstream Guards
  2nd Scots Guards
  1st Black Watch
  2nd Royal Munster Fusiliers
2nd Brigade (Bulfin):
  2nd Royal Sussex Regiment
  1st Loyal North Lancashire Regiment
  1st Northamptonshire Regiment
  2nd King's Royal Rifle Corps
3rd Brigade (Landon):
  1st Queen's Regiment
  1st South Wales Borderers
  1st Gloucestershire Regiment
  2nd Welch Regiment

Mounted Troops:
A Squadron 15th Hussars
1st Cyclist Company
Artillery:
25th Brigade (113th, 114th, 115th
  Batteries) RFA
26th Brigade (116th, 117th, 118th
  Batteries) RFA
39th Brigade (46th, 51st, 54th Batteries)
  RFA
43rd (How.) Brigade (30th, 40th, 57th
  Batteries) RFA
26th Heavy Battery RGA

2nd Division (Monro)

4th (Guards) Brigade (Scott-Kerr):
  2nd Grenadier Guards
  2nd Coldstream Guards
  3rd Coldstream Guards
  1st Irish Guards
5th Brigade (Haking):
  2nd Worcestershire Regiment
  2nd Oxford and Buckinghamshire
  Light Infantry
  2nd Highland Light Infantry
  2nd Connaught Rangers
6th Brigade (Davies):
  1st King's Regiment
  2nd South Staffordshire Regiment
  1st Royal Berkshire Regiment
  1st King's Royal Rifle Corps

Mounted Troops:
B Squadron 15th Hussars
2nd Cyclist Company
Artillery:
34th Brigade (22nd, 50th, 70th Batteries)
  RFA
36th Brigade (15th, 48th, 71st Batteries)
  RFA
41st Brigade (9th, 16th, 17th Batteries)
  RFA
44th (How.) Brigade (47th, 56th, 60th
  Batteries) RFA
35th Heavy Battery RGA

II Corps (Smith-Dorrien)
3rd Division (Hamilton)

7th Brigade (McCracken):
3rd Worcestershire Regiment
2nd South Lancashire Regiment
1st Wiltshire Regiment
2nd Royal Irish Rifles
8th Brigade (Doran):
2nd Royal Scots
2nd Royal Irish Regiment
4th Middlesex Regiment
1st Gordon Highlanders
9th Brigade (Shaw):
1st Northumberland Fusiliers
4th Royal Fusiliers
1st Lincolnshire Regiment
1st Royal Scots Fusiliers

Mounted Troops:
C Squadron 15th Hussars
3rd Cyclist Company
Artillery:
23rd Brigade (107th, 108th, 109th
   Batteries) RFA
40th Brigade (6th, 23rd, 49th Batteries)
   RFA
42nd Brigade (29th, 41st, 45th Batteries)
   RFA
30th (How.) Brigade (128th, 129th,
   130th Batteries) RFA
48th Heavy Battery RGA

5th Division (Fergusson)

13th Brigade (Cuthbert):
2nd King's Own Scottish Borderers
2nd Duke of Wellington's Regiment
1st Royal West Kent Regiment
2nd King's Own Yorkshire Light
Infantry
14th Brigade (Rolt):
2nd Suffolk Regiment
1st East Surry Regiment
1st Duke of Cornwall's Light
Infantry
2nd Manchester Regiment
15th Brigade (Gleichen):
1st Norfolk Regiment
1st Bedfordshire Regiment

1st Cheshire Regiment
1st Dorsetshire Regiment
Mounted Troops:
A Squadron 19th Hussars
5th Cyclist Company
Artillery:
15th Brigade (11th, 52nd, 80th Batteries)
   RFA
27th Brigade (119th, 120th, 121st
   Batteries) RFA
28th Brigade (122nd, 123rd, 124th
   Batteries) RFA
8th (How.) Brigade (37th, 61st, 65th
   Batteries)
108th Heavy Battery RGA

III Corps (Pulteney)
[formed in France, 31 August]
4th Division (Snow)

10th Brigade (Haldane):
  1st Royal Warwickshire Regiment
  2nd Seaforth Highlanders
  1st Royal Irish Fusiliers
  2nd Royal Dublin Fusiliers
11th Brigade (Hunter-Weston):
  1st Somerset Light Infantry
  1st East Lancashire Regiment
  1st Hampshire Regiment
  1st Rifle Brigade
12th Brigade (Wilson):
  1st King's Own (Royal Lancaster
  Regiment)
  2nd Lancashire Fusiliers
  2nd Royal Inniskilling Fusiliers
  2nd Essex Regiment

Mounted Troops:
B Squadron 19th Hussars
4th Cyclist Company
Artillery:
14th Brigade (39th, 68th, 88th Batteries) RFA
29th Brigade (125th, 126th, 127th Batteries) RFA
32nd Brigade (27th, 134th, 135th Batteries) RFA
37th (How.) Brigade (31st, 35th, 55th Batteries) RFA
31st Heavy Battery RGA

6th Division (Keir)

16th Brigade (Ingouville-Williams):
  1st Buffs
  1st Leicestershire Regiment
  1st King's Shropshire Light Infantry
  2nd York and Lancaster Regiment
17th Brigade (Doran):
  1st Royal Fusiliers
  1st North Staffordshire Regiment
  2nd Prince of Wales Leinster
  Regiment
  3rd Rifle Brigade
18th Brigade (Congreve):
  1st West Yorkshire Regiment
  1st East Yorkshire Regiment

2nd Sherwood Foresters
2nd Durham Light Infantry
Mounted Troops:
C Squadron 19th Hussars
6th Cyclist Company
Artillery:
2nd Brigade (21st, 42nd, 53rd Batteries) RFA
24th Brigade (110th, 111th, 112th Batteries)
38th Brigade (24th, 34th, 72nd Batteries) RFA
12th (How.) Brigade (43rd, 86th, 87th Batteries) RFA

24th Heavy Battery RGA

19th Infantry Brigade (Drummond):

  2nd Royal Welch Fusiliers

  1st Cameronians

  1st Middlesex Regiment

  2nd Argyll & Sutherland

  Highlanders

[formed from line-of-communication troops as an independent infantry brigade; subsequently incorporated into 6th Division]

IV Corps (Rawlinson)

[formed 10 October; temporarily disbanded 27 October)

7th Division (Capper)

20th Brigade (Ruggles Brice):

  1st Grenadier Guards

  2nd Scots Guards

  2nd Border Regiment

  2nd Gordon Highlanders

21st Brigade (Watts):

  2nd Befordshire Regiment

  2nd Green Howards

  2nd Royal Scots Fusiliers

  2nd Wiltshire Regiment

22nd Brigade (Lawford):

  2nd Queen's

  2nd Royal Warwickshire Regiment

  1st Royal Welch Fusiliers

  1st South Staffordshire Regiment

Mounted Troops:

  Northumberland Hussars

  7th Cyclist Company

Artillery:

  14th Brigade (C, F, T Batteries) RHA

  22nd Brigade (104th, 105th, 106th Batteries) RFA

  35th Brigade (12th, 25th, 58th Batteries) RFA

  3rd (Heavy) Brigade (111th, 112th [Heavy] Batteries) RGA

3rd Cavalry Division (Byng)

6th Cavalry Brigade (Makins):

  3rd Dragoon Guards

  1st Royal Dragoons

  10th Hussars

7th Cavalry Brigade (Kavanagh):

  1st Life Guards

  2nd Life Guards

  Royal Horse Guards

Artillery:

  15th Brigade (K Battery) RHA

APPENDIX B

British Army Organization

At the outbreak of war the British Expeditionary Force was organized into six infantry divisions and one cavalry division. By the end of 1914, as a consequence of general organizational changes and the arrival of new formations, the BEF comprised four army corps (eight infantry divisions), the Cavalry Corps (three small cavalry divisions) and the Indian Corps (two small infantry divisions, plus supporting cavalry). Territorial battalions had also begun to arrive in France, and were allocated directly to Regular Army formations as reinforcements.

Infantry

The infantry division, the key building block of all armies in 1914, contained elements of the three main arms (infantry, artillery, cavalry). The division's infantry component was made up of three brigades, each of four battalions, while the artillery comprised three field artillery brigades (54 18-pounders), one field howitzer brigade (18 4.5in. howitzers) and a heavy artillery battery (four 60-pounders). Supporting services included a cavalry squadron, two engineer companies, a signals company and a cyclist company, plus three field ambulances and four Army Service Corps transport companies. Commanded by a major-general (with a small divisional staff), an infantry division at full strength totalled 18,073 officers and men and 5,592 horses.

The 12 infantry battalions within a division were each commanded by a lieutenant-colonel, with an official strength of 30 officers and 977 men, although in peacetime this figure was often slightly exceeded (but would steadily diminish while on campaign). A battalion was divided into four companies (commanded by a major or captain), plus a small headquarters staff and a machine-gun section of two Maxim machine guns. Each company (six officers and 221 men) was divided into four platoons (commanded by a lieutenant/second lieutenant); they in turn were sub-divided into four sections of 12 men under the command of an NCO.

Artillery

Apart from a few independent heavy batteries that arrived during the battles of the Aisne and Ypres, all artillery was deployed at divisional level. The field gun and howitzer brigades (commanded by a lieutenant-colonel) were similar in strength and organization, each brigade comprising three six-gun batteries and an ammunition column. A battery (commanded by a major or captain) was made up of five officers and 193 men, plus 50 riding horses and 122 draught horses. Each battery was allotted 12 six-horse wagons and a single two-horse cart. The brigade ammunition column – providing small-arms as well as artillery ammunition – was commanded by a captain, along with two other officers and 155 men, plus 20 riding horses and 176 draught horses pulling 25 wagons and eight carts.

Cavalry

Five cavalry brigades were despatched to France in August 1914, four of the brigades organized as the Cavalry Division, the fifth acting independently. The establishment strength of the original Cavalry Division was 439 officers and 8,830 men, with 7,350 riding horses and 2,378 draught horses. The artillery component was provided by four batteries of horse artillery, totaling 24 13-pounder field guns. Each cavalry brigade within the division consisted of three regiments (commanded by a lieutenant-colonel), with each regiment divided into three squadrons (commanded by a major or captain), plus a small headquarters and a machine-gun section of two Vickers machine guns. The establishment strength of a cavalry regiment was 26 officers and 523 men.

ACKNOWLEDGEMENTS

A work of this nature is almost totally reliant on documentary material from the major British archives. I would thus particularly like to thank the Imperial War Museum (Department of Documents); the Liddell Hart Centre for Military Archives, King's College, London; The Liddle Collection, Brotherton Library, University of Leeds; and the National Archive, Kew. My gratitude extends to both the knowledgeable and highly efficient staffs of these institutions and to the many copyright holders who have given me permission to use material in this book.

I would also like to thank my agent, Andrew Lownie, and the editorial staff of Osprey, especially my editor, Marcus Cowper, and copy editors, Julie Frederick and Emily Holmes. The excellent maps were the work of Peter Bull.

SOURCE NOTES

Abbreviations: IWM (Imperial War Museum: Dept. of Documents), LHCMA (Liddell Hart Centre for Military Archives, King's College, London), LCBLUL (Liddle Collection, Brotherton Library, University of Leeds)

Introduction

1. Edmonds, *History of the Great War Based on Official Documents, Military Operations France and Belgium, 1914* (Vol. I), first (1922) edition, pp. 10–11, hereafter, Official History (I) or O. H. (I).
2. Liddell Hart, in French, 'Sir James Edmonds and the Official History', p. 70, in Bond (ed.) *The First World War and British Military History*. French provides a sympathetic yet critical account of Edmonds and his methods, but for a spirited defence of Edmonds, see Green, *Writing the Great War*.
3. Edmonds, in French, p. 73.
4. Official History (I), p. 182. While the battle was being fought, the forces involved were roughly numerically similar. During the afternoon, when the British were already retreating, lead elements of the German IV Reserve Corps began to arrive on the battlefield. After the British had withdrawn, the German 5th Division (III Corps) marched past Le Cateau but took no part in the battle. Map 11 of the Official History suggests that IV Reserve Corps and III Corps were fully engaged in the fighting, thus giving the false impression that the British faced odds of over two to one.
5. See, for example, Badsey, *Doctrine and Reform in the British Cavalry;* French and Holden Reid (eds.), *The British General Staff;* Gardner, *Trial by Fire;* Gooch, *The Plans of War;* Sheffield and Todman (eds.), *Command and Control on the Western Front;* Robbins, *British Generalship on the Western Front;* Samuels, *Command or*

Control?; Travers, *The Killing Ground.*

6.   Terraine, in Terraine (ed.), *General Jack's Diary*, p. 33.
7.   Cassar, *The Tragedy of Sir John French* (Newark: University of Delaware Press, 1985), p. 123.
8.   Bird, *Gentlemen, We Will Stand and Fight*, p. 177.

Prologue

1.   For C Squadron's engagement see the regimental war diary (NA WO 95/1112), Brereton, *A History of the 4th/7th Royal Dragoon Guards*; Bridges, *Alarms and Excursions*; Emden (ed.) *Tickled to Death to Go.*
2.   Bridges, in Brereton, p. 308.
3.   Thomas, in Hammerton (ed.), *I Was There*, p. 41.
4.   Worrell, in Ascoli, *The Mons Star,* p. 53.
5.   Osburn, *Unwilling Passenger,* p. 25.
6.   Chance, 'Draw Swords', p. 1, LCBLUL.
7.   See Lloyd, *A Trooper in the 'Tins'*, p. 99.
8.   Osburn, p. 24.

Chapter One

1.   Baring, *Flying Corps Headquarters*, p. 4.
2.   Boreham, in Dunn, *The War the Infantry Knew*, p. 1.
3.   Jack, in Terraine (ed.), *General Jack's Diary*, p. 22.
4.   Mills, *With My Regiment from the Aisne to La Bassée*, p. 5.
5.   Lloyd, *A Trooper in the 'Tins'*, p. 69.
6.   Ibid.
7.   Bolwell, *With a Reservist in France*, p. 3.
8.   McIlwain, Diary, p. 1, IWM.
9.   Boreham, p. 1.
10. Wilson, in C. E. Callwell, *Field Marshal Sir Henry Wilson* (Cassell, 1927), p. 158.
11. Kitchener, 'Instructions to Sir John French from Lord Kitchener', in O. H. (I), Appendix 8.
12. Haig, in Sheffield and Bourne, *Douglas Haig: War Diaries and Letters*, p. 56.
13. O'Neill, *The Royal Fusiliers in the Great War*, p. 33
14. Dillon, Letters, p. 4, IWM.
15. Montgomery, in Hamilton, *The Full Monty*, p. 49.
16. Spiers, 'The Regular Army', in Beckett and Simpson, *A Nation in Arms*, pp. 44–7.
17. Clouting, in Emden (ed.), *Tickled to Death to Go*, p. 24.
18. Osburn, *Unwilling Passenger*, p. 70.
19. Montgomery, p. 49.

20. Wolsey, in Travers, *The Killing Ground*, p. 39. For British officers, see also Simpson, 'The Officers', in Beckett and Simpson; Gardner, *Trial by Fire*, Chapter 1; Sheffield, *Leadership in the Trenches* (Basingstoke: Macmillan, 2000).
21. Money, in Simpson, p. 68.
22. Macleod, LHCMA, p. 48.
23. Ibid., p. 44
24. Figures from G. Hacker, 'War Diary of E. S. Hacker', p. 25, IWM.
25. O. H. (I), p. 31.
26. Baker-Carr, *From Chauffeur to Brigadier*, p. 11.
27. Baring, p. 10.
28. Ibid., p 12.

Chapter Two

1. Gordon-Lennox, in Craster (ed.), *'Fifteen Rounds a Minute'*, p. 23.
2. Ibid., pp. 23–4.
3. O'Neill, *The Royal Fusiliers in the Great War*, p. 33.
4. Strange, *Recollections of an Airman*, pp. 35–6.
5. Ibid., p. 39.
6. Grierson, in Raleigh, *The War in the Air* (1), pp. 177–8.
7. Slingsby, Diary, 14 August, LHCMA.
8. KOYLI War Diary, 20 August, PRO WO/95/1558.
9. Lucy, *There's a Devil in the Drum*, p. 77.
10. Lucy, p. 85.
11. Herbert, *Mons, Anzac and Kut*, p. 16.
12. Charteris, John, *At GHQ* (Cassell, 1931) p. 9 (the answer was 12). See also Gardner, *Trial by Fire*, p. 37, and Robbins, *British Generalship on the Western Front*, pp. 116–17.
13. Haldane, 'Shorncliffe Diary', 2 July 1912, IWM.
14. Samuels, *Command or Control?*, p. 3.
15. Spears, *Liaison 1914*, p. 74.

Chapter Three

1. Vivian, *The Phantom Brigade*, p. 101.
2. Beaumont, *Old Contemptible*, p. 28.
3. Ransome, *The Fine Fighting of the Dorsets*, p. 8.
4. Gleichen, *The Doings of the Fifteenth Infantry Brigade*, p. 15.
5. Figures from Bidwell and Graham, *Fire-Power*, p. 28.
6. See, in particular, Travers, *The Killing Ground*, and Samuels, *Command or Control?*

7. Crookenden, *The Cheshire Regiment in the Great War*, p. 4.
8. Spiers, 'Reforming the Infantry of the Line', in Raugh, *The British Army 1815–1914*, p. 303.
9. Kiggell, in Bidwell and Graham, p. 52.
10. Gooch, *The Plans of War*, pp. 34–5.
11. McMahon, in C. H. B. Pridham, *Superiority of Fire* (Thomas French, 1945), p. 56. In expert hands 'fifteen rounds a minute' was easily exceeded, one soldier achieving double that in test conditions.
12. Bidwell and Graham, p. 31. See also Balck, *Tactics* (I), p. 169.
13. Longley [Wagger], *Battery Flashes*, p. 38; Clouting, in Emden (ed.), *Tickled to Death to Go*, p. 23.
14. Archibald, pp. 73–4, IWM.
15. Ibid., p. 74.
16. Wynne, p. 23, LHCMA.
17. Ibid.
18. Barrow, *The Fire of Life*, pp. 143–4.
19. L. B. Oatts, *I Serve* (privately pub., 1966), p. 202.
20. For the Royal Scots Greys in 1914, see S. J. Hardy, *History of the Royal Scots Greys* (privately pub., 1928).
21. Maze, *A Frenchman in Khaki*, p. 19.
22. Gough, *Soldiering On*, p. 115.
23. Crowsley, Diary, 22 August, IWM.
24. Anglesey, *A History of British Cavalry*, Vol. 4, pp. 424–5. See also Badsey, 'Cavalry and the Breakthrough Doctrine', in Griffith, *British Fighting Methods in the Great War*; Haldane, 'Shorncliffe Diary', IWM.

Chapter Four

1. Rosinski, in Samuels, *Command or Control?*, p. 17.
2. Figures from Herrmann, *The Arming of Europe*, p. 234.
3. British officer, in Samuels, p. 79.
4. Samuels, p. 77.
5. Figures from Herrmann, p. 234.
6. See O. H. (I), pp. 71, 92.
7. Martin, *A Surgeon in Khaki*, p. 95. See also Mills [Platoon Commander], *With My Regiment from the Aisne to La Bassée*, p. 162; Hay, *Wounded and a Prisoner of War*, p. 48.
8. See Sheldon, *The German Army at Ypres 1914*, pp. xi–xii.
9. Lt. T. E. Davey, p. 4, NA CAB 45/196.
10. Zuber, *The Mons Myth*, p. 66.
11. Samuels, p. 83.
12. See Brose, *The Kaiser's Army*, pp. 159–65.
13. Ibid., p. 191.

14. Ibid., p. 164.
15. See Samuels, p. 77; Brose, p. 154.
16. In Tuchman, *August 1914*, p. 189.
17. Zuber, pp. 97–101; Brose, p. 201.
18. Brose, p. 190.
19. Strachan, *The First World War* Vol. I, p. 170.
20. Ibid., p. 180.
21. Zuber, *The Real German War Plan 1904–14* (History Press, 2011); Zuber, 'The Schlieffen Plan Reconsidered', in *War in History* (1999) vol. 6, no. 3, pp. 262–305; Strachan, op. cit., pp. 166–80; but see also Gross, 'There was a Schlieffen Plan', in *War in History* (2008) vol. 15, no. 4, pp. 389–431.

Chapter Five

1. Spears, *Liaison 1914*, pp. 147–9.
2. O. H. (I), p. 63.
3. Tower, p. 10, IWM.
4. Ibid., p. 9.
5. Wollocombe, p. 30, IWM.
6. Ibid., p. 31.
7. Ibid.
8. Tower, p. 11.
9. See Farndale, *History of the Royal Regiment of Artillery*, p. 15.
10. Sausmarez, 108th War Diary, p. 1, LCBLUL.
11. Beaumont, *Old Contemptible*, p. 34.
12. Horsefall and Cave, *Mons*, p. 87.
13. Zuber, *The Mons Myth*, p. 156 – figures from the regimental history, *Das Grenadier-Regiment Prinz Karl von Preussen … im Weltkriege*, by Ernst von Schoenfeldt.
14. Roupell, Diary, pp. 3–4, IWM. British rifle fire was never as unerringly accurate as many writers maintained; see, for example, Dunn, *The War the Infantry Knew*, p. 70 and Hanbury-Sparrow, *The Land-Locked Lake*, pp. 66–7.
15. Wynne, 'Experiences', p. 33, LHCMA.
16. Zuber, p. 138.
17. O. H. (I), p. 75; but see Vivian, *The Phantom Brigade*, pp. 164–70, and Wollocombe, p. 33.
18. Tower, p 11.
19. Ibid., p. 12.
20. O'Neill, *The Royal Fusiliers in the Great War*, p. 140; the O. H. (I) lists just over 100 (p. 76).
21. Brownlow, *The Breaking of the Storm*, pp. 40–1.

22. Hay [an Exchange Officer], *Wounded and a Prisoner of War*, pp. 48–9.
23. Casualty figures from O. H. (I), p. 80 – taken from the German General Staff's *Die Schlacht bei Mons*, pp. 33, 34; Zuber, p. 143, maintains a figure of 271 (unsourced).
24. Durand, pp. 5–6, IWM.
25. Farndale, p. 12.
26. Figures from O. H. (I), pp. 82, 83.
27. Some German casualty figures, in descending order: Horsefall and Cave (*Mons*, p. 105) – 'an estimated 10,000 casualties', without source; Brose (*Kaiser's Army*, p. 283) – 'almost 6,800', based on returns of regimental strengths before and after Mons; Keegan (*The First World War: An Illustrated History*, p. 88) – 'must have reached nearly 5,000', without source; Zuber (*Mons Myth*, p. 167) – 'no more than 2,000 casualties', based on casualty lists, drawn from regimental histories of main units and estimations from others.
28. O. H. (I), p. 83.
29. O. H. (I), p. 71.
30. Bloem, *The Advance from Mons* (1930).
31. Terraine, *Mons*, p. 94.
32. Zuber, p. 158.
33. Hay, p. 45.
34. French, in O. H. (I), p. 84.
35. Holmes, *The Little Field Marshal*, p. 217.

Chapter Six

1. Haig, in Sheffield and Bourne, *Douglas Haig: War Diaries and Letters*, p. 61.
2. Ibid., p. 63.
3. Ibid.
4. Ibid., p. 64. See also Sheffield, *The Chief*, pp. 72–4.
5. For BEF communications, see Priestley, *The Signal Service in the European War*.
6. Figures from Zuber, *The Mons Myth*, p. 175.
7. Brandis, *Die Stürmer von Douaumont*, in O. H. (I), p. 93.
8. Osburn, *Unwilling Passenger*, p. 38
9. Ibid.
10. Gleichen, *The Doings of the Fifteenth Infantry Brigade*, p. 28. See also Archibald, p. 88, IWM and Mowbray, p. 4, IWM.
11. For British shrapnel, see 'Some Lessons of the War', pt. 23, in NA WO 95/629, and Zuber, pp. 173, 255.
12. O. H. (I), p. 101.
13. Horsefall and Cave, *Mons*, p. 125. Good published accounts can be found in Bridges, *Alarms and Excursions*, pp. 81–3; Emden (ed.) *Tickled to Death to Go*, pp. 50–8; Osburn, pp. 40–7.
14. Chance, 'Draw Swords' p. 3, LCBLUL.

15. Grenfell, in Ascoli, *The Mons Star*, p. 83.
16. Figure from Badsey, *Doctrine and Reform in the British Cavalry*, p. 245; Emden, p. 56, puts forward a higher total of 234.
17. O. H. (I), p. 101.
18. de Lisle, in Badsey, p. 245; for Smith-Dorrien's scorn at de Lisle's assertion see Diary, p. 67, NA CAB/206.
19. Matterson, NA CAB 45/197.
20. Gleichen, letter to Smith-Dorrien, NA CAB 45/206.
21. O. H. (I), p. 105.
22. Ibid., for British casualties; Zuber, p. 193, estimates German casualties at 2,400.
23. Robertson, *From Private to Field Marshal*, p. 210.
24. Roupell, p. 5, IWM.
25. Lucy, *There's a Devil in the Drum*, pp. 118–19.
26. Ibid., p. 119.
27. Haig, in Sheffield, *The Chief*, p. 76. See also Hanbury-Sparrow, *The Land-Locked Lake*, p. 34.
28. Keppel, p. 6, NA CAB 45/196.
29. Ibid.
30. Brownlow, *The Breaking of the Storm*, p. 60
31. Wynne, 'Experiences', p. 56, LHCMA.
32. Owens, p. 26, IWM.
33. Brownlow, p. 66.
34. Strange, *Recollections of an Airman*, pp. 43–4.
35. See Badsey, *Doctrine and Reform in the British Cavalry*, p. 245.
36. Snow, 'Doings of the 4th Division', pp. 19–20, IWM. See also Osburn, p. 61.
37. Snow, p. 19.

Chapter Seven

1. Terraine (ed.), *General Jack's Diary*, pp. 32–3.
2. Stacke, *The Worcestershire Regiment*, p. 7.
3. O. H. (I), p. 135.
4. Ibid.
5. FSR (Part 1, Section 12, Para. 13, sub-para. iii), in Smith-Dorrien, *Memories of Forty-Eight Years' Service*, p. 403.
6. Becke, *Royal Regiment of Artillery at Le Cateau*, p. 20.
7. Wynne, 'Experiences', p. 64, LHCMA.
8. Ibid.
9. KOYLI War Diary, p. 14, NA WO95/1558.
10. Rolt, in Murphy, *History of the Suffolk Regiment*, p. 32.
11. Smith-Dorrien, ibid., p. 29.
12. For the deployment of the 15th Brigade RFA and 37th Battery, see Henning,

Jones (NA CAB 45/196); Nutt (NA CAB 45/197); MacLeod, pp. 80–1, LHCMA; Becke, pp. 23–4; Bidwell, *Gunners at War*, pp. 25–6.

13. Kinsman, NA CAB 45/196.
14. Lutyens, 'Account of the Battle of Le Cateau', p. 26, IWM.
15. Bond, *History of the KOYLI in the Great War*, Vol. III, p. 723. See also Helm, p. 4, IWM.
16. Headlam, 'Papers relating to 5th Div', IWM.
17. Bidwell, p. 18 [italics in original].
18. Snow, 'Doings of the 4th Division', p. 25, IWM.
19. Edmonds, 'Memoirs', Chapter XXIV, p. 3, LHCMA.
20. Hart, 'Narrative of the Retreat', NA CAB 45/196.
21. Montgomery, *Memoirs*, p. 32.
22. Montgomery, in B. Montgomery, *A Field-Marshal in the Family*, p. 159.
23. Hart, op. cit.
24. Kingsford, *Story of the Royal Warwickshire Regiment*, p. 132.
25. Snow, p. 29.
26. Brereton, pp. II–III, IWM [the maps in Becke and Farndale have the battery sited to the west of Haucourt].
27. Lattorf, in Cave and Sheldon, *Le Cateau*, p. 150.
28. Brownlow, *The Breaking of the Storm*, pp. 83–4.
29. Archibald, pp. 86–7, IWM.
30. Ibid., p. 87.
31. In Zuber, *The Mons Myth*, p. 248.
32. Hay, *Wounded and a Prisoner of War*, p. 67.
33. Ibid, pp. 67–8.
34. Ibid., p. 68.
35. Lucy, *There's a Devil in the Drum*, pp. 128–9.
36. Stacke, p. 9.
37. Johnston, in Astill (ed.), *Great War Diaries of Brigadier Alexander Johnston*, p. 10. See also Falls, *Royal Irish Rifles in the Great War*, pp. 7–8.

Chapter Eight

1. Gough, *The Fifth Army*, p. 28, in Gardner, *Trial by Fire*, pp. 56–7.
2. Nutt, NA CAB 45/197.
3. MacLeod, p. 82, LHCMA.
4. Ibid., p. 83.
5. In Zuber, *The Mons Myth*, p. 239.
6. Schacht, in Cave and Sheldon, *Le Cateau*, p. 52.
7. Lutyens, 'Lionel's Account of the Battle', p. 29, IWM.
8. Nutt, op. cit.
9. In Becke, *The Royal Regiment of Artillery at Le Cateau*, p. 48.

10. Headlam, 'Address to the Canadian Club, Winnipeg', 4/12/18, pp. 9–10, IWM; for similar 'amnesia' see 'Letters Home', 5/10/14, IWM.
11. Sausmarez, 108th Battery War Diary, p. 4, LCBLUL.
12. Ramsden, Letters, 30/9/14, IWM.
13. Wynne, 'Experiences', pp. 69–70, LHCMA.
14. See Cave and Sheldon, p. 53.
15. Sausmarez, op. cit.
16. Ibid.
17. Smith-Dorrien, *Memories of Fort-Eight Years' Service*, p. 406.
18. O. H. (I), p. 163.
19. Lutyens, p. 34.
20. Ibid., p. 35.
21. Henning, NA CAB 45/196.
22. MacLeod, p. 92.
23. Wynne, p. 72.
24. Ibid., p. 73.
25. Ibid., p. 74.
26. Heathcote, NA CAB 45/196.
27. Bond, KOYLI War Diary, p. 20, NA WO 95/1558. The Official History (I), p. 166, gives the time as 3.30 p.m., certainly too early.
28. Wynne, p. 79.
29. Ibid., pp. 81–2.
30. Zuber, p. 242.
31. Helm, p. 5, IWM.
32. Wollocombe, Diary, p. 45, IWM.
33. Tower, p. 18, IWM. For similar descriptions, see Lt Longman, in Foss, *The Royal Fusiliers*, p. 108; 2nd Lt Archibald, p. 88, IWM; and Lt-Col Bird, in Taylor, *The 2nd Royal Irish Rifles in the Great War*, p. 31.
34. Johnston, in Astill (ed.), *The Great War Diaries of Brigadier Alexander Johnston*, p. 12.
35. Lucy, *There's a Devil in the Drum*, pp. 141–2.
36. Nicholson, *History of the East Lancashire Regiment*, pp. 15–16.
37. Wirth, 'The Battle of Le Cateau', *RUSI Journal* (1920), 65:457, p. 186.
38. Edmonds, 'Memoirs', Chapter XXIV, p. 7, LHCMA.
39. Snow, 'Doings of the 4th Division', p. 45, IWM.
40. Ibid.
41. Wheeler, 'Report on Action of 26 August', 10th Brigade War Diary, NA WO 95/1477.
42. Hart, 'Narrative of the Retreat', NA CAB 45/196.
43. Montgomery, in Hamilton, *Monty: The Making of a General*, p. 79.
44. See Neish, NA CAB 45/197, and Falls, *The Gordon Highlanders in the First World War*, pp. 6–9.

Chapter Nine

1. Casualty figures from O. H. (I), p. 182, not including those missing who later rejoined their units, although, overall, the figure may be slightly inflated after some double-counting with casualties suffered on the 24th/25th – see Smith-Dorrien, letter to Becke, NA CAB 45/206. Cave and Sheldon, *Le Cateau* (p. 9), suggest a figure as low as 5,000.

2. Zuber, *The Mons Myth*, p. 257.

3. See Smith-Dorrien, *Memories of Forty-Eight Years' Service*, pp. 407–8; Fergusson, 'Notes of a Conversation with Lt-Gen. Sir Charles Fergusson', NA CAB 45/195; Headlam papers, IWM; Haldane, *A Brigade of the Old Army*, pp. 19–30.

4. Becke, *Royal Regiment of Artillery at Le Cateau*, p. 22.

5. Smith-Dorrien, p. 407.

6. Smith-Dorrien, Diary, 27 August, NA CAB 45/206.

7. Quoted in Gardner, *Trial by Fire*, pp. 61–2. See also Robbins, *British Generalship on the Western Front*, p. 117.

8. Owens, Diary, 27 August, IWM.

9. Smith-Dorrien, op. cit.

10. Roupell, Diary, p. 6, IWM.

11. Slingsby, letter 29 August, LHCMA.

12. Osburn, *Unwilling Passenger*, p. 69.

13. Tower, p. 19, IWM.

14. Lucy, *There's a Devil in the Drum*, pp. 150–1. See also Taylor, *The 2nd Royal Irish Rifles*, p. 35 (Colthurst kept his command for the time being).

15. Jack, in Terraine (ed.), *General Jack's Diary*, p. 42.

16. Baring, *Flying Corps Headquarters*, pp. 26–7.

17. Strange, *Recollections of an Airman*, p. 46.

18. Haldane, p. 37.

19. Montgomery, letter, 27 September, in Hamilton, *Monty: The Making of a General*, p. 80.

20. Bridges, *Alarms and Excursions*, pp. 87–8. See also Hutton, *August 1914*, for a full account of the St Quentin incident.

21. Osburn, p. 87.

22. Rees, pp. 6–7, IWM

23. Ibid.

24. Haig, I Corps Despatches, 24 September, NA WO95/588. Maxse was subsequently removed from command of the brigade.

25. French, Diary, 28 August 1914.

26. French, in Spears, *Liaison 1914*, pp. 295–6.

27. Kitchener, 31 August in O. H. (I), p. 473; see Appendix 22 for the full telegraphic exchange.

Chapter Ten

1.   Kitchener, in O. H. (I), p. 245.
2.   French, *1914*, p. 100.
3.   Kitchener, in Holmes, *The Little Field Marshal*, pp. 233–4.
4.   French, in O. H. (I), p. 245.
5.   Herbert, *Mons, Anzac and Kut*, p. 36.
6.   Ibid., p. 37.
7.   Osburn, *Unwilling Passenger*, p. 93.
8.   Baker-Carr, *From Chauffeur to Brigadier*, p. 30. See also Edmonds, 'Memoirs' Chapter XXIV, p. 14, LHCMA.
9.   Ibid.
10. Geiger, in Dunn, *The War the Infantry Knew*, p. 45.
11. Helm, p. 10, IWM.
12. McIlwain, Diary, 2 September, IWM.
13. Jack, in Terraine (ed.), *General Jack's Diary*, p. 47.
14. Brownlow, *Breaking of the Storm*, p. 133.
15. Richards, *Old Soldiers Never Die*, p. 31,
16. Forestier-Walker, 'Notes of II Corps' Experiences', p. 21, NA WO 95/629.
17. Haldane, *A Brigade of the Old Army*, p. 66.
18. McIlwain, Diary, 2 September.
19. Forestier-Walker, 'March Discipline', NA WO 95/1510.
20. Richards, p. 30.
21. Hyndson, *From Mons to the First Battle of Ypres*, p. 35.
22. Jack, p. 46.
23. Hanbury-Sparrow, *The Land-Locked Lake*, p. 48.
24. Ibid., pp. 51–2.
25. Spears, *Liaison, 1914*, p. 415.
26. Ibid., pp. 416–17.
27. Ibid, pp. 417–18

Chapter Eleven

1.   Bridges, *Alarms and Excursions*, p. 93.
2.   Mileage figures from O. H. (I), p. 492.
3.   Ibid., p. 260; casualty figures ibid., p. 262.
4.   Barrow, *The Fire of Life*, p. 144.
5.   Moltke, in O. H. (I), p. 266.
6.   Jack, in Terraine (ed.), *General Jack's Diary*, p. 48.
7.   Osburn, *Unwilling Passenger*, p. 117.
8.   Ibid., pp. 119–20.
9.   Haldane, *A Brigade of the Old Army*, p. 78. For similar views, see also, Mowbray, p.

16, IWM; Hanbury-Sparrow, *The Land-Locked Lake*, pp. 59–60; Jack, p. 49.

10.   Johnston, in Astill (ed.), *The Great War Diaries of Brigadier Alexander Johnston*, pp. 19-20.

11.   Ibid., pp. 21–2.

12.   Ibid., p. 22.

13.   Snow, 'Doings of the 4th Division', p. 66, IWM.

14.   Brereton, p. XVIII, IWM.

15.   Ibid.

16.   Patterson, 'War Diary', p. 14, LCBLUL.

17.   Smith-Dorrien, NA WO 95/629.

18.   Helm, p. 12, IWM.

19.   Gleichen, *The Doings of the Fifteenth Infantry Brigade*, p. 74.

20.   Robertson, *From Private to Field Marshal*, p. 213; just one of many similar euphemisms.

21.   Spencer, Diary, 9 September, IWM.

22.   Strange, *Recollections of an Airman*, p. 58.

23.   Zwehl, 'The VII German Reserve Corps at the Aisne' in *RUSI Journal*, Feb/Nov 1921 (66), p. 524.

24.   Operation Order No. 22, O. H. (I), Appendix 44.

25.   O. H. (I), p. 326.

Chapter Twelve

1.   Bloem, *The Advance from Mons*, pp. 181–2. See also O. H. (I), p. 330.

2.   Roupell, Diary, p. 17, IWM.

3.   Hyndson, *From Mons to the First Battle of Ypres*, pp. 49–50. See also Wylly, *The Loyal North Lancashire Regiment*, p. 9.

4.   Hyndson, pp. 52–3.

5.   Knight, Diary, 14 September, IWM.

6.   Rees, 'Personal Record', p. 19, IWM.

7.   O. H. (I), p. 342.

8.   Jeffreys, in Craster, (ed.), *'Fifteen Rounds a Minute'*, pp. 85–6. See also J. Gough, 'Memo on British and German Tactics', in I Corps Despatches, NA WO 95/588.

9.   Wynne, 'Experiences', p. 79, LHCMA.

10.   See, for example, Zuber, *The Mons Myth*, pp. 238, 241.

11.   Osborne-Smith, 18 September, I Corps Despatches, NA WO 95/588.

12.   Zuber, p. 238.

13.   Patterson, 'War Diary', p. 18, LCBLUL.

14.   O. H. (I), p. 360.

15.   Lucy, *There's a Devil in the Drum*, p. 169.

16.   Ibid., p. 189.

17. Richards, *Old Soldiers Never Die*, p. 98.
18. Jack, in Terraine (ed.), *General Jack's Diary*, p. 49. Of numerous other examples of exemplary bravery, see, for example, Matterson, NA CAB 45/197; Lutyens, pp 33–4, IWM.
19. French, in I Corps Despatches, NA WO 95/588.
20. Ibid.
21. Gleichen, *The Doings of the Fifteenth Infantry Brigade*, p. 82. See also Roupell, Diary, p. 14, IWM.
22. O. H. (I), p. 355.
23. Figures from O. H. (I), p. 356 and Farndale, *Royal Regiment of Artillery*, p. 63.
24. O. H. (I), p. 356.
25. Haldane, *A Brigade of the Old Army*, pp. 100–1. Elkington and Mainwaring had been dismissed after the St Quentin 'surrender', and Croucher (1st Royal Irish Fusiliers) was sacked by Smith-Dorrien at Haldane's request on 5 September. See also Haldane, Shorncliffe Diary, p. 215, IWM.
26. O. H. (I), p. 357.
27. Lucy, p. 178.
28. Ibid., pp. 179–80.
29. Ibid., p. 180.
30. Falls, *Royal Irish Rifles in the Great War*, p. 14.

Chapter Thirteen

1. French, Operational Order 26, O. H. (I), Appendix 49.
2. 'Notes based on Experiences Gained by the Second Corps', Pt 2, NA WO 95/629.
3. 'Memo on British and German tactics', Pt 4, I Corps Despatches, NA WO 95/588.
4. Johnston, in Astill (ed.), *Great War Diaries of Brigadier Alexander Johnston*, p. 25.
5. Martin, *A Surgeon in Khaki*, p. 105.
6. Haig, in Terraine, *White Heat*, (Sidgwick & Jackson, 1981) p. 105.
7. 'Notes based … ', Pt 6, op. cit.
8. Money, Diary, 30 Sept., LCBLUL.
9. 'Notes based …', Pt 22, op. cit.
10. Haig, 'Operations of the I Corps, 13 September to 16 October', p. 17, NA WO 95/588.
11. Strange, *Recollections of an Airman*, p. 64.
12. Ibid.
13. Baring, *Flying Corps Headquarters*, p. 48.
14. Haig, in Sheffield and Bourne, *Douglas Haig: War Diaries and Letters*, p. 71. See also Farndale, *Royal Regiment of Artillery*, pp. 63–6.
15. Mowbray, Diary, 1 October, IWM.

16. Wynne, 'Experiences', p. 69, LHCMA.
17. White, Diary, in Blewitt Papers, IWM.
18. Money, 4 October, op. cit.; see similar entry on 14 September.
19. Patterson, 'War Diary', p. 27, LCBLUL.
20. Owens, Diary, 16 September, IWM.
21. Osburn, *Unwilling Passenger*, pp. 133–4. See also O. H. (I), p. 398.
22. Johnston, p. 26.
23. Wyrall, *West Yorkshire Regiment in the Great War*, p. 12.
24. de Lisle, Report on Paissy, NA WO 95/588. See also reports by Congreve and Lomax NA WO 95/588, and 1918 interviews with captured W. Yorks officers (Grant-Dalton, Harrington, Henderson, Wilson) in NA CAB 45/142.
25. Bridges, *Alarms and Excursions*, pp. 96–7.
26. Haig, on Lomax's report, op. cit.
27. Osburn, p. 148 (italics in original).
28. 'Some Lessons of the War', NA WO 95/629.
29. Brownlow, *Breaking of the Storm*, p. 162. The officially recommended field of fire was actually around 300 yards, see 'British and German Tactics', p. 3, op. cit., and II Corps 'Notes based …' Pt 4, op. cit.
30. Patterson, p. 25.
31. McIlwain, Diary, p. 19, IWM.
32. Hesketh-Prichard, *Sniping in France* (Hutchinson, 1920) p. 16.
33. Dashwood, 1 October, NA CAB 45/195.
34. Forestier-Walker, II Corps 'Notes Based …', Pt 67, op. cit.
35. Rees, 'Personal Record', pp. 23–4, IWM.
36. Platoon Commander [Arthur Mills], *With My Regiment from the Aisne to La Bassée*, p. 47. For a sociological perspective, see Tony Ashworth, *Trench Warfare 1914–1918: The Live and Let Live System* (Macmillan, 1980).
37. Roupell, Diary, pp. 22–3, IWM.
38. Ibid., p. 23.
39. Ibid., p. 19.
40. McIlwain, p. 24.
41. Osburn, p. 170.
42. Smith-Dorrien, *Memories of Forty-Eight Years' Service*, pp. 425–6.

Chapter Fourteen

1. Burge, Letters, pp. 14–15, IWM.
2. Ibid., p. 20.
3. Butler, *A Galloper at Ypres*, p. 58.
4. Lloyd, *A Trooper in the 'Tins'*, p. 93.
5. Sansom, RFC Ypres report, NA CAB 45/142.
6. Rupprecht, Diary, 20 October, in Sheldon, *The German Army at Ypres*, p. 10.
7. Headlam, letter to Edmonds, 23 April 1923, NA CAB 45/182.

8. O.H (II), p. 75.
9. Johnston, in Astill (ed.), *Great War Diaries of Brigadier Alexander Johnston*, pp. 32–3.
10. Gough, 'Memo on British and German tactics', 27 September, I Corps, NA WO 95/588. See also, Beckett, *Johnnie Gough, VC* (Tom Donovan, 1989); and for tactics: Griffith, *Battle Tactics of the Western Front* (Yale, 1994); Samuels, *Command or Control?*
11. See Gardner, *Trial by Fire*, pp. 118–21; O. H. (II), p. 81; Gleichen, *The Doings of the Fifteenth Infantry Brigade*, pp. 109–12.
12. Watson, *Adventures of a Despatch Rider*, p. 174.
13. Smith-Dorrien, *Memories of Forty-Eight Years' Service*, p. 446 (fn.).
14. Headlam to Edmonds, letter of 2 April 1923, CAB 45/182.
15. O. H. (II), p. 96.
16. Montgomery, *Memoirs*, p. 33.
17. Montgomery, letter in Hamilton, *Monty: The Making of a General*, p. 88.

Chapter Fifteen

1. Operational Order No. 38, O. H. (II), Appendix 21. See also Gardner, *Trial by Fire*, pp. 153–4.
2. Kerrich, Diary, 20 October, LHCMA
3. Ibid.
4. O. H. (II) Maps, distances taken from Maps 14, 15.
5. O. H. (II), p. 164 (fn.).
6. Sutton, *A Record of His Life*, p. 67.
7. Olivant, NA CAB 45/141. See also Earle, NA CAB 45/140.
8. McIlwain, Diary, 20 October, IWM.
9. Rees, 'A Personal Record', p. 33, IWM.
10. Knight, Diary, 24 October, IWM.
11. Rees, pp. 33–4.
12. Dillon, Letters, p. 35, IWM.
13. Ibid., pp. 35–6.
14. Hyndson, *From Mons to the First Battle of Ypres*, pp. 77–80.
15. Bulfin, Diary, p. 26, NA CAB 45/140.
16. Sheldon, *The German Army at Ypres*, p. 150.
17. Baker-Carr, *From Chauffeur to Brigadier*, p. 49.
18. Butler, *A Galloper at Ypres*, pp. 118–19.
19. Raleigh, *The War in the Air*, p. 346.
20. Jeffrey, in Craster (ed.), *'Fifteen Rounds a Minute'*, p. 118. The incident was widely observed on both sides; see Bolwell, *With a Reservist in France*, p. 84, and Sheldon, p. 153.
21. RFC at Ypres, NA CAB 45/142, but see also WO 95/706 for infantry continuing to fire on RFC aircraft with roundels during November 1914.
22. Haig, in Sheffield and Bourne, *Douglas Haig: War Diaries and Letters*, p. 75.

23. Figures from O. H. (II), p. 248.
24. Lloyd, *A Trooper in the 'Tins'*, p. 102
25. Home, *The Diary of a World War I Cavalry Officer*, p. 31.

Chapter Sixteen

1. Figures from O. H. (II), p. 86. See also Gardner, *Trial by Fire*, pp. 125–6.
2. Johnston in Astill (ed.), *The Great War Diaries of Alexander Johnston*, p. 38.
3. Ibid., p. 39.
4. Ibid.
5. Smith-Dorrien, report to GHQ, 22/10/14 (G 312), NA WO 95/629.
6. Ibid.
7. Ibid.
8. Dunn (ed.), *The War the Infantry Knew*, p. 80.
9. Lucy, *There's a Devil in the Drum*, p. 219.
10. Ibid., p. 220.
11. Smith-Dorrien, Diary, p. 92, NA CAB 45/206.
12. Mills [Platoon Commander], *With My Regiment from the Aisne to La Bassée*, p. 159. See also Dillon, Letters, p. 41, IWM; Mowbray, Diary, p. 52, IWM.
13. Helm, p. 24, IWM.
14. Robertson, *From Private to Field Marshal*, p. 217.
15. Forestier-Walker, Expenditure of Artillery Ammunition, NA WO 95/629. See also Beckett, *Ypres*, pp. 113–15.
16. Devenish, *A Subaltern's Share in the War*, p. 38. See also J. Bremner (Diary, IWM), whose 115th Heavy Battery RGA was regularly firing 100 rounds per day in November.
17. Roe, in Downham (ed.), *Diary of an Old Contemptible*, p. 57. See also, Richards, *Old Soldiers Never Die*, pp. 46, 48–9; Lucy, p. 236.
18. Ibid., p. 58.
19. Forestier-Walker, NA WO 95/629.
20. Wilson, Diary, 25 October, in Holmes, *The Little Field-Marshal*, p. 247.
21. Lucy, pp. 248–9.
22. Ibid., p. 249. British Lyddite (from Lydd, where it was developed) was a high explosive made from picric acid and had a particularly distinctive yellow colour.
23. War Diary, 27 October, in Taylor, *The 2nd Royal Irish Rifles*, p. 56.
24. Maude, in C. E. Callwell, *The Life of Sir Stanley Maude* (Constable, 1920), p. 185.
25. O. H. (II), p. 217.
26. Ibid., p. 218 (Indian casualty figures, p. 218).
27. Helm, IWM, p. 25.
28. Ibid.
29. Ibid., p. 26.
30. Ibid.

31. Figures from O. H. (II), p. 222.
32. Gleichen, *The Doings of the Fifteenth Infantry Brigade*, p. 134.
33. Watson, *Adventures of a Despatch Rider*, p. 198.

Chapter Seventeen

1. O. H. (II), p. 282.
2. Ibid.
3. Artillery figures from O. H (II), p. 259 and Beckett, *Ypres*, p. 123.
4. See Farndale, *History of the Royal Regiment of Artillery*, p. 81.
5. Johnston, in Astill (ed.), *Great War Diaries of Brigadier Alexander Johnston*, p. 61.
6. Hamilton, *The First Seven Divisions*, p. 276.
7. See, Gardner, *Trial by Fire*, pp. 213–14, and Beckett, p. 155.
8. Rice, Letter to Edmonds, 6 November 1922, NA CAB 45/141. Rice suggests that Capper had not consulted his senior staff officer on the siting of his trenches.
9. Hamilton, p. 279.
10. Bulfin, Diary, p. 30, NA CAB 45/140.
11. O. H. (II), p. 305.
12. Home, *Diary of a World War I Cavalry Officer*, p. 36.
13. Marshall, in *The History of the Welch Regiment*, p. 320.
14. Ibid.
15. O. H. (II), p. 317. Privately, Edmonds was scathing on what he considered (surely unjustly) as the 'running away' of the Welch Regiment: 'The 2/Welch cleared out in front of Ypres, leaving the Queen's to be massacred' – Edmonds, War Papers (VI/8), LHCMA.
16. Rees, 'A Personal Record', p. 40, IWM
17. Blewitt, p. 3, IWM.
18. Hyndson, *From Mons to the First Battle of Ypres*, p. 94.
19. See Bolwell, *With a Reservist in France*, pp. 88–9, for the argument between the two COs.
20. Figures in Sheldon, *The German Army at Ypres*, p. 175.
21. Lomax, in O. H. (II), p. 322.
22. Baines, 'Personal account of 31 October', p. 4, IWM.
23. Ibid., p. 5.
24. Ibid., p. 7.
25. Bulfin, p. 30.
26. Haig, in Holmes, *The Little Field Marshal*, p. 251.
27. Charteris, in Terraine, *Douglas Haig, The Educated Soldier*, p. 114.
28. Leach, 'Account of Gheluvelt battle', p. 11, NA CAB 45/140 (Leach maintains the SWB had regained their trenches along the sunken road; the Worcestershires claim the SWB were clinging on at the edge of the chateau).

29. Senhouse Clarke, 'A Short Account', p. 2, NA CAB 45/140.
30. Ibid, p. 3.
31. Senhouse Clarke, 'Action of A Company at Gheluvelt', NA CAB 45/140;
    Stacke, *The Worcestershire Regiment*, p. 34.
32. O. H. (II), p. 329.
33. See Sheldon, p. 174.
34. Senhouse Clarke, 'Action of A Company', op. cit.
35. Blewitt, p. 4.
36. Bulfin, pp. 31–2.
37. Baines, p. 10.
38. Ibid.
39. Dillon, Letters, p. 25, IWM.
40. Holmes, *The Little Field Marshal*, p. 251.
41. Stacke, comment on Gheluvelt, NA CAB 45/141.
42. Stacke, *The Worcestershire Regiment*, p. 35.
43. Hankey, letter to Stacke, NA CAB 45/140.
44. Figures from O. H. (II), p. 339.
45. Rees, p. 38.
46. Johnston, in Astill (ed.), p. 50.
47. Ibid.
48. See Hyndson, pp. 105–6; Wylly, *The Loyal North Lancashire Regiment*, p. 18.
49. See Sheldon, p. 333.
50. Thorne, 'Account of Attack by Prussian Guard', NA CAB/141.
51. Jeudwine, letter to Edmonds, 22 April 1923, NA CAB 45/182.
52. McIlwain, Diary, IWM, p. 39.
53. Baines, in Crosse, *A Record of H. M. 52nd Light Infantry*, p. 85.
54. O. H. (II), p. 448.

Epilogue

1. Figures from O. H. (II), p. 466.
2. Hyndson, *From Mons to the First Battle of Ypres*, p. 111. The 1st North Lancs were back in action on 21 December 1914, leading an attack near Givenchy that cost them six officers and 408 other ranks casualties, the regimental history concluding: 'The battalion was brought out of action by 2nd Lieutenant J. G. W. Hyndson.'
3. Helm, p. 28, IWM.
4. Lucy, *There's a Devil in the Drum*, p. 285.
5. Ibid., pp. 293–4.

BIBLIOGRAPHY

UNPUBLISHED SOURCES

Imperial War Museum (Department of Documents)
Papers of:
Anonymous account of battle of Mons (2304), Royal Fusiliers
Major-General S. C. M. Archibald, Royal Field Artillery
Lieutenant-Colonel C. S. Baines, Oxford and Bucks Light Infantry
Commander H. P. Baylis, Royal Navy Volunteer Reserve
Lieutenant-Colonel R. Blewitt, Royal Field Artillery
Corporal J. Bremner, Royal Garrison Artillery
Major C. L. Brereton, Royal Field Artillery
Lieutenant-Colonel N. O. Burge, Royal Marines
Lieutenant-Colonel T. B. Butt, King's Own Yorkshire Light Infantry
Major-General A. R. Chater, Royal Marines
Bombardier S. W. Crowsley, Royal Horse Artillery
Lieutenant-Colonel H. M. Dillon, Oxford and Bucks Light Infantry
Brigadier-General Alan Durand, Royal Field Artillery
Captain C. H. Gaskell, Wiltshire Regiment
Lieutenant E. S. Hacker, Army Service Corps
General Aylmer Haldane, 10th Infantry Brigade
Private D. Harrop, Duke of Wellington's Regiment
Major-General John Headlam, CRA 5th Division
Colonel Cyril Helm, Royal Army Medical Corps
Private Samuel Knight, Welch Regiment
Major E. G. Lutyens, Royal Field Artillery
Sergeant John McIlwain, Connaught Rangers
Captain W. G. Morritt, East Surrey Regiment
Major John Mowbray, Royal Field Artillery
Captain H. B. Owens, Royal Army Medical Corps

Lieutenant-Colonel J.V. Ramsden, Royal Field Artillery
Brigadier-General H. C. Rees, Welch Regiment
Brigadier-General G. R. P. Roupell, East Surrey Regiment
Major-General T. D. O. Snow, GOC 4th Division
Lieutenant-Colonel A.V. Spencer, Oxford and Bucks Light Infantry
Lieutenant-Colonel K. F. B. Tower, Royal Fusiliers
Lieutenant-Colonel T. S. Wollocombe, Middlesex Regiment
Second-Lieutenant N. L. Woodroffe, Irish Guards

Liddell Hart Centre for Military Archives, King's College, London
Papers of:
Brigadier-General C. R. Ballard, Norfolk Regiment
Brigadier-General J. E. Edmonds, Official Historian
Brigadier-General W. A. F. Kerrich, Royal Engineers
Colonel R. MacLeod, Royal Field Artillery
Captain H. L. Slingsby, King's Own Yorkshire Light Infantry
Captain G. C. Wynne, King's Own Yorkshire Light Infantry

Liddle Collection, Brotherton Library, University of Leeds
Papers of:
Captain Roger Chance, 4th Royal Dragoon Guards
Lieutenant Kenneth Hooper, East Lancashire Regiment
Major-General R. C. Money, Cameronians (Scottish Rifles)
Captain C. J. Patterson, South Wales Borderers
Brigadier-General C. de Sausmarez, Royal Garrison Artillery
Major G. N. Stockdale, West Yorkshire Regiment

National Archive, Kew
CAB 45 series (Official History material):
CAB 45/129; CAB 45/140; CAB 45/141; CAB 45/142; CAB 45/157; CAB 45/182;
  CAB 45/195; CAB 45/196; CAB 45/197; CAB 45/206.
WO 95 series (War Diaries and related material):
WO 95/588; WO 95/629; WO 95/668; WO 95/706; WO 95/1112; WO 95/1439; WO
  95/1477; WO 95/1482; WO 95/1488; WO 95/1510; WO 95/1558.

OFFICIAL/SEMI-OFFICIAL WORKS, REGIMENTAL & DIVISIONAL HISTORIES
(Place of publication London unless stated otherwise)
Balck, William, *Tactics*, Vols. I and II (Fort Leavenworth, Kansas: US Cavalry Association,
  1911 and 1914)
Becke, A. F., *The Royal Regiment of Artillery at Le Cateau, Wednesday 26th August, 1914* (R.
  A. Institution, 1919)
Bond, R. C., *History of the KOYLI in the Great War* (P. Lund, Humphries, 1926)
Brereton, J. M., *A History of the 4th/7th Royal Dragoon Guards* (privately pub., 1982)

Crookenden, Arthur, *The History of the Cheshire Regiment in the Great War* (Chester: W. H. Evans, 1935)

Crosse, R. B., *A Record of H. M. 52nd Light Infantry in 1914* (Warwick: Spennell Press, 1956)

Edmonds, J. E. (comp.), *History of the Great War Based on Official Documents: Military Operations France and Belgium 1914*, Vols. I and II (Macmillan, 1922, 1925)

Falls, Cyril, *The Royal Irish Rifles in the Great War* (Aldershot: Gale and Polden, 1925)

Falls, Cyril, *The Gordon Highlanders in the First World War*, Vol. IV (Aberdeen: University Press, 1958)

Farndale, Martin, *History of the Royal Regiment of Artillery: Western Front 1914–18* (R. A. Institution, 1986)

Field Service Pocket Book 1914 (HMSO [David and Charles Reprint, 1971])

Field Service Regulations Part I Operations (HMSO)

Foss, Michael, *The Royal Fusiliers* (Hamish Hamilton, 1967)

Hamilton, Ernest W., *The First Seven Divisions* (Hurst and Blackett, 1918; original ed., 1916)

Husey, A. H. and Inman, D. S., *The Fifth Division in the Great War* (Nisbet, 1921)

Kingsford, C. L., *The Story of the Royal Warwickshire Regiment* (Country Life, 1921)

Longstaff, F.V. and Hilliard A., *The Book of the Machine Gun* (Hugh Rees, 1917)

Mockler-Ferryman, A. F., *The Oxfordshire and Buckinghamshire Light Infantry Chronicle* (Eyre and Spottiswoode, n.d. [1920])

Murphy, C. C. R., *The History of the Suffolk Regiment, 1914–1927* (Hutchinson, 1928)

O'Neill, H. C., *The Royal Fusiliers in the Great War* (Heinemann, 1922)

Pearse, H.W. and Sloman, H. S., *The History of the East Surrey Regiment* Vol. II (Medici, 1923)

Priestley, R. E., *The Signal Service in the European War of 1914 to 1918* (Chatham, Kent: Mackay, 1921)

Raleigh, Walter, *The War in the Air: Being the Story of the Part Played in the Great War by the Royal Air Force*, Vol. I (Oxford: Clarendon Press, 1922)

Ransome, A. L., *The Fine Fighting of the Dorsets* (privately published, n.d)

Schwink, Otto, *Ypres 1914: An Official Account Published by Order of the German General Staff* (Constable, 1919)

Stacke, H. FitzMaurice, *The Worcestershire Regiment in the Great War* (Kidderminster: Cheshire and Sons, n.d. [1928])

Taylor, James W., *The 2nd Royal Irish Rifles in the Great War* (Dublin: Four Courts Press, 2005)

Welch Regiment 1914–18, The History of (Cardiff: The Western Mail and Echo, 1932)

Wylly, H. C., *The Loyal North Lancashire Regiment* Vol. II 1914–1919 (RUSI, 1933)

Wyrall, Everard, *The West Yorkshire Regiment in the War 1914–1918* (Bodley Head, 1924)

MEMOIRS, DIARIES AND OTHER FIRST-PERSON ACCOUNTS

Astill, Edwin (ed.), *The Great War Diaries of Brigadier-General Alexander Johnston 1914–1917* (Barnsley, S.Yorkshire: Pen and Sword, 2007)

Baker-Carr, C. D., *From Chauffeur to Brigadier* (Ernest Benn, 1930)

Baring, Maurice, *Flying Corps Headquarters 1914–1918* (Buchan and Enright, 1985; original ed., 1920)

Barrow, George de S., *The Fire of Life* (Hutchinson, 1942)

Beaumont, Harry, *Old Contemptible* (Hutchinson, 1967)

Bloem, Walter, *The Advance from Mons 1914* (Peter Davies, 1930)

Bolwell, F. A., *With a Reservist in France* (Routledge, 1917)

Bridges, Tom, *Alarms and Excursions: Reminiscences of a Soldier* (Longmans, 1938)

Brownlow, C. A. L., *The Breaking of the Storm* (Methuen, 1917)

Butler, Patrick, *A Galloper at Ypres* (T. Fisher Unwin, 1920)

Callwell, C. E., *Experiences of a Dug-Out* (Constable, 1920)

Chapman, Guy (ed.), *Vain Glory* (Cassell, 1937)

Corbett-Smith, A., *The Retreat from Mons* (Cassell, 1916)

Craster, J. M. (ed.), *Fifteen Rounds a Minute: The Grenadiers at War, August to December 1914* (Macmillan, 1976)

Devenish, G. W., *A Subaltern's Share in the War* (Constable, 1917)

Downham, Peter (ed.), *Diary of an Old Contemptible* (Barnsley, S. Yorkshire: Pen and Sword, 2004)

Dunn, J. C. (ed.), *The War the Infantry Knew 1914–19* (Cardinal, 1989; original ed., 1938)

Emden, Richard van (ed.), *Tickled to Death to Go: Memoirs of a Cavalryman in the First World War* (Staplehurst, Kent: Spellmount, 1996)

French, Viscount, *1914* (Constable, 1914)

Gillespie, A. D., *Letters from Flanders* (Smith Elder, 1916)

Gleichen, A. E. W., *The Doings of the Fifteenth Infantry Brigade August 1914 to March 1915* (Edinburgh: Blackwood, 1917)

Gough, Hubert, *Soldiering On* (Arthur Barker, 1954)

Haldane, Aylmer, *A Brigade of the Old Army 1914* (Arnold, 1920)

Hammerton, John (ed.), *I Was There*, Vol. I (Amalgamated Press, 1914–15)

Hanbury-Sparrow, A. A., *The Land-Locked Lake* (Arthur Barker, n.d. [1932])

Hay, M. V. [an Exchange Officer], *Wounded and a Prisoner of War* (Edinburgh, 1916)

Herbert, Aubrey, *Mons, Anzac and Kut* (Arnold, 1919)

Home, Archibald, *The Diary of a World War I Cavalry Officer* (Tunbridge Wells, Kent: Costello, 1985)

Hyndson, J. G. W., *From Mons to the First Battle of Ypres* (privately pub., 1932)

Hodgson, C. F., *From Hell to the Himalayas* (Westville, S. Africa: King and Wilks, 1983)

Kluck, Alexander von, *The March on Paris and the Battle of the Marne 1914* (Arnold, 1920)

Lloyd, R. A., *A Trooper in the 'Tins'* (Hurst and Blackett, 1938)

Longley, C. W. [Wagger], *Battery Flashes* (New York: Dutton, 1916)

Lucy, J. F., *There's a Devil in the Drum* (Faber, 1938)

Martin, Arthur A., *A Surgeon in Khaki* (Arnold, 1915)

Maze, Paul, *A Frenchman in Khaki* (Heinemann, 1934)

Mills, Arthur [Platoon Commander], *With My Regiment from the Aisne to La Bassée* (Heinemann, 1915)

Montgomery, Lord, *Memoirs* (Collins, 1958)

Osburn, Arthur, *Unwilling Passenger* (Faber, 1932)

Powell, E. Alexander, *Fighting in Flanders* (New York: Scribners, 1914)

Richards, Frank, *Old Soldiers Never Die* (Anthony Mott, 1983; original ed., 1933)

Robertson, William, *From Private to Field Marshal* (Constable, 1921)

Samson, Charles Rumney, *Fights and Flights* (Ernest Benn, 1930)

Sheffield, Gary and Bourne, John (eds.), *Douglas Haig War Diaries and Letters 1914–18* (Weidenfeld, 2005)

Smith-Dorrien, Horace, *Memories of Forty-Eight Years' Service* (Murray, 1925)

Snow, Dan and Pottle, Mark (eds.), *The Confusion of Command: The Memoirs of Lieutenant-General Sir Thomas D'Oyly Snow* (Frontline, 2011)
Spears, E. L., *Liaison 1914: A Narrative of the Great Retreat* (Heinemann, 1930)
Stewart, Herbert A., *From Mons to Loos, Being the Diary of a Supply Officer* (Edinburgh: Blackwood, 1917)
Strange, L. A., *Recollections of an Airman* (Hamilton, 1933)
Sutton, R. V., *Richard Vincent Sutton, A Record of His Life* (privately published, n.d.)
Terraine, John (ed.). *General Jack's Diary* (Cassell, 2000; original ed., 1964)
Vivian, A. P. G., *The Phantom Brigade* (Ernest Benn, 1930)
Watson, W. H. L., *Adventures of a Despatch Rider* (Edinburgh: Blackwood, 1915)

SECONDARY SOURCES

Anglesey, Marquis of, *A History of British Cavalry*, Vol. 4 (Leo Cooper, 1996)
Ascoli, David, *The Mons Star* (Harrap, 1981)
Badsey, Stephen, *Doctrine and Reform in the British Cavalry 1880–1918* (Aldershot: Ashgate, 1988)
Beckett, Ian F. W., *Ypres The First Battle, 1914* (Harlow: Pearson, 2006)
Bidwell, Shelford, *Gunners at War: A Tactical Study of the Royal Artillery in the Twentieth Century* (Arrow, 1972)
Bidwell, Shelford, and Graham, Dominick, *Fire-Power: British Army Weapons and Theories of War 1904–1945* (Allen and Unwin, 1982)
Bird, Antony, *Gentlemen, We Will Stand and Fight: Le Cateau 1914* (Ramsbury, Wiltshire: Crowood, 2008)
Brose, Eric Dorn, *The Kaiser's Army: The Politics of Military Technology in Germany During the Machine Age* (Oxford: OUP, 2001)
Brown, Ian Malcom, *British Logistics on the Western Front, 1914–1919* (Praeger, 1998)
Cave, Nigel, and Sheldon, Jack, *Le Cateau, 26 August 1914* (Barnsley, S. Yorkshire: Pen and Sword, 2008)
Clarke, Dale, *British Artillery 1914–19: Field Army Artillery* (Oxford: Osprey, 2004)
Cornish, Paul, *Machine Guns and the Great War* (Barnsley, S. Yorkshire: Pen and Sword, 2009)
Gardner, Nikolas, *Trial by Fire: Command and the British Expeditionary Force in 1914* (Praeger, 2003)
Gooch, John, *The Plans of War: The General Staff and British Military Strategy c. 1900–1916* (Routledge, 1974)
Grayson, Richard S., *Belfast Boys: How Unionists and Nationalists Fought and Died Together in the First World War* (Continuum, 2009)
Green, Andrew, *Writing the Great War: Sir James Edmonds and the Official History 1915–1948* (Frank Cass, 2003)
Hamilton, Nigel, *Monty: The Making of a General 1887–1942* (Hamish Hamilton, 1981)
Hamilton, Nigel, *The Full Monty: Montgomery of Alamein 1887–1942* (Allen Lane, 2001)
Hearn, Peter, *Flying Rebel: The Story of Louis Strange* (HMSO, 1994)
Herrmann, David G., *The Arming of Europe and the Making of the First World War* (Princeton, NJ: Princeton University Press, 1996)
Holmes, Richard, *The Little Field Marshal: A Life of Sir John French* (Weidenfeld, 2004; original ed., 1981)
Holmes, Richard, *Riding the Retreat: Mons to the Marne 1914 – Revisited* (Pimlico, 2007)

Horsefall, Jack, and Cave, Nigel, *Mons 1914* (Barnsley, S. Yorkshire: Pen and Sword, 2000)

Hutton, John, *August 1914: Surrender at St Quentin* (Barnsley, S. Yorkshire: Pen and Sword, 2010)

Macdonald, Lynn, *1914* (Michael Joseph, 1987)

Mead, Peter, *Eye in the Sky: A History of Air Observation and Reconnaissance for the Army 1785–1945* (HMSO, 1983)

Messenger, Charles, *Call to Arms: The British Army 1914–18* (Weidenfeld, 2005)

Montgomery, Brian, *A Field-Marshal in the Family* (Constable, 1973)

Nash, D. B., *Imperial German Army Handbook 1914–1918* (Ian Allen, 1980)

Robbins, Simon, *British Generalship on the Western Front 1914–18: Defeat into Victory* (Routledge, 2006)

Samuels, Martin, *Command or Control?: Command, Training and Tactics in the British and German Armies 1888–1918* (Frank Cass, 1995)

Sheffield, Gary, *The Chief: Douglas Haig and the British Army* (Aurum, 2011)

Sheldon, Jack, *The German Army at Ypres 1914* (Barnsley, S. Yorkshire: Pen and Sword, 2010)

Showalter, Dennis E., *Tannenberg: Clash of Empires* (N. Haven, CT: Archon Books, 1991)

Simpson, Keith, *The Old Contemptibles: A Photographic History of the British Expeditionary Force, August to December 1914* (Allen and Unwin, 1981)

Smithers, A. J., *The Man Who Disobeyed: Sir Horace Smith-Dorrien and his Enemies* (Leo Cooper, 1970)

Strachan, Hew, *The First World War Volume I: To Arms* (Oxford: OUP, 2001)

Strong, Paul, and Marble, Sanders, *Artillery in the Great War* (Barnsley, S. Yorkshire: Pen and Sword, 2011)

Terraine, John, *Mons: The Retreat to Victory* (Batsford, 1960)

Terraine, John, *Douglas Haig: The Educated Soldier* (Hutchinson, 1963)

Travers, Tim, *The Killing Ground: The British Army, the Western Front and the Emergence of Modern Warfare 1900–1918* (Routledge, 1993)

Tuchman, Barbara, *August 1914* (Constable, 1962)

Woodward, David, *Armies of the World 1854–1914* (Sidgwick and Jackson, 1978)

Zuber, Terence, *The Mons Myth: A Reassessment of the Battle* (Stroud, Glos.: The History Press, 2010)

ARTICLES AND SEPARATE CHAPTERS

Badsey, Stephen, 'Cavalry and the Development of the Breakthrough Doctrine', in Paddy Griffith, *British Fighting Methods in the Great War* (Frank Cass, 1996)

Bailey, Jonathan, 'British Artillery in the Great War', in Paddy Griffith, *British Fighting Methods in the Great War* (Frank Cass, 1996)

Barr, Niall, 'Command in Transition from Mobile to Static Warfare, August 1914 to March 1915', in Gary Sheffield and Dan Todman, *Command and Control on the Western Front: The British Army's Experience 1914–18* (Stroud, Glos.: Spellmount, 2007)

Broad, C. N. F., 'The Development of Artillery Tactics', *Journal of the Royal Artillery*, XLIX, 1922–3, pp. 62–81

Bruce, Jack, 'The War in the Air: The Men and Their Machines', in Hugh Cecil and Peter H. Liddle, *Facing Armageddon: The First World War Experienced* (Leo Cooper, 1996)

French, David, 'Sir James Edmonds and the Official History: France and Belgium', in Brian Bond, *The First World War and British Military History* (Oxford: Clarendon Press, 1991)

Gooch, John, 'A Particularly British Institution: The British General Staff in the Era of the Two World Wars', in David French and Brian Holden Reid, *The British General Staff: Reform and Innovation c. 1890–1939* (Frank Cass, 2002)

Holmes, Richard, 'The Last Hurrah: Cavalry and the Western Front, August–September 1914', in Hugh Cecil and Peter H. Liddle, *Facing Armageddon: The First World War Experienced* (Leo Cooper, 1996)

Kuhl, General von, 'The Operations of the British Army August–September 1914', *RUSI Journal* 1921 (66), p. 293

Philpott, William, 'The General Staff and the Paradoxes of Continental War', in David French and Brian Holden Reid, *The British General Staff: Reform and Innovation c. 1890–1939* (Frank Cass, 2002)

Sheffield, Gary, 'Officer–Man Relations, Discipline and Morale in the British Army of the Great War', in Hugh Cecil and Peter H. Liddle, *Facing Armageddon: The First World War Experienced* (Leo Cooper, 1996)

Simpson, Keith, 'The Officers', in Ian Beckett and Keith Simpson, *A Nation in Arms: A Social Study of the British Army in the First World War* (Donovan, 1990)

Spiers, Edward M., 'Rearming the Edwardian Artillery', *Journal of the Society for Army Historical Research*, 57 (1981), pp. 167–76

Spiers, Edward M., 'Reforming the Infantry of the Line, 1900–1914 ', *Journal of the Society for Army Historical Research*, 57 (1981)

Spiers, Edward M., 'The Regular Army in 1914', in Ian Beckett and Keith Simpson, *A Nation in Arms: A Social Study of the British Army in the First World War* (Donovan, 1990)

Strachan, Hew, 'The British Army, its General Staff and the Continental Commitment, 1904–14', in David French and Brian Holden Reid, *The British General Staff: Reform and Innovation c. 1890–1939* (Frank Cass, 2002)

Todman, Dan, and Sheffield, Gary, 'Command and Control in the British Army on the Western Front', in Gary Sheffield and Dan Todman, *Command and Control on the Western Front: The British Army's Experience 1914–18* (Stoud, Glos.: Spellmount, 2007)

Wirth, Alfred, 'The Battle of Le Cateau', *RUSI Journal*, 1920, pp. 185–7

Zwehl, General von, 'The VII German Reserve Corps at the Aisne', *RUSI Journal*, 1921, 66, p. 519

INDEX